# Learn Well This Tablet

# Learn Well This Tablet

*A Commentary on the Tablet of Aḥmad*

by

H. Richard Gurinsky

George Ronald
Oxford

George Ronald, *Publisher*
*www.grbooks.com*



*A catalogue record for this book is available from the British Library*

ISBN 0–85398–444–1

Typeset by Stonehaven Press LLP, Knoxville, Tennessee
Printed and bound in Great Britain by Biddles Ltd
*www.biddles.co.uk*

# Contents

*Acknowledgements* . . . . . . . . . . . . . . . . . . . . . . . x
*Introduction by Todd Lawson* . . . . . . . . . . . . . . . . . . . . xii

**Section One: The Story of Aḥmad**

1 The Story of Aḥmad . . . . . . . . . . . . . . . . . . . . . 1
2 Prologue: O Aḥmad! . . . . . . . . . . . . . . . . . . . . 12
3 Arise and Teach the Cause of God: Bahá'u'lláh's Call in the Tablet of Aḥmad . . . 15
4 A Special Potency and Significance . . . . . . . . . . 18
5 Themes in the Tablet of Aḥmad . . . . . . . . . . . . . 20

**Section Two: The Opening Paragraph**

6 He is the King . . . . . . . . . . . . . . . . . . . . . . . . 22
7 He is the King: The Báb . . . . . . . . . . . . . . . . . 28
8 The Nightingale of Paradise . . . . . . . . . . . . . . . 31
9 The Tree of Eternity . . . . . . . . . . . . . . . . . . . . 38
10 The Tree of Eternity: Symbol of the Covenant . . . . . . . . . . . . . . . 41
11 Holy and Sweet Melodies . . . . . . . . . . . . . . . . . 42
12 The Glad Tidings . . . . . . . . . . . . . . . . . . . . . . 45
13 The Nearness of God . . . . . . . . . . . . . . . . . . . 50
14 The Believers in the Divine Unity . . . . . . . . . . . 54
15 Divine Unity: The Historical Context . . . . . . . . . 59
16 Divine Unity: Bahá'í Teachings . . . . . . . . . . . . . 62
17 The Presence of the Generous One . . . . . . . . . . 66
18 His Holy Court . . . . . . . . . . . . . . . . . . . . . . . 70
19 Informing the Severed Ones . . . . . . . . . . . . . . . 73

20 The Seat of Sanctity
and This Resplendent Beauty . . . . . . . . . . . . . 77
21 The King, the Glorious, the Peerless . . . . . . . . . 80
22 The Lovers . . . . . . . . . . . . . . . . . . . . . . . . . . . . . . 84
23 The Seat of Sanctity . . . . . . . . . . . . . . . . . . . . . 87
24 The Seat of Sanctity: The Covenant . . . . . . . . . . 91
25 The Most Great Beauty . . . . . . . . . . . . . . . . . . . 94

**Section Three: The Station of Bahá'u'lláh**

26 The Promised One Foretold
in the Books of the Messengers . . . . . . . . . . . 97
27 Through Whom Truth
Shall be Distinguished from Error . . . . . . . . 101
28 The Wisdom of Every Command
Shall be Tested . . . . . . . . . . . . . . . . . . . . . . . . 106
29 The Wisdom of Every Command
is Made Clear . . . . . . . . . . . . . . . . . . . . . . . . 113
30 The Tree of Life . . . . . . . . . . . . . . . . . . . . . . . 120
31 The Fruits of God . . . . . . . . . . . . . . . . . . . . . . 124

**Section Four: Twin Manifestations**

32 Bear Thou Witness . . . . . . . . . . . . . . . . . . . . . 130
33 There is No God but God . . . . . . . . . . . . . . . . 131
34 Verily He is God:
The Historical Connection . . . . . . . . . . . . . . 133
35 Verily He is God
and There is No God but Him . . . . . . . . . . . 135
36 He is God: His Word of Affirmation . . . . . . . . . 140
37 He is God and There is No God but Him:
Him Whom God Shall Make Manifest . . . . . 146
38 The True One from God . . . . . . . . . . . . . . . . . 150
39 To Whose Commands
We are All Conforming . . . . . . . . . . . . . . . . 154

40 O People be Obedient .................... 158
41 O People be Obedient: The Covenant ....... 161
42 The King of the Messengers .............. 164
43 The Mother Book ........................ 169

## Section Five: This Clear Message

44 The Call and the Clear Message ........... 174
45 The Call and the Clear Message:
Historical Perspective ................. 179
46 Deliver This Clear Message ............... 183
47 Choose the Path to Your Lord ............ 186

## Section Six: The First Warning

48 If Ye Deny These Verses ................. 191
49 O Assemblage of False Ones .............. 195

## Section Seven: The Bounties of Bahá'u'lláh's Love

50 Counsels ................................ 198
51 Forget Not My Bounties (I) ............... 200
52 Forget Not My Bounties (II) .............. 204
53 The Wonders of My Munificence
and Bounty .............................. 209
54 While I am Absent ....................... 211
55 My Distress and Banishment .............. 215
56 This Remote Prison
and the Nearness of God ................ 221
57 Be Thou So Steadfast in My Love .......... 224
58 Even If ................................. 226
59 A Flame of Fire to My Enemies ........... 229
60 The Fire of the Love of God .............. 233
61 Teach Ye the Cause of God ............... 235
62 Burn Away the Veil of Self ............... 238

63 Be Not of Those Who Doubt (I) . . . . . . . . . . . . 240
64 Be Not of Those Who Doubt (II) . . . . . . . . . . . 242
65 Affliction in My Path . . . . . . . . . . . . . . . . . . . . . 247

**Section Eight: The Paths of Delusion**

66 The Paths of Delusion . . . . . . . . . . . . . . . . . . . . 251
67 Their Superstitions Have Become Veils . . . . . . 254

**Section Nine: The Second Warning**

68 Be Thou Assured in Thyself (I) . . . . . . . . . . . . . 257
69 Be Thou Assured in Thyself (II) . . . . . . . . . . . . 259
70 He Who Turns Away from This Beauty . . . . . . . 261

**Section Ten: Learn Well This Tablet**

71 Learn Well This Tablet . . . . . . . . . . . . . . . . . . . 264
72 The Reward of a Hundred Martyrs . . . . . . . . . 266
73 A Service in Both Worlds . . . . . . . . . . . . . . . . . 273
74 Be of Those Who are Grateful . . . . . . . . . . . . . 275

**Section Eleven: The Promise of Divine Assistance**

75 Steps in Spiritual Problem-Solving . . . . . . . . . . 278
76 Read This Tablet with Absolute Sincerity . . . . . 283
77 The Promise of Divine Assistance . . . . . . . . . . . 288
78 The Merciful, the Compassionate . . . . . . . . . . 297
79 The Lord of All the Worlds . . . . . . . . . . . . . . . 299
80 Epilogue: O Aḥmad! . . . . . . . . . . . . . . . . . . . . 302

*Bibliography* . . . . . . . . . . . . . . . . . . . . . . . . . . . . . 305
*Notes and References* . . . . . . . . . . . . . . . . . . . . . 308

This book is dedicated
in loving memory
of my father
David H. Gurinsky, PhD

# Acknowledgements

My beloved husband, shortly after becoming a Bahá'í in the early 1970s, became intensely interested in the Tablet of Aḥmad and began chanting, studying and researching it following a deepening given by Hand of the Cause Zirkrullah Khadem. Over the years, many of the friends contributed to Richard's understanding of the Tablet of Aḥmad and therefore to the writing of this book. As he neared the completion of the book he talked to me about how he might write the acknowledgement. Unfortunately, a few months after he sent the book to be published he passed away unexpectedly before the acknowledgement could be written. I am left without knowledge of all the wonderful people Richard consulted during the process of writing the book. Please know that our heartfelt thanks go out to each of you who shared your time and insights and provided help to Richard as he composed this book.

However, in the last two and half years that Richard and I worked together diligently on his book, there were people who provided assistance who I feel Richard would have wanted acknowledged. Those friends are Brent Poirier, Dr Khazeh Fananapazir, Jack McCants, and Bobby Mitchell, without whose love, encouragement and assistance Richard often told me, his book would have been difficult to finish. I believe that Richard, who loved his children very much, would have wanted them to be acknowledged in his book. They are Elissa Gurinsky Chavez, Kevin Gurinksy, Samara Gurinsky Barbeux, and David Gurinsky. I wish also to acknowledge the contribution of Wendi Momen of George Ronald Publisher, and Dr Todd Lawson, who worked on the book after Richard's untimely passing. As a result of these friends' efforts, Richard's book is not just a deepening on the Tablet of Ahmad but a loving and beautifully written education of the Faith.

I am also grateful to the National Spiritual Assembly of the Bahá'ís of the United States for permission to quote the article 'A Flame of Fire – The Story of the Tablet of Aḥmad' by A. Q. Faizi from *Bahá'í News* and to the late Mr Adib Taherzadeh for permission to quote from *The Revelation of Bahá'u'lláh*, vol. 2.

I am reminded that there is a singular acknowledgement which cannot be omitted and this is Richard's love for Bahá'u'lláh and service to His cause. As you read the book, this loving dedication to the changeless cause of God will show forth.

Linda Gurinsky
June 2000

# Introduction

This is a remarkable study of one of the best loved prayers of Bahá'u'lláh. It is remarkable because it seems to be the first attempt at a line by line commentary on the text of a prayer that is not only much loved but also held by Bahá'ís to have a special power or efficacy. The late author of the work at hand, it seems, was the only person who saw the importance of such a detailed and intensive study. This work is remarkable also, and more importantly, because of the many insights into the prayer that are brought forth during the course of it. In many cases these comments, explanations and contextualizations have an uncanny authority about them, uncanny because the author apparently had no knowledge of Arabic, the language in which the prayer was revealed. This excellent discussion of the Tablet of Aḥmad also draws our attention to the importance of the Guardian's exhortations to the Bahá'ís about the study of Islam:

> [The Bahá'ís] must strive to obtain, from sources that are authoritative and unbiased, a sound knowledge of the history and tenets of Islám – the source and background of their Faith – and approach reverently and with a mind purged from preconceived ideas the study of the Qur'án which, apart from the sacred scriptures of the Bábí and Bahá'í Revelations, constitutes the only Book which can be regarded as an absolutely authenticated Repository of the Word of God. They must devote special attention to the investigation of those institutions and circumstances that are directly connected with the origin and birth of their Faith, with the station claimed by its Forerunner, and with the laws revealed by its Author.[1]

Because Islam is such a vast complex of historical, political, religious and linguistic – that is to say, cultural – phenomena, it may help us in our pursuit of this goal to recognize several distinct but interrelated streams of influence. First, of course, is the Qur'án itself, a book that has had incalculable influence not only on world history and literature but also on the Bahá'í Faith. One may also use the more inclusive category of scripture so that the nearly equally important corpus of Islamic Tradition (*ḥadíth/akhbár*) be included. Within this category we may choose to study more fully and in greater depth those passages in the Tablet of Aḥmad that are either direct quotations or slight variations of Quranic verses and material from the Ḥadíth.

The second major stream of influence for a study of the relationship between the Bahá'í Faith and Islam would be the distinctive history, from genesis through all its developments, of Shí'í Islam. Here, those passages touching upon the fulfilment of prophecy and martyrdom are particularly germane. Of course, it goes without saying that in order to appreciate this minor tradition one must acquire some familiarity with the major tradition of Islam as such, as suggested in the above quotation from Shoghi Effendi. In this connection, the interested student may wish to pursue a private study of such categories as prophethood, revelation and even history as these are understood within the greater Islamic tradition.

The third stream of influence important in the study of the Tablet of Aḥmad is Sufism or Islamic mysticism. This tradition is invoked in the distinctive vocabulary of the Tablet of Aḥmad, especially with the image of 'detachment', 'wine', 'manifestation, the word 'Nightingale' and the various allusions to certain phrases mentioned by Richard Gurinsky in his text especially esteemed within the Sufi tradition such as 'we all come from God and unto Him do we return'; which, while originally a Quranic verse, was nonetheless taken up by the Sufis as a formula, much like a mantra, to be chanted repeatedly in the quest of purification and attainment.

At chapter 5, for example, he has drawn our attention to the Quranic references in the Tablet of Aḥmad (e.g. 'in which the wisdom of every command is tested'). But the notion of 'reference' here is much too pallid a concept. It must always be held in mind that the sacred literature of Islam is more akin to a sacred person than a text as usually understood in the West. The Qur'án is more like a being than a thing. Indeed, this is brought out in the frequently cited analogy between Islam and Christianity in which the Qur'án is likened not to the Gospels but to Jesus in order to underline the particular mood of Islamic piety. Thus reading the sacred scriptures of Islam is to partake of something quite beyond a mere textual reality. It follows that any allusions to the text, particularly in such a context as a prayer, is meant to convey much more than mere familiarity or knowledge of the scripture: it is intended to invoke the divine reality carried by the scripture and to allow the reader to participate in such a reality to however limited a degree. As is well known, the Bahá'í sacred writings are radiated with Quranic verses and Traditions. It was the deft and compelling manner in which the sacred literature of Islam was honoured by the Báb and Bahá'u'lláh (and later 'Abdu'l-Bahá and Shoghi Effendi) that in fact attracted many to the new Faith. So, for example, when in the Tablet of Aḥmad it is promised 'God hath ordained for the one who chants it, the reward of a hundred martyrs', the vocabulary employed here is directly related to the Islamic theophany of the Qur'án through the use of the Arabic word *qara*, 'to intone', which is, in fact, widely recognized in Islam as the first idea to be revealed in the Qur'án (a word derived from it) in the form of the imperative verb 'Recite!' (*iqra'*, cf. Qur'án 98:1). Its use may stimulate to life in the mind of the listener the idea of a new revelation.

But a more unmistakable claim for such a revelation is found in the explicit designation of the Báb as 'King of the Messengers' (where the Báb's station is identified with the divine in the word Sulṭán) and the Bayán as the Mother Book. In addition to the commentary offered at chapter 44, it is important for readers to know that the Quranic term Mother Book (*umm al-kitáb*, Qur'án 3:7; 13:39; 43:4) has a special significance in the Islamic tradition. The Qur'án as we have it in book form is held to be a reflection or version of the archetypal and transcendent textual Source that is beyond the ability of humans to access. This Mother Book has never come to earth, has never been revealed to humankind in its completeness. So when Bahá'u'lláh designates the Báb's revelation as the Mother Book, He is making a very dramatic and perhaps shocking claim: not only was the Báb a divine messenger like Moses, Jesus and Muḥammad, but He ranks above them as their Sulṭán, their 'King' (cf. the use of the same word in the opening of the Tablet: 'He is King, the All-Knowing, the Wise' and Gurinsky's persuasive, lucid and penetrating commentary on this in chapters 6, 7 and 21). And not only are His writings sacred revelation but they are in fact none other than that heretofore unapproachable Source known to Muslims as the Umm al-Kitáb. The important paradox here is that even though the Báb's writings seem to have come last in a long chronological chain of dispensations, in reality these same writings are in fact *the* Source for all other revelations that have come before and thus have a priority over them that perhaps transcends our current notions of time and history.

From the point of view of religious history, the claim of Bahá'u'lláh to be the Promised One of all religions is intimately connected to and conditioned by the strong messianic theme in Shí'ism. As the Guardian has said in his introduction to *God Passes By*, the history of the Bahá'í Faith is essentially a history of the transformation of 'a heterodox and seemingly negligible offshoot of the Shaykhí school of the Ithná-'Asharíyyih sect of Shí'ah Islám into a world religion . . .'[2] From this viewpoint, Shí'í messianism may be thought to have been universalized by Bahá'u'lláh's Revelation. This is not to suggest that there is no messianism in Sunní Islam. But by comparison, the Shí'í tradition may be seen as a special tradition devoted to the expression and exploration of the timeless religious motif of messianism. Thus when in the Tablet of Aḥmad Bahá'u'lláh speaks of 'that Most Great Beauty foretold in the Books of the Messengers', the distinctively Shí'í interpretation of Islam would appear to scholars to have been invoked.

Both logically and paradoxically, such a fulfilment of expectation depends for its fruition upon concealment. So, just as messianism and the appearance of the Promised One has been a continuously contemplated and hoped-for event in Shí'í Islam, it has been influential on the historical plane – in the development of specifically Shí'í theology in tandem with its partner concept, concealment or absence. In the Shí'í world this absence has acquired enormous importance and its own distinctive terminology. So when Bahá'u'lláh refers to His own absence (*ghaybatí*), He is aware of the power the word will have upon His predominately Shí'í audience. Thus in addition to the extremely valuable textual analysis or practical reading given by Richard Gurinsky in chapter 56, it is important that the reader know that the Arabic words 'my absence' (ghaybatí) are destined to resonate with a reader from the Iranian Shí'í tradition in a particularly profound and powerful way. The words cause an immediate association with the tragic history of Shí'ism and the persecution of the Imáms, which eventually resulted in the last one having to remain hidden and separated from his passionately devoted community. Absence here also suggests its opposite: manifestation, fulfilment. Thus Bahá'u'lláh seamlessly appropriates the religious ethos and verve of an entire history and culture with the use of a single word.

The period between concealment and manifestation in Shí'ism is the period of expectation or waiting for the Hidden Imám to appear. As such this period has a special status: the community of the Shí'a are taught to endure the suffering occasioned by the absence of godly rule on earth with certain hope of the appearance of their Master. Another way of expressing 'certain hope' is the English verb 'to await' or 'to wait for'. So in Shí'ism piously awaiting the appearance of the Hidden Imam is an element of devotion and steadfastness.

Unfortunately, this waiting entails suffering so that suffering is highly esteemed in Shí'ism as a way of testifying publicly and before God to the depth of one's faith and steadfastness. The word 'martyr' (derived from a Greek word meaning 'witness') is a translation of the Arabic *shahíd*. And in the Islamic tradition, whether Shí'í or Sunní, there is no act more highly esteemed than the testimony to one's faith. The verbal formula for this testimony is of course the *shaháda* (which is also the same word for 'martyrdom') or Testimony: 'There is no god but God and Muḥammad is His Messenger' (*lá iláha illá 'lláh Muḥammadu rasúlu'lláh*). Gurinsky takes up this topic in chapter 33. Here he points out that in the Islamic tradition, living a life of obedience and devotion to Islam is also seen as a form of testifying or bearing witness to the truth of Islam. But it should be pointed out that in the Qur'án those who have died or been slain in the way of God are designated as witnesses/*shuhadá* who have born witness to the truth of their faith in the most ultimate of terms. In Shí'ism martyrdom also enjoys a special significance. This is most readily exemplified in the annual 'passion plays' or *Ta'ziyehs,* enacted throughout the world wherever Shí'í Muslims reside, in which the tragic death of Ḥusayn, the Prophet Muḥammad's grandson, is reenacted with extraordinary devotion and in the midst of audiences of men and women who welcome the opportunity to 'suffer with' (cf. the word *ta'ziyeh* – consolation) their beloved Imám and his family and small entourage when they were slaughtered by the deceitful and venal enemies who represented the claims of the Umayyad Caliph Yazíd. But note the special way these images and motifs have been presented by Bahá'u'lláh in the discussion of the 'path of God' in chapter 48 and 'witness' in Chapter 46.

With regard to the spoken formula of the shahráda, Bahá'u'lláh also invokes its power in the Tablet of Aḥmad when He says 'verily He is God and there is no God but Him'. It is certain that no Muslim hearing these words would not also supply the missing 'and Muḥammad is the Apostle of God'. Thus Bahá'u'lláh once again identifies His Cause with the sacred Cause of Islam, in effect saying: 'There is no God but God and the Báb is His Messenger, just as Muḥammad was His Messenger.'

Finally, it is important to note the references to the Islamic mystical lexicon, if not tradition, throughout the Tablet of Aḥmad. Here the ideas of 'Beauty', 'Divine Presence', 'manifestation', 'detachment', 'wine' and 'Nightingale' stand out as key terms. Sufism began, in some ways, as a reaction to what appeared to be an exaggerated emphasis on the part of official Islam on the law or the *sharí'a*: those normative practices prescribed frequently in general terms in the Qur'án but later 'fleshed out' by the legal establishment in Islamic lands. The Sufis (some of whom were also members of this legal establishment) may be identified as those persons who felt that too much emphasis was being put on the letter of the law and not enough on its spirit. In time, Sufism would become the predominant feature of Islam, especially after the 13th century, when Muslims began to establish distinct Sufi orders throughout Islamdom in order to compensate for the clear and heartbreaking failure of the official Caliphate to meet the needs of the people and to protect them from destructive forces, most recently in the form of the Mongol invasions. In the process of this social and political development mystical writings and poetry would acquire a wider and wider audience. It is now that Shí'ism begins to express itself through a lexicon of more or less agreed upon mystical technical terminology amongst which the most important, not only for a study of the 'genetic code' of the Bahá'í Faith but also for Islam itself, are precisely such words and ideas as 'presence' and 'manifestation'. It is Sufism that insisted upon the necessity of love for a full understanding of the law. It is Sufism that insisted upon 'intuition' or mystical knowledge '*'irfán*' as an unerring guide to Truth. This terminology was employed by Shí'í theologians to speak of love for the Imám and knowledge of the Imám. Thus the words 'Thou hast created me to know Thee and to worship Thee' in the Short Obligatory Prayer have an important and essential history that Bahá'ís have been taught by Shoghi Effendi to study in order that they might better understand more fully the significance of the Bahá'í Revelation. There is no space here to go into these and other traces of Islamic mysticism. Interested readers are invited to consult such standard reference works as the *Encyclopedia of Religion* or the *Encyclopedia of Islam* in order to begin a study of the intimate and profound connection between the Bahá'í Faith and Sufism.

Richard Gurinsky, as a result of his deep devotion and profound spirituality, has offered us in the form of the present book, a firm foundation for the further exploration of the connections between the Faith and Islam. There are places in the text, however, where the lack of familiarity with the Arabic leads our author to conclusions that may be thought erroneous. In chapter 7, in his discussion of the Nightingale of Paradise, he rightly points out that the Nightingale is a symbol of sacrifice in the Islamicate poetic tradition but he does not add that the actual Arabic word, translated by the Guardian as 'nightingale', is in reality the word for dove or pigeon (*warqa*). As far as I know, the theme of sacrifice has not been associated with this species; rather the soothing cooing of the dove is the important element to be kept in mind here, together with the standard topos of the dove as a symbol of the soul. It would be churlish, however, to say that the reading offered by Richard here was 'wrong'. Certainly the motif of sacrifice for divine beauty is one of the guiding metaphors of the Bahá'í ethos. Spiritual insight appears to be independent of the dictionary rather than coterminous with it.

Unfamiliarity with the Islamic religious tradition may also be behind the somewhat problematic identification of 'the believers in the Divine Unity' (*al-muwaḥḥidún*) with the Bábís. As such, this may be thought a specious identification because the quality of perfectly affirming simultaneously immanent and transcendent Divine Unity has been a religious desideratum of Islam from a very early period. Frequently the term *muwaḥḥid*, 'affirmer or believer in the Divine Unity' has been adopted by religious reformers who by using it are implying that others who call themselves Muslim may not be fully and correctly Muslim (cf. for example the famous 'Wahhábi' movement of the 18th century. They were know as Wahhábiya only from the outside, as it were. They thought of themselves precisely as the 'Believers in Divine Unity', *al-muwaḥḥidún*). Clearly, as divine unity is such a cardinal element of the Islamic tradition, no Muslim would ever willingly classify himself as anything but a 'believer in the Divine Unity'.

But these very minor points do not obscure the real value the present work has for those interested in the 'compositions' of Bahá'í. Our author would be amongst the first to disclaim for his work completeness or thoroughness. But in the absence of such an unattainable ideal, *Learn Well this Tablet* will repay many times over the effort made to engage with the astonishing depth of its interpretations, readings and insights. One word of warning to close with: the Tablet of Aḥmad is simultaneously dependent on and independent of the Islamic tradition. The various streams or seams of cultural and historical content which our author draws to our attention should not lead us to conclude that the Tablet of Aḥmad does not have a proper audience outside of the Islamicate realm. The most dramatic demonstration of this assertion is obviously the book itself. It is the work of someone born into an non-Islamicate culture, unschooled in the religion of Islam or its major languages. Yet the author has demonstrated that this prayer properly belongs to the world, showing that within the body of the Islamic vocabulary and presuppositions, the heart that beats is first and foremost a human one.

Todd Lawson<br>Montreal<br>May 2000

## *Section 1: The Story of Aḥmad*

# 1

# The Story of Aḥmad

Mírzá Aḥmad Yazdí was born around 1805 in the city of Yazd, Persia, to a very wealthy and influential family. Early in his youth he developed a passion for mysticism, which quickly became the dominating force of his life. His goal, the intense yearning of his heart, was to find the Qá'im, the Promised One of Islam. While he was still an adolescent Aḥmad began to practise a rigorous discipline of fasting and prayers and even secluded himself from friends and family. This led to a serious clash of wills with his family, who strongly objected to his ascetic lifestyle. Refusing to be thwarted in his spiritual search, Aḥmad decided to leave home. Early one morning he packed some of his clothes, pretended to go to the public bath and set off on his own.

He had been told that there were men who claimed to know special prayers which, if repeated many times, were supposed to guide the devotee to his heart's desire. Dressed as a dervish, Aḥmad travelled from village to village looking for a spiritual guru who would guide him on the path of truth and share his secret desire. He was so eager to reach his goal that whenever anyone recommended a new prayer or ritual for him to follow, he would carry it out with devotion and zeal. But none of these practices brought him any closer to the object of his quest.

Aḥmad gave up searching in Persia and set out for India, the land of mystics, eventually settling in Bombay. Continuing his quest, he was told that if he washed himself, dressed in absolutely clean clothes, prostrated himself and repeated the Quranic verse 'There is no God but God' twelve thousand times, he was sure to be guided to his Beloved. Aḥmad was so sincere and eager to find the Qá'im that he did this not once but several times. Yet he found nothing, the goal of his life went unfulfilled and he became disillusioned. None of the many mystics he had met had been able to guide him to his heart's desire.

Abandoning his quest, Aḥmad returned to Persia, settling in Ká<u>sh</u>án. Here he married and started his own business as a cloth-maker, soon becoming a very successful businessman. But the desire to find the Qá'im still burned strongly in his heart.

Most of what we know about Aḥmad's life is drawn from the record of his spoken chronicle. His story continues in his own words:

> Some time passed, and the news of the Báb from <u>Sh</u>íráz reached many areas including Ká<u>sh</u>án. A strong urge was created in me to investigate this message. I made enquiries through every channel, until one day I met a traveller in the caravanserai. When I enquired of him, he said 'If you are a seeker of truth proceed to Ma<u>sh</u>had where you may visit a certain Mullá 'Abdu'l-<u>Kh</u>áliq-i-Yazdí who can help you in your investigations.'
>
> After hearing this, I set off on my journey early next day. I walked all the way to Ṭihrán and from there to Ma<u>sh</u>had. [The distance between Ká<u>sh</u>án and Ma<u>sh</u>had is approximately 500 miles.] However, upon arrival I became ill and had to convalesce for two months in that city. On recovering, I called at the home of Mullá 'Abdu'l-<u>Kh</u>áliq . . .[3]

When I reached the house, I knocked at the door and the servant of the house came forth. Holding the door ajar, he asked me, 'What do you want?' 'I must see your Master,' I answered. The man went back into the house and then the Mullá himself came out. He admitted me to his house and when we stood face to face I explained to him all that had happened to me. When I finished, he at once grasped my arm and told me, 'Do not say such things here!' and he pushed me out of his house. There was no end to my sorrows. Heartbroken and utterly astounded I said to myself, 'Are all my efforts in vain? To whom shall I turn? Whom shall I approach? . . . But I will never leave this man. I will persist till such time as he will open his heart to me and will guide me to the right path of God. It is incumbent upon the one who searches to drain the bitter cup of hardship.' The next morning I was at the door of the same house. I knocked harder than the previous day. This time the Mullá himself came to the door and the moment he opened it, I said, 'I will not go away. I will not leave you until you tell me the whole truth.' This time he found me earnest and true. He became sure that I had not been at his door to spy or cause difficulties for him and his friends.[4]

. . . he then told me to meet him that night in the mosque of Gawhar-Shád where he would put me in touch with someone who could tell me the whole truth.

I went to the mosque in the evening, but after attending the prayers and listening to him preach, I lost him because of the crowds. The next morning, I arrived at his house and explained what had happened. He instructed me to go to the mosque of Pír-Zan that evening and promised that he would send someone there to meet me and take me to the appointed place. Guided by the man who met me in the mosque, after walking some distance I passed through a corridor into the courtyard of a house and went upstairs into a room. I saw a venerable figure who occupied the seat of honour. Mullá 'Abdu'l-Kháliq, who was standing at the door, intimated to me that this great man was the one he wanted me to meet. This was no less a person than Mullá Ṣádiq-i-Khurásání.[5]

After attending a few meetings I was enabled to recognize and acknowledge the truth of the Message of the Báb. Afterwards, Mullá Ṣádiq instructed me to return to my wife and family in Káshán and resume my work. He also advised me not to teach the Faith unless I found a hearing ear.[6]

> When I reached Káshán, everyone asked what had happened that I had left everything so abruptly. I told them: 'My longing for pilgrimage was too great to resist, and I was right.' What else could take me away from my work, my house and my family except that innermost yearning? The instant I heard these words from the traveller there was no more patience left in me.[7]

Aḥmad settled down again in Ká<u>sh</u>án. He soon discovered another believer, Ḥájí Mírzá Jání, who was the first person in Ká<u>sh</u>án to accept the Báb. The two shared many joyous hours together.

The rapid spread of the Faith of the Báb was causing an uproar throughout Persia. The authorities, fearful of the Báb's rising influence, held Him under house arrest. The government then ordered that the Báb be brought to the capital city of Ṭihrán. The route passed through Ká<u>sh</u>án. Ḥájí Mírzá Jání, who was an influential merchant, paid a large sum of money to the guards who were escorting the Báb to permit him to host the Báb in his own home. Aḥmad was invited to Ḥájí Mírzá Jání's home to meet the Báb. A few mullás were also there to question Him:

> One of the Mullás faced the Báb and said, 'We have heard that a certain young man in <u>Sh</u>íráz has claimed to be the Báb. Is it true?' 'Yes,' answered the Báb. 'And does he reveal verses, too?' said the same man. The Báb responded, 'And We reveal verses, too.'
>
> Aḥmad has further said: 'This clear and courageous answer was sufficient for anyone who had ears to hear and eyes to see and find the whole truth immediately. His beautiful face and His powerful words and presence sufficed all things. But when they served tea and a cup was offered to the Báb, He immediately took it, called the servant of the same Mullá and very graciously gave it to him. The day after, the very same humble servant came to me and with great sorrow deplored the stupidity of his

> master. A little explanation as to the station of the Báb brought him to our fold and our number grew to be three.[8]

The Báb was imprisoned for the remainder of His ministry. Because the clerics and the authorities were unable to stop the spread of His Faith, they ordered that He be put to death. On 9 July 1850 the Báb was executed. Two and a half years later, the government, now fearful of the influence of Bahá'u-'lláh, exiled Him to Baghdád.

As the years passed the number of believers in Káshán grew and with growth came persecution. The clerics of the city incited the local people to attack and plunder the homes of the Bábís. Aḥmad, too, came under attack:

> One day, a number of ruffians attacked the believers and took all our possessions, they even broke all doors and windows. I hid myself in the wind tower [ventilation shaft] of the house and remained there for forty days. The friends brought me food and water in secret.
>
> Since it became difficult to live in Káshán, I set off for Baghdád. It was about five years since Bahá'u'lláh had taken up residence in that city. On the way, I met a stranger who was also travelling. Both of us indicated that our destination was Karbilá. Throughout the journey we conducted ourselves as Muslims and prayed according to Muslim rites. On our arrival in Baghdád, I walked in the direction of the house of Bahá'u'lláh. I found that my friend was also going in the same direction, and soon I discovered that he was also a Bábí! We had both dissimulated our faith.
>
> After being admitted to the house of Bahá'u'lláh, I attained His presence.[9]

Those who were admitted into the presence of Bahá'u'lláh often reported that they were overwhelmed by His majesty and glory. Aḥmad was no exception. He says that Bahá'u'lláh brought him to his senses with a humorous remark: 'He turned to me and said "What a man! He becomes a Bábí and then goes and hides in the wind tower!"'[10]

'Forget not My bounties,' Bahá'u'lláh later wrote to Aḥmad in his now famous Tablet. Having spent 25 years searching and in deprivation, Aḥmad now enjoyed the immeasurable bounty of living in close proximity to his Lord, the supreme Manifestation of God. Bahá'u'lláh showered His infinite love and tender care on the sincere and devoted Aḥmad:

> I remained in Baghdád for six years and worked as a hand-weaver. During this period my soul was bountifully nourished from His glorious presence and I had the great honour to live in the outer apartment of His blessed house.[11]

> How innumerable, how great and how immensely mighty were the events of those years. Our nights were filled with memorable episodes. Joyful and at times sorrowful were our experiences, yet beyond the power of anyone to describe. For example one day as the Blessed Beauty was walking, a certain government officer approached Him and reported that one of His followers had been killed and his body thrown on the river bank. The Tongue of Power and Might replied, 'No one has killed him. Through seventy thousand veils of light We showed him the glory of God to an extent smaller than a needle's eye; therefore, he could not more bear the burden of his life and has offered himself as a sacrifice.'[12]

Speaking of those glorious days in Baghdád, the historian Nabíl, who was also one of the companions of Bahá'u'lláh during those years, exclaimed, 'O, for the joy of those days . . .'[13] Another man who met Aḥmad reports that the bounties Aḥmad received from Bahá'u'lláh went far beyond merely being in His presence and living next to Him:

> He became the recipient of [Bahá'u'lláh's] bounties and favours. Once he told me that he had beheld the innermost Beauty of the Blessed Perfection. He was speaking the truth, because he had a Tablet in the handwriting of Bahá'u'lláh

> which testified that Aḥmad had gazed upon His hidden Beauty.[14]

Aḥmad continued to enjoy the inestimable bounty of being in the presence of his Lord until Bahá'u'lláh's banishment to Constantinople in April of 1863. Although Aḥmad begged Bahá'u'lláh to be permitted to go with Him, Bahá'u'lláh did not choose to take Aḥmad with Him on this new exile. To his great sorrow, Aḥmad was among those whom Bahá'u'lláh asked to remain behind in Ba<u>gh</u>dád:

> . . . I was basking in the sunshine of Bahá'u'lláh's presence until the Sulṭán's decree for Bahá'u'lláh's departure to Constantinople was communicated. It was thirty-one days after Naw-Rúz that the Blessed Beauty went to the Garden of Najíb Pá<u>sh</u>á. [This garden is now known as the Garden of Riḍván. It was there that Bahá'u'lláh declared to His family and close companions that He was the Promised One of God.] On that day the river overflowed and they had to open the lock gates to ease the situation. On the ninth day the flooding subsided and Bahá'u'lláh's family left the house in Ba<u>gh</u>dád and went to the Garden. Immediately after their crossing, however, the river began to swell again and the lock gates had to be re-opened. On the twelfth day Bahá'u'lláh left for Constantinople. Some of the believers accompanied Him and some including this servant had to remain in Ba<u>gh</u>dád. At the time of His departure, all of us were together in the Garden. Those who were to remain behind were standing on one side. His blessed Person came to us and spoke words of consolation to us. He said that it was better that we remain behind. He also said that He had allowed some to accompany Him, merely to prevent them from making mischief and creating trouble.
>
> One of the friends recited the following poem of Sa'dí in a voice filled with emotion and deep sorrow:
>
> 'Let us shed tears as clouds pour down in the spring;
> Even the stones wail when lovers part.'

> Bahá'u'lláh responded, 'These words were truly meant for today.'[15]

Aḥmad remained in Bag͟hdád, comforting the friends and teaching the newly declared Cause of God with great devotion. But separation from his Lord proved too much for him to bear. After a few years he left Bag͟hdád with the intention of visiting Bahá'u'lláh, who had been banished again. After less than four months in Constantinople, Bahá'u'lláh had been sent by the government to the city of Adrianople, in the northwest corner of the Ottoman empire. When Aḥmad reached Constantinople en route to Adrianople, he received the Tablet in Arabic from Bahá'u'lláh now known as the Tablet of Aḥmad. In the final, untranslated, paragraph of this Tablet, Bahá'u'lláh intimates to Aḥmad that he should return to Bag͟hdád. Aḥmad recounts his response to this precious Tablet:

> I received the Tablet of 'The Nightingale of Paradise' and reading it again and again, I found out that my Beloved desired me to go and teach His Cause. Therefore I preferred obedience to visiting Him.[16]

Aḥmad, ever faithful to his Lord, returned to Persia without visiting Bahá'u'lláh and began teaching the Bábí families the truth of Bahá'u'lláh's claim to be the Promised One of the Báb, 'Him Whom God shall make manifest'. He travelled throughout Persia, dedicating himself to the teaching work. Through his persistent efforts many Bábís were enabled to recognize the station of Bahá'u'lláh and became strong Bahá'ís. Aḥmad's life is a shining example of sacrifice and devotion. Hand of the Cause Mr Faizi extols him in these words:

> Aḥmad became the embodiment of his own Tablet. Such persistence, undaunted spirit, tenacity and steadfastness as his are hardly to be found in any annals of the Cause.[17]

His was not an easy task. In addition to the hardships of travelling on foot, Aḥmad often faced the scepticism of the Bábís. Sometimes he was even confronted by outright hostility:

> I left Ṭihrán for Khurásán and spoke to many concerning the advent of 'Him Whom God shall make manifest'. I went to Furúgh [a city in the province of Khurásán] in the garb of a dervish, and spoke about 'Him Whom God shall make manifest' to Mullá Mírzá Muḥammad and his brothers. In the course of our discussions they became aggressive and fiercely assaulted me. In the struggle which ensued they broke my tooth. When the fighting had stopped and emotions subsided, I resumed the discussion, saying that the Báb had specifically mentioned that 'Him Whom God shall make manifest' would appear by the name of Bahá. They promised to accept the claims of Bahá'u'lláh should I be able to verify my statement. I asked them to bring the Writings of the Báb to me. They made an opening in the wall and took out all the Writings which were hidden for fear of the enemy.[18] As soon as I opened one of them, we found a passage which indicated that 'He Whom God shall make manifest' would bear the name of Bahá. They happily embraced the Faith of Bahá'u'lláh and I left them and travelled to other towns.[19]

These brothers became distinguished Bahá'ís and were staunch defenders of the infant Cause of God.

Aḥmad continued teaching throughout the province of Khurásán. He then decided to return to Baghdád to teach but on the way he became sick and had to abandon the journey. While in Ṭihrán, he was recognized by some of the mullás from Káshán, who alerted the authorities to the presence of the 'Bábí' in their city. Aḥmad was arrested. The young officer who was put in charge of the case insisted that Aḥmad recant his Faith. Aḥmad recalls:

> At that moment I was at the height of my faith and enthusiasm and never for one moment even thought of recanting.[20]

Aḥmad insisted that he was not a Bábí but a Bahá'í. He was imprisoned but during his incarceration the officer's wife suddenly fell seriously ill. The officer became extremely frightened and promised Aḥmad that if his wife recovered he would set Aḥmad free. Three days later he fulfilled his promise. Disregarding the possible consequences to himself, he escorted Aḥmad to the city gate and released him.

Once freed, Aḥmad continued teaching and travelling through the villages of Persia and eventually settled in the province of Fars in southern Persia, where he lived for nearly 25 years. His simple home became a haven for travelling teachers who visited the region.

Aḥmad lived a very long life and was always of service to whoever needed help or assistance. An account of his later years relates:

> . . . he used to carry with him the original Tablet which is in the handwriting of the Blessed Beauty . . . He was a very simple man, pure and truthful . . . He was ninety-six years of age when he arrived at Munj, but was in the utmost health and vigour. He spent most of his time in reading the Holy Writings, especially his own Tablet which he chanted very often.[21]

Aḥmad's wife had died many years earlier. He had a married daughter living in Ṭihrán who was very anxious to have her father come and stay with her but apparently he was not enthusiastic about going. In spite of her letters to him and to the friends in the area, it took years and a recurrence of persecution against the Bahá'ís before Aḥmad finally agreed to be taken to Ṭihrán.

> . . . the waves of persecution spread all over Persia, the friends in their love and admiration for Aḥmad endeavoured to protect him against fatal attacks and after long consultations, they suggested to him that he immediately leave that

> forlorn and forsaken corner of the country for a more populated centre. Wherever Aḥmad went, the friends suggested the same thing to him. He was so well known . . . that his mere presence would cause agitation amongst the bigoted Muslims . . . After changing many places of residence many times, he settled in Ṭihrán . . . After having lived one century always enjoying good health, he passed on to the presence of his Beloved in 1905 in Ṭihrán.[22]

Near the end of his life Aḥmad entrusted his Tablet to his grandson Jamál. Jamál was a devoted Bahá'í and he later gave the original Tablet to the Trustee of the Ḥuqúqu'lláh. Shoghi Effendi, the Guardian of the Faith, sent this original Tablet as a gift to the archives of the Bahá'ís of the United States on the occasion of the Intercontinental Conference of 1953.

## 2

# Prologue: O Aḥmad!

As we have seen, Hand of the Cause Mr Faizi provided an important insight into the life of Aḥmad:

> Aḥmad became the embodiment of his own Tablet. Such persistence, undaunted spirit, tenacity and steadfastness as his are hardly to be found in any annals of the Cause.[23]

Aḥmad's life and these outstanding qualities make Aḥmad a very special individual and an example to all Bahá'ís, most importantly, perhaps, because Aḥmad chose to respond to Bahá'u'lláh's call to him in this Tablet. The Guardian is reported to have said that making choices is a quality of one's soul.[24] If this is true, then choosing to accept Bahá'u'lláh, choosing to turn one's heart and mind to Him, choosing to be obedient to the laws and teachings and choosing to arise and serve the Cause of God are all prime examples of the exercise and development of this quality of the soul. We note that in the Tablet of Aḥmad Bahá'u'lláh counsels us, 'whosoever desireth let him choose the path to his Lord'.

From the account of Aḥmad's life we know that he chose, at an early age, to dedicate his life to searching for the Promised One. He chose never to give up his search in spite of all the setbacks, disappointments and hardships he experienced. When, after a quarter of a century of search, he finally learned of the Promised One, Aḥmad chose to accept the Báb. He then chose to teach the Cause of the Báb. Later Aḥmad chose to visit Bahá'u'lláh in Baghdád. He chose to accept Bahá'u'lláh as his Lord even before Bahá'u'lláh had declared His station publicly. Aḥmad then chose to obey Bahá'u'lláh and remain behind in Baghdád when Bahá'u'lláh was exiled to Constantinople. When his heart could no longer stand being separated from Bahá'u'lláh, Aḥmad decided to visit Him in Adrianople. En route, Aḥmad received this Tablet from Bahá'u'lláh and chose to read it over and over again. Aḥmad reports that once he found out what Bahá'u'lláh's purpose was in sending him the Tablet and what Bahá'u'lláh desired of him, he chose to be obedient to the instructions he was given. Rather than completing his journey to visit Bahá'u'lláh, Aḥmad travelled to Persia to teach Bahá'u'lláh's Cause to the Bábís. After arriving in Persia, Aḥmad chose to spend his life travelling and teaching the Cause of Bahá'u'lláh. It is not easy to find another record of such a faithful, dedicated believer who wanted so ardently to be with his Lord, who so willingly gave it up to serve the Cause and who was happy and content to do so.

We may infer that it was through the choices that he made that Aḥmad became the embodiment of his own Tablet. Mr Faizi mentions Aḥmad's persistence, his undaunted spirit, his tenacity and his steadfastness. Aḥmad chose to persist, both in his search for the Promised One and in his teaching efforts. His undaunted spirit illustrates his attitude towards life, which was a conscious choice on his part. His tenacity and steadfastness also demonstrate Aḥmad's choice to be faithful to Bahá'u'lláh and to be tenacious in serving His Cause.

All of these characteristics, taken together, describe a person of true heroism. In this sense, the life of Aḥmad mirrors that of characters in heroic literature. In such stories, the hero undertakes a quest of epic proportions. To accomplish his quest, he must embark upon a journey, fraught with obstacles and hardships. He encounters difficulties which overwhelm him and he is nearly defeated in his quest. Somehow, reaching deep into himself, he finds the strength and courage to continue, in spite of the impossible odds against him. By reaching into himself for what may be his last effort, the hero attains victory over himself and over all the forces that oppose him. In so doing the hero is enabled to achieve the object of his quest. In some stories the hero unlocks a secret mystery which was hidden and had been unattainable in past ages. The result of his heroism is often that he paves the way for others to attain goodness, to find the path of true happiness and to be blessed for the rest of their lives.

When we study the life of Aḥmad, we find that his life exemplifies this heroic pattern. What, may we ask, is the blessing that he has conferred upon the rest of us?

There may be many answers to this question. Perhaps Aḥmad unlocked the spiritual potency of the Tablet. By choosing to become the embodiment of his own Tablet, Aḥmad may have opened the spiritual bounties that Bahá'u-'lláh enshrined within it. By responding to Bahá'u'lláh's call in this Tablet and by demonstrating that it could be done, Aḥmad's heroism and virtues may have released the floodgates of blessings which continuously pour out upon every believer who turns his heart to Bahá'u'lláh and recites the Tablet of Aḥmad with sincerity. By the example of his own life, Aḥmad has shown us that these divine bounties, which Bahá'u'lláh promises to us in this Tablet, are available in abundance to everyone who believes and who asks Bahá'u'lláh to receive His bounties. As Christ exhorted us, 'Ask, and ye shall receive.' And as Bahá'u'lláh counsels us in the Tablet of Aḥmad, 'Forget not My bounties . . . These favours have We bestowed upon thee as a bounty on Our part and a mercy from Our presence, that thou mayest be of those who are grateful.'

We may conclude that it is the example of Aḥmad's life which has paved the way for all of us who have followed him. Each of us, to the best of our abilities, can 'Learn well this Tablet', can choose to respond to Bahá'u'lláh's call to us and can choose the path of obedience and service to our Lord.

# 3

# Arise and Teach the Cause of God: Bahá'u'lláh's Call in the Tablet of Aḥmad

Bahá'u'lláh revealed the Tablet of Aḥmad a year or two after His arrival in Adrianople and some two years after His declaration that He was the One promised by the Báb. At the time, most of the Báb's followers in Persia were unaware of the claim of Bahá'u'lláh. In addition, the enemies of Bahá'u'lláh were spreading falsehoods throughout the Bábí community that Azal, the half-brother of Bahá'u'lláh, was the real successor of the Báb and that Bahá'u'lláh was an impostor. Consequently, there was great confusion within the Bábí community in Persia as to who was the true successor of the Báb.

During this early period of His exile in Adrianople, Bahá'u'lláh sent several of His trusted disciples back to Persia to teach the Bábís the truth about His claim to be the One who was promised by the Báb.[25] Aḥmad was one of these chosen teachers. Aḥmad reports that when he received this Tablet, he read it many times and 'found out that my Beloved desired me to go and teach His Cause'.[26] Instead of continuing on his journey to visit Bahá'u'lláh in Adrianople, he walked back to Persia and immediately began travelling around the country teaching the Bábís the truth of Bahá'u'lláh's claim.

Several features of Aḥmad's story merit our attention. Foremost among them is Aḥmad's obedience to the teaching mission Bahá'u'lláh entrusted to him. Aḥmad tells us he studied his Tablet until he discovered its purpose and once he found out what Bahá'u'lláh was calling him to do, he immediately arose to carry out the bidding of his Lord. This is even more significant considering that Aḥmad could no longer bear being separated from Bahá'u'lláh at the time he received this Tablet. Aḥmad's decision to give up his intention to visit Bahá'u'lláh and return to Persia to teach suggests that within this Tablet Bahá'u'lláh placed a great power. Such was this power that it also enabled Aḥmad to carry out his arduous teaching mission for the rest of his long life.

Another aspect of this story is Aḥmad's age and the very long distances he walked. Aḥmad was not a young man when he decided to leave Baghdád and visit Bahá'u'lláh. Since Aḥmad was born about 1805 and he received the Tablet in 1865 or thereabouts, we know that Aḥmad was about 60 years old when Bahá'u'lláh sent the Tablet to him. Aḥmad had just walked the entire distance from Baghdád to Constantinople[27] – more than 1100 miles or 1700 kilometres – when he received this Tablet. Adrianople is another 160 miles, 260 kilometres, from Constantinople. However, Aḥmad did not choose this easier path. Instead, he directed his steps to Persia. From Constantinople, Aḥmad walked another 1400 miles, 2240 kilometres, to reach his destination. Such a feat is almost unimaginable today, although, of course, it was more common in the 19th century. Yet once he arrived in Persia, Aḥmad did not rest. He continued walking around the country, teaching the Bábís.

Aḥmad arose to teach the Bábís because he responded to Bahá'u'lláh's call to him in the Tablet of Aḥmad. Bahá'u'lláh did not request that Aḥmad visit Him so that He might give Aḥmad His personal instructions. Aḥmad knew that Bahá'u'lláh had a serious purpose in sending him such a weighty Tablet. That Bahá'u'lláh sent Aḥmad this Tablet while he was travelling, rather than waiting for Aḥmad to visit Him, suggests that Bahá'u'lláh may have also been communicating a sense of urgency.

With this in mind, we may, like Aḥmad, read the Tablet many times to find those phrases and words which indicate Bahá'u'lláh's purpose. The more we do this, the clearer it becomes that much of the Tablet of Aḥmad may be viewed as a call to teach and that one of its major themes, therefore, is teaching the Cause of God.

We also see that it was Aḥmad's obedience to Bahá'u'lláh's call to him in this Tablet that makes Aḥmad's life and his service to the Cause of God so memorable and noteworthy. In another Tablet Bahá'u'lláh declares, 'To assist Me is to teach My Cause.'[28] The call to teach will never fade away. Bahá'u'lláh tells us that it is an eternal call. In the Tablet of Aḥmad Bahá'u'lláh admonishes each one of us in these words:

> Whosoever desireth, let him turn aside from this counsel and whosoever desireth let him choose the path to his Lord.

It was Aḥmad's choice to respond to this call of Bahá'u'lláh by arising to teach His Cause. On a personal level, then, it is up to each of us to search our hearts, to decide for ourselves what our response to Bahá'u'lláh's call will be and then to arise to carry out this service like Aḥmad, with the utmost determination, tenacity and steadfastness.

# 4

# A Special Potency and Significance

In a letter written on his behalf, Shoghi Effendi has emphasized that the Tablet of Aḥmad has been 'invested by Bahá'u'lláh with a special potency and significance':

> These daily obligatory prayers, together with a few other specific ones, such as the Healing Prayer, the Tablet of Aḥmad, have been invested by Bahá'u'lláh with a special potency and significance, and should therefore be accepted as such and be recited by the believers with unquestioned faith and confidence, that through them they may enter into a much closer communion with God, and identify themselves more fully with His Laws and precepts.[29]

Our purpose in studying the Tablet of Aḥmad, therefore, should be to help us draw closer to God and to Bahá'u'lláh and help us obey His teachings more carefully. Let us first consider what the 'special potency and significance' of this Tablet might be.

What could have caused Aḥmad to give up his deep desire to be with Bahá'u'lláh, to obey Him and to return to Baghdád? What could have so comforted his heart that he no longer felt the need to be with Bahá'u'lláh? Bahá'u'lláh intimated to Aḥmad that he should return to Baghdád – surely Bahá'u'lláh was not punishing Aḥmad because of his desire to be with Him. Accounts of other devoted believers show that Bahá'u'lláh was very willing to let them visit Him. Aḥmad's obedience, his devotion, his steadfastness and his dedication to the teaching mission Bahá'u'lláh had given to him were exceptional and we may reasonably expect that Bahá'u'lláh would have rewarded Aḥmad for this. If this was so, and Bahá'u'lláh did not invite Aḥmad to visit Him, then what was his reward?

We may infer that the spirit of love that Bahá'u'lláh placed within this Tablet is so great that it comforted Aḥmad's heart and empowered him to carry out the mission he had been given. Shoghi Effendi emphasizes that we should accept the special potency and significance of this Tablet so that we may 'enter into a much closer communion with God'. Surely Aḥmad did this. Thus we may also infer that it is the 'special potency' of this Tablet which enabled Aḥmad to more fully commune with Bahá'u'lláh and feel close to Him. It may be this special spirit that was Aḥmad's reward for his obedience and his willingness to forego his ardent desire to be with Bahá'u'lláh.

If this is so, it gives us a valuable insight into the tremendous significance of this Tablet and its implications for our own lives.

# 5

# Themes in the Tablet of Aḥmad

Through our repeated reading and study of the Tablet of Aḥmad we find that certain themes emerge and are emphasized. In the Tablet of Aḥmad these various themes seem to be interwoven throughout its verses. During one reading of this Tablet it may seem that a particular word or phrase indicates a specific theme. At a later time we may be surprised to discover that this same theme is echoed in another word or phrase elsewhere in the Tablet. Through our use and study of the Tablet of Aḥmad over a long period we may continue to marvel at the power of the words Bahá'u'lláh used to create this very special Tablet. The unlimited creative power of the Word of God is so vast that no matter how many times we study this Tablet, we can continue to find new meanings and significance in it.

The following is a list of themes that appear to be included in the Tablet of Aḥmad. This list is not meant to be definitive but is presented merely to help focus the reader's attention on ideas and concepts discussed in the commentary and to highlight the richness of the text. To study this Tablet is to undertake a concise course in the fundamental verities of the Bahá'í Faith.

## Themes in the Tablet of Aḥmad

- The teaching mission Bahá'u'lláh entrusted to Aḥmad, as reported by Aḥmad in his own study of his Tablet

- The call to arise and teach the Cause of God
- The call to service to the Cause of God
- The fulfilment by Bahá'u'lláh of prophecies in the Qur'án, the Old and New Testaments and other sacred scriptures
- The true station of Bahá'u'lláh
- The true station of the Báb
- The twin Manifestations of God
- The Covenant of God and the twin, twofold duties of recognition and obedience, and obedience and steadfastness
- The requirements of faith for the individual
- The consequences of turning away 'from this Beauty' and rejecting the revealed Word of God
- The love of Bahá'u'lláh for everyone
- The infinite bounties of Bahá'u'lláh's love and the immeasurable bounty of His Presence
- The nature of steadfastness
- The appropriate response to the enemies of the Cause of God
- The appropriate response to tests and difficulties
- Reliance upon God
- The condition of the people of the world
- The value of studying and reciting the Tablet regularly
- The promise of divine assistance
- The application of the Tablet to one's personal situation

# *Section 2: The Opening Paragraph*

## 6

## He is the King

*He is the King, the All-Knowing, the Wise!*

The Tablet of Aḥmad begins with the invocation 'He is the King, the All-Knowing, the Wise!' An invocation is a call to God to plead for His blessing, His help, His guidance, His inspiration and His protection. Is this opening phrase of the Tablet of Aḥmad simply an invocation to God or does it have greater significance?

Let us begin by considering the fact that Bahá'u'lláh's words are the revealed Word of God. Bahá'u'lláh tells us that every word of His Tablets is, by its nature, endowed with unlimited creative power.[30] He explains that the potency of this creative power means that each word of His Tablets has the capacity to create new meaning, unfold new knowledge and cause new wonders to appear in the physical world. This suggests that the opening phrase of the Tablet of Aḥmad may be much more than simply an introductory invocation.

Let us examine the phrase 'He is the King'. To whom does 'the King' refer? To God or to Bahá'u'lláh?

It is important to note that it is the usual practice in Islamic works to begin by invoking God in some way or another and that the way He is invoked is connected with the specific contents of the text that follows. It appears that this pattern has been repeated in the Tablet of Aḥmad.

'He is the King' may have several, simultaneous meanings. It may refer *both* to God *and* to Bahá'u'lláh. It may also refer to the Báb (see chapter 7).

We in the West are accustomed to thinking and making comparisons in terms of 'either/or'. We tend to judge everything we read, say and do as either right or wrong, for or against, good or bad. When we attempt to understand the Word of God, however, such an approach is extremely limiting. It prevents us from recognizing essential relationships and it veils us from seeing new spiritual meanings.

Bahá'u'lláh tells us that the meaning of the Word of God 'can never be exhausted'.[31] He also warns us that we must look beyond the literal meaning of the Word of God if we want to comprehend its inner, spiritual significance:

> In such utterances, the literal meaning, as generally understood by the people, is not what hath been intended.[32]

Bahá'u'lláh often attributes different meanings to the same phrase, an approach which is *inclusive*. A prime example is the *Book of Certitude*. In it Bahá'u'lláh gives numerous examples of scriptural verses that have multiple levels of meaning. For instance, in introducing the symbolism of the terms 'sun' and 'moon' as used in the holy scriptures, Bahá'u'lláh says:

> By the terms 'sun' and 'moon', mentioned in the writings of the Prophets of God, is not meant solely the sun and moon of the visible universe. Nay rather, manifold are the meanings they have intended for these terms.[33]

Later in this same book, Bahá'u'lláh quotes this sacred verse:

> We speak one word, and by it we intend one and seventy meanings; each one of these meanings we can explain.[34]

Notice that in both of the above quotations, the key verb is 'intend' *(murád)*. These verses tell us that when we study the Word of God we should expect to find many levels of meaning present. Thus when we analyze the writings of Bahá'u'lláh we should *expect* that He has intended there to be many levels of significance to His words. 'Abdu'l-Bahá reinforces this point:

> . . . the Words of God have innumerable significances and mysteries of meanings – each one a thousand and more.[35]

It is for us to discover the hidden treasures concealed in the ocean of His utterances.

Extending this idea further, often the meaning of a *spiritual* concept depends on our point of view and the particular frame of reference we use to analyze the concept. Thus the meaning we derive from a particular verse may depend on exactly what it is we are trying to understand and may also depend on the particular situation to which we are applying the spiritual concept. Therefore each verse may have many simultaneous levels of meaning, all of which are equally valid.

As we begin our study of the Tablet of Aḥmad, we must ever keep in mind the importance of simultaneous levels of meaning. We cannot possibly hope to gain insights into the various meanings of the verses of this Tablet if we suppose that Bahá'u'lláh intended only one meaning for each verse. However, if we allow ourselves to approach these verses with the understanding that Bahá'u'lláh intended the words He used to encompass many levels of meaning simultaneously, we will be filled with wonder when we discover new implications and meanings contained within the same phrase.

Let us return to the opening phrase of the Tablet of Aḥmad. At one level its significance depends on whether we are thinking about God or whether we are thinking about Bahá'u'lláh. For example, in one of His prayers Bahá'u'lláh gives us an indication of the mystery inherent in any discussion of the names and attributes of God. Since these names and attributes apply equally to God and to His Manifestation, in this passage Bahá'u'lláh shows us that it is impossible to differentiate between those names which apply to God and those which apply to the Manifestation:

> Glory be to Thee, O my God! My face hath been set towards Thy face, and my face is, verily, Thy face, and my call is Thy call, and my Revelation Thy Revelation, and my self Thy Self, and my Cause Thy Cause, and my behest Thy behest, and my Being Thy Being, and my sovereignty Thy sovereignty, and my glory Thy glory, and my power Thy power.[36]

On the one hand 'He is the King' most certainly refers to God, as may be seen in such phrases as:

> Praise be to God, the All-Possessing, the King of incomparable glory, a praise which is immeasurably above the understanding of all created things, and is exalted beyond the grasp of the minds of men.[37]

On the other hand, 'He is the King' may also refer to Bahá'u'lláh Himself. For example, in His Tablet to the Kings Bahá'u'lláh refers to Himself as the 'King of Kings':

> Ye are but vassals, O kings of the earth! He Who is the King of Kings hath appeared, arrayed in His most wondrous glory.[38]

The phrase 'He is the King' may thus be regarded as a declaration by Bahá'u'lláh that He is the King of Kings, the Promised One of all ages.

At the same time, 'He is the King' may also signify that Bahá'u'lláh's advent fulfils innumerable prophecies from the sacred scriptures of the past concerning this promised Day of God. One of these specific prophecies is the promise of the coming of the 'King of glory', which is found in Psalm 24 of the Hebrew Bible:

> Lift up your heads, O ye gates; even lift them up, ye everlasting doors; and the King of glory shall come in.Who is this King of glory? The Lord of hosts, he is the King of glory.[39]

The 'Lord of Hosts', Shoghi Effendi points out, refers specifically to Bahá'u'lláh.[40] In one of His Tablets Bahá'u'lláh affirms this truth:

> The Promised Day is come and the Lord of Hosts hath appeared. Rejoice ye with great joy by reason of this supreme felicity.[41]

Thus we may infer that when Bahá'u'lláh opens the Tablet of Aḥmad by proclaiming that 'He is the King', in one sense He is asserting that He is the Lord of Hosts, the King of glory promised by David in his psalms.

Another significant prophecy concerning 'the King' is the promise of the appearance of the 'King of the day of reckoning' mentioned in the fourth verse of the opening chapter of the Qur'án:

> In the Name of God, the Compassionate, the Merciful
> Praise be to God, Lord of the worlds!
> The compassionate, the merciful!
> King of the day of reckoning.[42]

The Báb prophesied that the 'King of the Day of Reckoning' would be manifested in the year 1280 AH, that is, 1863, which is the year of Bahá'u'lláh's declaration.[43] In this sense, Bahá'u-'lláh's affirmation that 'He is the King' may be seen as His declaration to both the Bábí and Muslim communities that He is indeed the One promised by Muḥammad in the very beginning of the Qur'án, the 'King of the day of reckoning'.

In yet another sense, 'He is the King' may be viewed as a proclamation of the unrivalled power and supreme authority of the Revelation of Bahá'u'lláh. It is a variation of the powerful affirmation 'He is God'. 'He is God' is often used in the Bahá'í writings to denote the triumph of the Cause of God, in this most holy Dispensation, over all the forces of opposition and denial leagued against it (see the discussion in chapter 36). Both phrases – 'He is God' and 'He is the King' – affirm that God has established His Cause upon an unassailable foundation. They also symbolize the appearance of the long awaited Kingdom of God on earth, promised to humankind in all the holy scriptures. For example in the New Testament we find:

> Behold, the tabernacle of God is with men, and he will dwell with them, and they shall be his people, and God himself shall be with them, and be their God.[44]

We see, then, that the phrase 'He is the King, the All-Knowing, the Wise!' is much more than an invocation to God. It refers simultaneously to God and Bahá'u'lláh and may also refer to the Báb. 'He is the King' is an extremely important symbol. In opening the Tablet of Aḥmad with this declaration, Bahá'u-'lláh introduces several very significant concepts all at once. He asserts that this is the Promised Day of God, the Day when 'God himself shall be with [men]'; He affirms that He is the Promised One of God, the King of Kings, the King of glory, and the King of the day of reckoning. In so doing, He proclaims that He is, indeed, the One promised in all the holy scriptures of the past, the Promised One of all ages. With His affirmation 'He is the King' Bahá'u'lláh announces, in unequivocal terms, the establishment of the Kingdom of God on earth and the triumph of the Cause of God. With this invocation Bahá'u'lláh issues His call to all the religious communities of the world to recognize Him as the One who was promised to them by God in their sacred scriptures.

# 7

# He is the King: The Báb

*He is the King, the All-Knowing, the Wise!*

The opening invocation of the Tablet of Aḥmad may also refer to the Báb. This can be seen from the Tablet itself. Bahá'u'lláh, glorifying the station of the Báb, declares: 'Verily, He is the King of the Messengers'. The Arabic for 'He is the King', '*Huwa as-Sulṭán*', is the same in both of these phrases. *Ḥakím* is the Arabic word translated as 'the Wise'. *Ḥakím* is also used by Bahá'u'lláh to describe the Báb. Later in the Tablet Bahá'u'lláh refers specifically to the Báb when He says 'the ordinances of God which have been enjoined in the Bayán by the Glorious, the Wise One'; the Báb is the author of the Bayán. Again, *ḥakím* is the Arabic word translated here as 'the Wise One'. In this sense, therefore, 'the King' and 'the Wise' of the opening invocation may refer to the Báb, 'the Wise One' who is 'the King of the Messengers' (see the discussion in chapter 42).

There is an intimate and indissoluble link between Bahá'u'lláh's Revelation and that of the Báb. Bahá'u'lláh refers to the Báb as 'My Previous Manifestation'[45] and to Himself as the reappearance of the Báb in His new Name:[46]

> . . . I am His Well-Beloved, the revelation of His own Self, though My name be not His name.[47]

The Báb, in turn, wrote that He had sacrificed Himself wholly for the sake of Bahá'u'lláh and that the purpose of everything

He had written was to prepare the people to recognize and accept Bahá'u'lláh. For example, He cries out to Bahá'u'lláh:

> O Thou Remnant of God! I have sacrificed myself wholly for Thee; I have accepted curses for Thy sake, and have yearned for naught but martyrdom in the path of Thy love. Sufficient witness unto me is God, the Exalted, the Protector, the Ancient of Days.[48]

Bahá'u'lláh, on His part, expressed His desire to sacrifice Himself in the path of the Báb:

> . . . We stand, life in hand, wholly resigned to His will; that perchance, through God's loving kindness and His grace, this revealed and manifest Letter may lay down His life as a sacrifice in the path of the Primal Point, the most exalted Word.[49]

Nabíl, the well-known Bahá'í historian, points out that the love between Bahá'u'lláh and the Báb was so great that each was unwilling for the other to suffer alone:

> The Báb, whose trials and sufferings had preceded, in almost every case, those of Bahá'u'lláh, had offered Himself to ransom His Beloved from the perils that beset that precious Life; whilst Bahá'u'lláh, on His part, unwilling that He who so greatly loved Him should be the sole Sufferer, shared at every turn the cup that had touched His lips. Such love no eye has ever beheld, nor has mortal heart conceived such mutual devotion. If the branches of every tree were turned into pens, and all the seas into ink, and earth and heaven rolled into one parchment, the immensity of that love would still remain unexplored, and the depths of that devotion unfathomed.[50]

It is not possible to study the Tablet of Aḥmad without discussing the intrinsic connection between the Revelations of the Báb and Bahá'u'lláh. It is surely no accident that the opening phrase may apply to both the Báb and Bahá'u'lláh. It clearly illustrates Bahá'u'lláh's emphasis on the fundamental and sublime link between Himself and the Báb.

If we take the view that 'He is the King' refers to Bahá'u-'lláh, then the Tablet of Aḥmad may be seen as a proclamation by Bahá'u'lláh to the followers of the Báb that they must now prove their belief in the Báb by recognizing Bahá'u'lláh as the One promised by their Lord. At the same time, if we view the opening invocation as referring to the Báb, we may infer that Bahá'u'lláh is paying homage to the Báb by revealing this important Tablet in His name and in His honour.

## 8

# The Nightingale of Paradise

*Lo, the Nightingale of Paradise*
*singeth upon the twigs of the Tree of Eternity,*
*with holy and sweet melodies*

In the previous chapters we saw that the opening invocation 'He is the King' may have several meanings. Significantly, the opening phrase, 'Lo, the Nightingale of Paradise singeth', may also have multiple levels of meaning. In one sense the 'Nightingale of Paradise'[51] may refer to Bahá'u'lláh Himself. This can be seen later in the Tablet of Aḥmad when Bahá'u-'lláh, speaking about Himself, says, 'Thus doth the Nightingale utter His call unto you from this prison.' At the time He revealed this Tablet Bahá'u'lláh was imprisoned in Adrianople. Thus in the sense that the Nightingale of Paradise is Bahá'u-'lláh Himself, the opening paragraph of the Tablet of Aḥmad may be seen as Bahá'u'lláh's majestic and joyous proclamation of His own advent.

In another sense the 'Nightingale of Paradise' may also refer to the Báb. This may be seen from a verse in the Kitáb-i-Aqdas in which Bahá'u'lláh refers to the Báb as the 'Nightingale'. In this passage, after quoting from the writings of the Báb, Bahá'u'lláh says:

> Thus hath the Nightingale sung with sweet melody upon the celestial bough, in praise of its Lord, the All-Merciful. Well is it with them that hearken.[52]

Notice how similar this verse is to the opening phrase of the Tablet of Aḥmad. In this sense, then, it is the Báb who is the Nightingale of Paradise, 'proclaiming to the sincere ones' and joyfully announcing the advent of Bahá'u'lláh's Revelation.

If we take the view that the Nightingale of Paradise is the Báb, then God has created a profound spiritual interplay between the voice of the Báb and the voice of Bahá'u'lláh. If the Báb is seen to be the Nightingale of Paradise, then we may view the Báb as the speaker of the first two paragraphs of the Tablet of Aḥmad. In this sense, it is the Báb who is proclaiming Bahá'u'lláh's advent in the opening paragraph and testifying to Bahá'u'lláh's greatness in the second when He says, 'Verily this is that Most Great Beauty foretold in the Books of the Messengers.' From this point of view, the speaker then appears to shift to Bahá'u'lláh, who, in the following two paragraphs testifies to the truth of the Báb's Revelation and the greatness of His station when He declares that, 'Verily, He is the King of the Messengers'.

We see, then, that in the first two opening phrases of the Tablet of Aḥmad, 'He is the King' and 'Lo, the Nightingale of Paradise singeth', Bahá'u'lláh is revealing a profound mystery to us. He appears to be telling us that He and the Báb are spiritually inseparable. In the sense that these two phrases may refer simultaneously to both the Báb and Bahá'u'lláh, then we cannot say that these verses are only about the Báb or only about Bahá'u'lláh. Recall that the Tablet of Aḥmad was revealed in Adrianople, at a time when Bahá'u'lláh was proclaiming that He was the return of the Báb. In this promised day God has sent us, in rapid succession, twin Manifestations. To see one is to see them both. To hear the voice of one is to hear the voice of the other. To recognize one requires us to accept the other. And to accept the divine teachings of one is to accept the divine teachings of the other, for not only are they inseparable but their writings are likewise inseparable. This appears to be one of the powerful messages of the Tablet of Aḥmad. Not only does Bahá'u'lláh honour the Báb and testify to the greatness of His station, He also affirms that if we recognize the Báb, then we must also recognize Bahá'u'lláh because we cannot fully recognize the Báb without also recognizing Bahá'u'lláh. Conversely, in recognizing Bahá'u'lláh, we must also fully accept the Báb and the greatness of His station because our recognition of Bahá'u-'lláh will be incomplete without our recognition of His immediate predecessor.

On yet another level, Bahá'u'lláh's evocation of the image of the 'Bird of Heaven' or the 'Nightingale of Paradise' symbolizes the voice of the Spirit of God speaking through His chosen Manifestation in every age. It is important to recognize that we can never distinguish between the voice of the Holy Spirit and the voice of the Manifestation (see the discussion on divine unity in chapter 16). Thus we may say that it is the voice of the Holy Spirit which is singing on the Tree of Eternity and proclaiming the advent of the Promised One of God. Or we may say that it is the voice of every Messenger of God who is singing on the Tree of Eternity proclaiming Bahá'u'lláh's advent and testifying to His greatness.

The symbolism of the Manifestation of God as the Nightingale of Paradise also appears to allude to the legend of the mystic nightingale that sacrifices itself on the altar of love. The story concerns the bird's all-consuming love and search for the white rose. When the nightingale finally finds the object of its quest, it is overcome with longing for its heart's desire. Heedless of danger, it dives towards the rose. A thorn pierces the bird's breast and its blood dyes the rose crimson. The nightingale takes off in its final flight, soaring higher than it has ever flown before. In its passion, it sings its farewell love song to the rose, a song more beautiful and sweeter than any it has yet sung.

Bahá'u'lláh's designation of Himself and the Báb as the Nightingales of Paradise may symbolize the willingness of both to sacrifice their lives in their love for God. Certainly, the martyrdom of the Báb proved His willingness to sacrifice His own life in the path of Bahá'u'lláh, while Bahá'u'lláh fully demonstrated His own willingness to sacrifice His life in His years of service to the Cause of the Báb and in His own 40–year ministry. Bahá'u'lláh alludes to His own sufferings in the path of God in the Tablet of Aḥmad. Assuring Aḥmad of His bounties and His love, He counsels him: 'Remember . . . My distress and banishment in this remote prison.'

In another Tablet Bahá'u'lláh describes His willingness to take on the sufferings of the world:

> I never passed a tree but Mine heart addressed it saying: 'O would that thou wert cut down in My name, and My body crucified upon thee.'[53]

Returning to our discussion of the Tablet, the word 'lo' calls 'attention to an amazing sight'.[54] Bahá'u'lláh calls our attention to the singing of the Nightingale of Paradise on the Tree of Eternity. In other words, it seems that He is urging every reader of this Tablet to see with his own eyes that the Promised One of God, symbolized by the Nightingale, has finally appeared and He is not silent. He is pouring forth His divine melodies, summoning the people of the earth to the Kingdom of God. Nightingales are well known both for the sweetness of their singing and for how insistently and persistently they sing. The symbolism of the Nightingale of Paradise may thus signify both the sweetness of Bahá'u'lláh's words and the insistence of His call.

Viewed in its historical context, the 'singing' of the Nightingale of Paradise may represent the public proclamation of Bahá'u'lláh's God-given station and His world-redeeming mission. In another sense, the 'singing' of the Nightingale may signify Bahá'u'lláh's announcement to the Bábí community that the One promised by the Báb has appeared and is proclaiming His mission to them.

The image of the singing of the Nightingale on the Tree

of Eternity is also suggestive of the return of springtime, evoking an image of the return of the birds after a long, desolate winter. The cheerful, sweet singing of such birds announces the end of winter, the arrival of warm, fragrant, sunny days and the emergence of new life. In this sense, the singing of the Nightingale is a sign of the reappearance of the divine springtime, a well-known theme in the writings of Bahá'u'lláh. In a Tablet celebrating the Festival of Riḍván, the anniversary of the declaration of His mission, He says:

> The Divine Springtime is come, O Most Exalted Pen, for the Festival of the All-Merciful is fast approaching. Bestir thyself, and magnify, before the entire creation, the name of God, and celebrate His praise, in such wise that all created things may be regenerated and made new. Speak, and hold not thy peace.[55]

The image of the Nightingale of Paradise singing the melodies of God appears throughout Bahá'u'lláh's writings. In some passages He refers to the 'Bird of Heaven', in others to the 'Dove of Eternity' and in still other instances to the 'Nightingale of Utterance'. Each time Bahá'u'lláh invokes this image, nuances of meaning emerge and give us glimpses of its power and significance. One such example is the following:

> . . . the Nightingale of Utterance hath warbled its melody upon the highest branch of true understanding. Verily, He Who was hidden in the knowledge of God and is mentioned in the Holy Scriptures hath appeared.[56]

Another example is this passage from the *Book of Certitude*:

> Such are the strains of the celestial melody which the immortal Bird of Heaven, warbling upon the Sadrih of Bahá, poureth out upon thee, that, by the permission of God, thou mayest tread the path of divine knowledge and wisdom.[57]

In His Tablet to the Sháh of Persia we find this soul-stirring and inspiring passage:

> O King! Wert thou to incline thine ears unto the shrill voice of the Pen of Glory and the cooing of the Dove of Eternity, which on the branches of the Lote-Tree beyond which there is no passing, uttereth praises to God, the Maker of all Names and the Creator of earth and heaven, thou wouldst attain unto a station from which thou wouldst behold in the world of being naught save the effulgence of the Adored One, and wouldst regard thy sovereignty as the most contemptible of thy possessions, abandoning it to whosoever might desire it, and setting thy face toward the Horizon aglow with the light of His countenance.[58]

In another passage nearly identical to the opening of the Tablet of Aḥmad, Bahá'u'lláh connects the Nightingale of Paradise with the affirmation 'He is the King, the All-Knowing, the Wise!' He says:

> . . . hearken unto the sweet warblings of the Bird of Heaven singing upon the twigs of the Tree of eternity: Verily there is none other God but Me, the All-Knowing, the All-Wise.[59]

In yet another striking passage, Bahá'u'lláh, in majestic terms, sets forth His divine mission:

> Thus doth the Holy Reed intone its melodies, and the Nightingale of Paradise warble its song, so that He may infuse life eternal into the mortal frames of men, impart to the temples of dust the essence of the Holy Spirit and the heavenly Light, and draw the transient world, through the potency of a single word, unto the Everlasting Kingdom.[60]

We see, then, that the image of the Nightingale of Paradise singing on the Tree of Eternity may symbolize the appearance of the Promised One of God. Bahá'u'lláh seems to be asserting that He is the representative and mouthpiece of God on earth, that His call is the call of God and that His word is the Word of God.

# 9

# The Tree of Eternity

*Lo, the Nightingale of Paradise*
*singeth upon the twigs of the Tree of Eternity,*
*with holy and sweet melodies*

The 'Tree of Eternity' appears to be a variation of the expressions the 'divine Lote-Tree', 'Sadratu'l-Muntahá' and the 'Tree of Divine Revelation', all of which are used by the Báb and Bahá'u'lláh to designate the appearance of the Manifestation of God. For example, in one of His Tablets Bahá'u'lláh declares:

> Through His potency the Trees of Divine Revelation have yielded their fruits, every one of which hath been sent down in the form of a Prophet, bearing a Message to God's creatures . . .[61]

The symbolism of the sacred tree signalizing the advent of the new Manifestation appears in many forms throughout the world's holy scriptures. For example, the opening chapters of the Book of Genesis in the Hebrew Bible speak of both the 'tree of the knowledge of good and evil' and the 'tree of life'.[62] 'Abdu'l-Bahá explains that the 'tree of good and evil signifies the human world' while 'the tree of life is the highest degree of the world of existence: the Word of God, and the Supreme Manifestation', i.e. Bahá'u'lláh.[63]

Numerous other examples using the symbolism of the holy tree can be found throughout the scriptures. Moses received

His Revelation from the Burning Bush, while Buddha was given supreme enlightenment at the sacred Bodhi Tree. Isaiah prophesied the appearance of the promised One in the phrase 'a Branch shall grow out of His roots'.[64] In the New Testament, Christ, alluding to the progression of divine Revelation, declared that 'every good tree bringeth forth good fruit'.[65] The Qur'án, describing the station of Muḥammad, refers to the 'Sadratu'l-Muntahá' ('Sidrah-tree'), the 'Tree beyond which there is no passing'.[66] The Báb also refers to Himself as 'the Tree beyond which there is no passing, the blessed Lote-Tree'.[67] Similarly, Bahá'u'lláh uses both terms, 'Divine Lote-Tree' and 'Sadratu'l-Muntahá', to describe His Manifestation.[68] He also refers to Himself as the 'Tree of the world of existence'.[69]

We see that the use of the sacred tree to represent the advent of God's appointed Manifestation is not a new concept. It has been an essential part of religious symbolism throughout the ages. Summarizing this point, the Báb explains that this tree is the Tree of God that has brought forth His Messengers and has revealed the holy scriptures:

> That which is intended by 'Revelation of God' is the Tree of divine Truth that betokeneth none but Him, and it is this divine Tree that hath raised and will raise up Messengers, and hath revealed and will ever reveal Scriptures.[70]

The Báb then asserts that it is this sacred Tree of God that will bring forth 'Him Whom God shall make manifest', Bahá'u-'lláh:

> From eternity unto eternity this Tree of divine Truth hath served and will ever serve as the throne of the revelation and concealment of God among His creatures, and in every age is made manifest through whomsoever He pleaseth . . . and when Him Whom God shall make manifest will shine forth, it will be through Him that He will vindicate the truth of His Faith . . .[71]

That the Nightingale of Paradise is singing on 'the twigs' of the Tree of Eternity reinforces this theme. In one sense this indicates that the tree of divine Revelation is the Nightingale's true home, a symbol that Bahá'u'lláh is, indeed, a Messenger of God. The Arabic word for twigs used in this phrase is '*afnán*'. In the Bahá'í writings the word 'Afnán' is used to designate the relatives of the Báb. This suggests at least two possibilities. On one level it lends further weight to the idea that the Báb is the Nightingale of Paradise. Secondly, in the sense that Bahá'u'lláh is the Nightingale of Paradise, His use of '*afnán*' to specify 'the twigs' of the Tree of Eternity seems to imply that He is related spiritually to the Báb, perhaps an allusion to the fact that Bahá'u'lláh is the lawful successor of the Báb. At the same time, it also suggests that Bahá'u'lláh is related to the tree of divine Revelation itself, a successor in the line of God's holy Prophets.

From this discussion we may surmise that by declaring that the Nightingale of Paradise is singing on the Tree of Eternity, Bahá'u'lláh is asserting that He is the promised fruit of the tree of divine Revelation, 'Him Whom God shall make manifest', the one promised by the Báb in His writings.

## 10

# The Tree of Eternity: Symbol of the Covenant

*Lo, the Nightingale of Paradise*
*singeth upon the twigs of the Tree of Eternity,*
*with holy and sweet melodies*

The appearance from age to age of God's appointed Messenger is the eternal promise of God to humankind. In the Book of Genesis God promised Abraham:

> I will establish my covenant between me and thee and thy seed after thee in their generations for an everlasting covenant, to be a God unto thee, and to thy seed after thee.[72]

This covenant is described in the Bahá'í writings as the greater or ancient covenant of God, the promise of continual divine guidance through the periodic appearance on earth of God's Messengers and Prophets.

As to the significance of the 'Tree of Eternity' in the Tablet of Aḥmad, 'Abdu'l-Bahá uses the term 'Tree' to refer specifically to 'the Tree of His Covenant'.[73] In another passage 'Abdu'l-Bahá, speaking about the Tree of Life, says: 'This Tree of Life is the Book of the Covenant.'[74]

This suggests that the 'Tree of Eternity' may also symbolize the eternal covenant of God. The singing of the Nightingale of Paradise on the Tree of Eternity may thus be understood as an affirmation by Bahá'u'lláh that His advent is the renewal of this ancient covenant of God with all humanity.

## 11

# Holy and Sweet Melodies

*Lo, the Nightingale of Paradise*
*singeth upon the twigs of the Tree of Eternity,*
*with holy and sweet melodies*

The Tablet of Aḥmad was revealed in the initial years of Bahá'u'lláh's public proclamation of His divine mission. Having kept silent during His entire ten-year exile in Baghdád about His true station and the magnitude of His world-redeeming mission, Bahá'u'lláh began systematically to spread far and wide the glad tidings of His claim to be the one promised by the Báb and the redeemer of all humankind. The 'singing' of the Nightingale of Paradise, as previously mentioned, may thus be seen as a symbol of the proclamation of Bahá'u'lláh's God-given mission to the peoples of the world. In a stirring passage He counsels:

> Unstop, then, the ear of thine heart that thou mayest hearken unto the speech of the Divine Lote-Tree that hath been raised up in truth by God, the Almighty, the Beneficent. Verily, this Tree . . . calleth aloud and summoneth all men unto the Sadratu'l-Muntahá and the Supreme Horizon. Blessed is the soul that hath gazed on the Most Mighty Sign, and the ear that hath heard His most sweet Voice, and woe to whosoever hath turned aside and done wickedly.[75]

The 'singing' of the Nightingale of Paradise may also be understood as an allusion to the revelation of divine verses, the holy and creative Word of God. In the *Book of Certitude*, Bahá'u'lláh explains that the revelation of divine verses is the mightiest testimony and surest proof of true prophethood:

> . . . nothing greater than these verses hath ever appeared, nor will ever be made manifest in the world![76]

The revelation of divine verses, He says, 'pertaineth to God Himself':

> It is, in its essence, and will ever so remain, the Bread which cometh down from Heaven. It is God's supreme testimony, the clearest evidence of His truth, the sign of His consummate bounty, the token of His all-encompassing mercy, the proof of His most loving providence, the symbol of His most perfect grace. He hath, indeed, partaken of this highest gift of God who hath recognized His Manifestation in this Day.[77]

The phrase 'with holy and sweet melodies' may be understood as another allusion to the significance of Bahá'u'lláh's divinely revealed verses. Throughout His writings Bahá'u'lláh urges us to 'taste the sweetness' of the words He has revealed. This sweetness is expressive of the creative and soul-stirring power of His words, a power which is an inherent property of the Word of God. Through its potency our hearts are moved, transformed and recreated. It is a gift to be highly treasured. In one of His prayers Bahá'u'lláh writes:

> Number me not with them who read Thy words and fail to find Thy hidden gift which, as decreed by Thee, is contained therein, and which quickeneth the souls of Thy creatures and the hearts of Thy servants.[78]

Elsewhere Bahá'u'lláh describes the effect that this quickening power can have on the heart of a sincere seeker:

> Were any man to ponder in his heart that which the Pen of the Most High hath revealed and to taste of its sweetness,

> he would, of a certainty, find himself emptied and delivered from his own desires, and utterly subservient to the Will of the Almighty. Happy is the man that hath attained so high a station, and hath not deprived himself of so bountiful a grace.[79]

Bahá'u'lláh says that the sweetness of His words can attract the hearts and cause them to become steadfast in His love. This may be one reason why He has enjoined on the believers the obligation to read from His writings every day:

> Whoever hath tasted the sweetness of those words will never consent to transgress the bounds which God hath fixed, neither will he turn his gaze towards any one except his Well-Beloved.[80]

Thus Bahá'u'lláh exhorts us not to ignore this divine favour, this 'highest gift of God'. He lovingly counsels us to listen to the sweetness of the melodies that the Nightingale of Paradise is singing from its perch on the Tree of Eternity. In other words, He seems to be advising us to recognize that He is revealing the divine Word of God, whose potency and sweetness can alone assure the hearts and quench the thirst of all who are seeking the river of life from the hand of the Beloved.

# 12

# The Glad Tidings

*proclaiming to the sincere ones*
*the glad tidings of the nearness of God*

Who are 'the sincere ones'?

The Bahá'í writings provide clarification. The writings indicate that the test of sincerity is an individual's response to the claim of Bahá'u'lláh. For example, consider the writings of the Báb. He constantly and repeatedly urges His followers to prepare themselves for Bahá'u'lláh's advent, for 'Him Whom God shall make manifest'. More specifically, He asserts that those who recognize Bahá'u'lláh are the only ones who are truly sincere:

> Indeed those who will bear allegiance unto Him Whom God shall make manifest are the ones who have grasped the meaning of that which hath been revealed in the Bayán; they are indeed the sincere ones . . .[81]

In His writings, Bahá'u'lláh adds:

> They whose eyes are illumined with the light of understanding will perceive the sweet savours of the All-Merciful, and will embrace His truth. These are they who are truly sincere.[82]

From these passages we see that Bahá'u'lláh's proclamation to 'the sincere ones' may be understood as His call to the followers of the Báb, announcing that He is the one whose advent was promised to them by their Lord.

What is the significance of the phrase 'the glad tidings of the nearness of God'?

When we study the Arabic words and phrases Bahá'u'lláh used in the Tablet of Aḥmad, we find many references to the writings of the Báb as well as unmistakable allusions to verses and prophecies in the Qur'án. This is especially evident in the opening paragraph of the Tablet. It is in this paragraph that Bahá'u'lláh paves the way for the clear, emphatic declaration of His station and mission, which follows immediately after this paragraph. We find that each phrase in this paragraph is designed to evoke an image that stirs our hearts and creates a longing desire to be with our Lord. The words themselves are clear signs that the Nightingale of Paradise is joyfully announcing that the divine promise has been fulfilled and that the day of reunion with our Lord has, at long last, arrived.

The Arabic words Bahá'u'lláh chose for each one of these phrases

> the glad tidings of the nearness of God
> the Presence of the Generous One
> the message which hath been revealed by God
> the seat of sanctity and . . . this resplendent Beauty

allude to specific Islamic verses and prophecies and point to particular verses in the writings of the Báb. All these allusions and references revolve around one theme: the promise of the coming of the great day of the Lord and the appearance of the Promised One Himself.

In the Tablet of Aḥmad, the Arabic for 'proclaiming the glad tidings' is *tubashshiru*. The word usually used in Bahá'í scripture to describe the Báb is *mubashshir*, herald or 'giver of the glad tidings'. Thus *tubashshiru* appears to have the clear implication that we are now being given the glad tidings which the 'giver of glad tidings', the Báb, had foretold in His writings.

Another aspect of the 'glad tidings' is connected with the story of Joseph in the Hebrew Bible and, more particularly, in the Qur'án. The Báb, on the night of His declaration, revealed the first chapter of His commentary on the Súrih of Joseph in the Qur'án.[83] In His commentary, called the Qayyúmu'l-Asmá', the Báb alludes to Bahá'u'lláh and calls Him the 'true Joseph'.[84] He also announces the glad tidings of His future advent. For example, He says:

> . . . announce unto them the joyful tidings that following this mighty Covenant there shall be everlasting reunion with God in the Paradise of His good-pleasure, nigh unto the Seat of Holiness.[85]

On one level, we see that the phrase, 'proclaiming . . . the glad tidings (*tubashshiru*)', may allude to this commentary of the Báb and, therefore, may indicate that the promised advent of these glad tidings has now been fulfilled.

In the story of Joseph, Joseph is placed in the well by his brothers and left to die. He is found by some travellers. In the Quranic story, when Joseph is found, the person who finds him cries out, 'Good news! ('Glad tidings!') This is a youth!'[86] Much later, Jacob, the father of Joseph, is in Egypt with his other sons. After all these years, Jacob has not found his son Joseph and is still despondent. At this point, the Qur'án says, a person comes to Jacob with 'the good tidings' that Joseph is alive and well.[87]

From this story, we see that there may be several meanings of the Arabic word *tubashshiru* to which Bahá'u'lláh alludes when He uses the phrase 'proclaiming . . . the glad tidings'. On one level, it may signify the proclamation of the glad tidings made by the Báb in His commentary on this chapter of the Qur'án. It may also allude to the glad tidings that were proclaimed to Jacob when he learned that his long-lost son was alive.

In one of His Tablets Bahá'u'lláh calls Himself the 'Divine

Joseph'.[88] In this sense, each one of us is Jacob, ever searching for our divine Joseph, the beloved of our hearts. We may thus infer that in the phrase 'proclaiming to the sincere ones the glad tidings of the nearness of God' Bahá'u'lláh is giving us the glad tidings that He is truly near to us and is knocking at the door of our hearts.

Bahá'u'lláh, in one of His Tablets, alludes to many elements of the story of Joseph and calls Himself 'this Youth':

> Say: Barter not away this Youth, O people, for the vanities of this world or the delights of heaven. By the righteousness of the one true God! One hair of Him excelleth all that is in the heavens and all that is on the earth. Beware, O men, lest ye be tempted to part with Him in exchange for the gold and silver ye possess. Let His love be a storehouse of treasure for your souls . . .[89]

We see that Bahá'u'lláh here draws a parallel between Himself and Joseph. Recall that Joseph, after being found in the well, was sold 'for a paltry price'.[90] He was then taken to Egypt, effectively exiled from his homeland. Just as Joseph was protected by God, so too did God protect Bahá'u'lláh and deliver Him from the hands of His enemies. The Tablet of Aḥmad was revealed in Adrianople, 'the remote prison', where Bahá'u'lláh had been sent after Constantinople. In this sense, *tubashshiru* may signify the proclamation of the glad tidings that the Youth of Heaven, Bahá'u'lláh, is alive and well, safe in the bosom of God's unfailing protection. Furthermore, there appears to be even another layer of significance implied. In the phrase 'proclaiming . . . the glad tidings of the nearness of God', Bahá'u'lláh is giving the glad tidings (*tubashshiru*) that, in spite of being physically so far away, He is, in reality, very near to Aḥmad, indeed to each one of us. The significance of this concept is that the 'clear message' of the Tablet of Aḥmad appears to be that Bahá'u'lláh is urging Aḥmad and us to partake of the priceless bounties of His nearness and His presence and stating that His physical absence is irrelevant.

In another sense, 'the glad tidings of the nearness of God' may also be understood as the inception of the Kingdom of God on earth, which has been inaugurated through the Revelation of Bahá'u'lláh. The establishment of the Kingdom of God on earth is Bahá'u'lláh's divine mission. '. . . sit ye not silent,' 'Abdu'l-Bahá urges us, 'carry to men's ears the glad-tidings of the Kingdom, spread far and wide the Word of God.'[91]

Thus we see that the phrase 'proclaiming . . . the glad tidings' has many allusions to the story of Joseph in the Hebrew Bible and in the Qur'án. The phrase 'proclaiming . . . the glad tidings' also appears to refer to the Báb, the 'giver of glad tidings' and to specific passages in His writings. All these references and allusions confirm that Bahá'u'lláh is the Promised One of God and that His advent fulfils the divine promises. The 'clear message' of the Tablet of Aḥmad is that Bahá'u'lláh is the best beloved of our hearts, whose love and presence we are all seeking.

# 13

# The Nearness of God

*proclaiming to the sincere ones*
*the glad tidings of the nearness of God*

Some people question whether the Bahá'í Faith has a concept of a personal God. If they understood the spiritual significance of Bahá'u'lláh's assertion of 'the nearness of God', the Bahá'í belief in a personal God would be clearly demonstrated.

The 'glad tidings of the nearness of God' may, in one sense, be understood as an allusion by Bahá'u'lláh to the fulfilment of certain prophecies in both the Bible and the Qur'án concerning the great day of the coming of the Lord. When we study these scriptural references, they usually contain a contrast between nearness and remoteness. Many people consider the day of the Lord to be quite remote, both in time and place: the idea that the Lord will appear on earth and that humankind will stand before Him is too overwhelming or implausible for most people to accept. Yet many of the holy scriptures emphasize the day of the coming of the Lord and promise that it will happen. It may be because God knew people would have such a hard time accepting the reality of this event that He repeatedly cautioned the believers of all faiths to prepare themselves for it.

It seems this is the fulfilment of these various promises that Bahá'u'lláh announces in the Tablet of Aḥmad through the phrase 'the glad tidings of the nearness of God'. Let us consider some examples of such promises and warnings. In the New Testament, Paul warns the Christians to be ready, that the day of the Lord is not as far distant as they may imagine:

> Love worketh no ill to his neighbour: therefore love is the fulfilling of the law. And that, knowing the time, that now it is high time to awake out of sleep: for now is our salvation nearer than when we believed. The night is far spent, the day is at hand: let us therefore cast off the works of darkness, and let us put on the armour of light.[92]

In the Hebrew Bible Joel also cautions the Jewish people to be ready for the day of the Lord, telling them that it is near at hand:

> Blow ye the trumpet in Zion, and sound an alarm in my holy mountain: let all the inhabitants of the land tremble: for the day of the Lord cometh, for it is nigh at hand . . .[93]

This verse begins with the blowing of the trumpet. In scriptural prophecies, this trumpet blast is supposed to announce the appearance of the promised Day of God. In one of His Tablets, Bahá'u'lláh declares:

> The Trumpet hath been blown, and lo, all eyes have stared up with terror, and the hearts of all who are in the heavens and on the earth have trembled, except them whom the breath of the verses of God hath quickened, and who have detached themselves from all things.[94]

Similarly, the Qur'án alerts the believers that the promised day of the Lord, which the people imagine to be far away, is quite near:

> Be thou patient therefore with becoming patience;
> They forsooth regard that day as distant,
> But we see it nigh:
> The day when the heavens shall become as molten brass,
> And the mountains shall become like flocks of wool . . .[95]

These references to the heavens becoming like molten brass and the mountains becoming like flocks of wool are found quite frequently in verses speaking about the promised day. Bahá'u'lláh refers specifically to these signs in some of His Tablets. For example, He says:

> Witness how ye gainsay His signs! . . . Say: Will ye not recognize how the mountains have become like flocks of wool, how the people are sore vexed at the awful majesty of the Cause of God?[96]

In the Hebrew Bible, the New Testament and the Qur'án we find explicit references to a divine event that people imagine to be far removed from them in time and place. The scriptures advise the people to be ready for this great event and to expect it soon. The Qur'án contains many verses which warn the people to prepare themselves for the great day of the Lord. Many of these verses either allude to the nearness of God or associate this advice with the word nearness or its synonyms. For example, we find:

> But as to him who shall enjoy near access to God,
> His shall be repose, and pleasure, and a garden of delights.[97]

> And when the leaves of the Book shall be unrolled,
> And when the Heaven shall be stripped away,
> And when Hell shall be made to blaze,
> And when Paradise shall be brought near,
> Every soul shall know what it hath produced.[98]

> On that day will we cry to Hell, 'Art thou full?' And it shall say, 'Are there more?'
>
> And not far from thence shall Paradise be brought near unto the Pious:
>
> – 'This is what ye have been promised: to every one who hath turned in penitence to God and kept his laws;
>
> Who hath feared the God of Mercy in secret, and come to him with a contrite heart:

Enter it in peace: this is the day of Eternity.'
There shall they have all that they can desire: and our's will it be to augment their bliss . . .[99]

And put me not to shame on the day when mankind shall be raised up,
The day when neither wealth nor children shall avail,
Save to him who shall come to God with a sound heart:
When Paradise shall be brought near the pious . . .[100]

In one of His Tablets, Bahá'u'lláh declares:

> Is there any doubt concerning His signs? Open ye your eyes, and consider His clear evidence. Paradise is on your right hand, and hath been brought nigh unto you, while Hell hath been made to blaze. Witness its devouring flame. Haste ye to enter into Paradise, as a token of Our mercy unto you, and drink ye from the hands of the All-Merciful the Wine that is life indeed.[101]

From this discussion we see that 'the nearness of God' appears to be an allusion by Bahá'u'lláh to all the prophecies in the Qur'án, the New Testament and the Hebrew Bible concerning the nearness of the promised Day of God. In this sense, 'the glad tidings of the nearness of God' is Bahá'u'lláh's affirmation that through His appearance all these momentous prophecies have, at long last, been fulfilled. Through His grace and bounty, He has brought us near to Him. He is offering us the paradise of His love and is inviting us to enter therein in His name, the God of mercy.

# 14

# The Believers in the Divine Unity

*calling the believers in the Divine Unity*
*to the court of the Presence of the Generous One*

Who are 'the believers in the Divine Unity'?

One possibility is that the phrase refers to all true Muslims, as they are 'believers' in divine unity. Another is that the phrase refers to the followers of the Báb. They were awaiting the appearance of 'Him Whom God shall make manifest', the one whose advent had been promised by the Báb. At the time this Tablet was revealed in Adrianople, the Bábís were either unaware of or misinformed about the claim of Bahá'u'lláh.

The Tablet of Aḥmad was revealed about two years after Bahá'u'lláh's declaration of His divine mission in the Garden of Riḍván in April 1863. This momentous announcement came on the eve of His departure from Ba<u>gh</u>dád. Within six months of His arrival in the capital city of the Sulṭán, Constantinople, He was sent to Adrianople, which was located in the extreme northwest corner of the Ottoman empire (the 'remote prison'). Owing to the great distances involved and the absence of means of communication, it was a time when most of the Báb's followers in Persia had not yet heard Bahá'u'lláh's claim to be 'Him Whom God shall make manifest'.

It was during these early years of Bahá'u'lláh's exile in Adrianople that He sent His most trusted disciples back to Persia to teach the Bábís the truth of His Revelation. Adib Taherzadeh, in *The Revelation of Bahá'u'lláh*, explains the situation of the Bábí community of Persia at that time:

Ever since the days of Bahá'u'lláh in Baghdád, the great majority of believers in Persia had increasingly turned to Him as the focal point of the Bábí community . . .

. . .[But] there were those who were corrupt and egotistical and who longed for leadership. A few such men in various towns in Persia made mischief among the believers . . . These men congregated around Mírzá Yaḥyá [the half-brother of Bahá'u'lláh] . . .

. . . [F]rom the early days in Baghdád, men such as these were spreading highly complimentary remarks about Mírzá Yaḥyá within the Bábí community in Persia. They circulated unfounded reports about his greatness and claimed that he was the successor to the Báb, that all the Writings of Bahá'u-'lláh had emanated from Mírzá Yaḥyá, and that Bahá'u'lláh had usurped his position and forced him to hide himself away . . .

However, most Bábís who had been able to meet Mírzá Yaḥyá were struck by his ignorance and cowardice. These men had no doubt about the station of Bahá'u'lláh and were convinced that Mírzá Yaḥyá was merely a figure-head appointed by the Báb for the purpose of diverting attention from Bahá'u'lláh. But those who had not attained the presence of Bahá'u'lláh were often confused by rumours and controversy among the Bábís concerning the position of Mírzá Yaḥyá . . .

When we look at the state of the Bábí community at that time, we realize that Bahá'u'lláh had assigned a tremendous task to Muníb and other teachers, namely, the reorientation of that community and its transformation into a world community . . . The declaration of the station of Bahá'u'lláh as 'Him Whom God shall make manifest' in the gatherings of the friends was the most exciting and challenging event since the inception of the Faith [of the Báb] two decades before . . .

Through the creative influence of the *Súriy-i-Aṣḥáb* and other Tablets revealed in this period, and through the dedicated labours of some outstanding teachers of the Faith, the community throughout Persia was gradually cleansed

> from the ills which Mírzá Yaḥyá and his supporters had inflicted upon it . . . This process, begun in 1864, took two to three years, during which time the great majority of the Bábís in Persia joined the community of the Most Great Name.
>
> Ḥájí Mírzá Ḥaydar-'Alí has made an interesting observation on the number of Bábís who entered the Cause of Bahá'u'lláh . . . [T]he Báb guided the people of the *Bayán* for six years. He constantly gave the glad-tidings of the appearance of 'Him Whom God shall make manifest', prepared His followers for His coming, focused their attention on His greatness and glory, sowed the seed of His love in their hearts . . . Consequently, when Bahá'u'lláh manifested His Cause, about ninety-nine per cent of the Bábí community recognized Him and embraced His Cause . . .
>
> The mission of Muníb and other teachers whom Bahá'u'lláh sent to Persia during the early years of His sojourn in Adrianople was primarily to teach the members of the Bábí community.[102]

The Tablet of Aḥmad is Bahá'u'lláh's call to Aḥmad to arise and teach these Bábís. The Báb refers to those who have recognized Him and embraced the truth of His Revelation, the Bábís, as 'the believers in the Divine Unity'. In the Persian Bayán He declares:

> There is no paradise, in the estimation of *the believers in the Divine Unity*, more exalted than to obey God's commandments . . .[103]

That Bahá'u'lláh uses the identical phrase, 'calling the believers in the Divine Unity', suggests that He is addressing His call directly to the Bábís, as well as to others.

Of all the commandments revealed by the Báb, the most fundamental, the most important and the one that runs like a continuous thread through His writings is His constant exhortation to His followers to prepare themselves to recognize 'Him Whom God shall make manifest' as soon as He reveals Himself. It is not possible to read, for example, the Persian Bayán without finding reference to this theme.

The Báb explains that the whole purpose of His Revelation is to enable His followers to recognize Bahá'u'lláh:

> Take good heed of yourselves, for the sum total of the religion of God is but to help Him [Him Whom God shall make manifest] . . .[104]

> And know thou of a certainty that every letter revealed in the Bayán is solely intended to evoke submission unto Him Whom God shall make manifest . . .[105]

He warns His followers of the consequences should they fail to recognize Bahá'u'lláh:

> Say, God shall of a truth cause your hearts to be given to perversity if ye fail to recognize Him Whom God shall make manifest; but if ye do recognize Him God shall banish perversity from your hearts . . .[106]

> O congregation of the Bayán, and all who are therein! Recognize ye the limits imposed upon you, for such a One as the Point of the Bayán Himself hath believed in Him Whom God shall make manifest, before all things were created.[107]

The Báb considered this teaching to be so fundamental and vital that He defined paradise as recognition of Bahá'u'lláh:

> And know thou of a certainty that by Paradise is meant recognition of and submission unto Him Whom God shall make manifest . . .[108]

We may thus infer that when the Báb exhorts 'the believers in the Divine Unity' to obey His commandments and says that this obedience is the most exalted paradise, He is alluding to their recognition of Bahá'u'lláh. In like manner, we may conclude that when Bahá'u'lláh calls 'the believers in the Divine Unity to the court of the Presence of the Generous One' He is alerting the followers of the Báb that now is time to fulfil this essential commandment of the Báb and to enter paradise by recognizing Him.

15

# Divine Unity: The Historical Context

*calling the believers in the Divine Unity*
*to the court of the Presence of the Generous One*

Muḥammad taught the doctrine of divine unity. The teachings of divine unity centre around an enlightened and mature concept of God. The concept of divine unity is that God is supreme over all of creation, that He is absolutely perfect in every respect and that He completely transcends His creation. This was a new and revolutionary concept of divinity when Muḥammad introduced it. Although Abraham taught the fundamental doctrine of monotheism, the belief in one God, religions up to the time of Muḥammad held an anthropomorphic view of God; that is, God was seen as an extension of a human being. For example, Hinduism developed many images of the various aspects of divinity, all of which are expressed in human form. This typified the way human beings thought about God. Similarly, traditional Judaeo-Christian beliefs still hold to a concept of God that cast Him in the form of a human being. The image of God as an old man with a white beard immediately comes to mind. A serious flaw of many anthropomorphic conceptions of God is that He is often depicted as less than perfect.

The anthropomorphic view of God contrasts sharply with the Islamic and Bahá'í belief in a divine being who is transcendent. The belief in a God who completely transcends His creation, who is absolutely perfect and who is one in His essence and His attributes is known as divine unity in both

Islamic and Bahá'í scriptures. It is called *tawḥíd* in Islam and is at the very core of all Islamic belief.[109] A person who achieves this level of belief is known as *muwaḥḥid*, a believer in divine unity.

The concept of *tawḥíd* brings significant elements into the religion of God. On a fundamental level, it reaffirms the essential and timeless doctrine of monotheism, demolishes all concepts of idols as deities and refutes all notions of pantheism. The essential concept of *tawḥíd* is that 'the one true God' completely transcends His creation. The Qur'án describes this idea:

> . . . for there is no God but one God . . .[110]

> This is God your Lord. There is no God but He, the creator of all things: therefore worship Him alone; – and He watcheth over all things.
>
> No vision taketh in Him, but He taketh in all vision: and He is the Subtile, the All-informed.[111]

> Say: All is from God . . .[112]

We see that the Qur'án establishes the oneness and transcendence of a divine being who is clearly the ruler and creator of all that is.

The Báb affirmed the Islamic concept of divine unity. For example, He says:

> Immeasurably exalted art Thou, O my God, above the endeavours of all beings and created things to praise Thee and recognize Thee. No creature can ever comprehend Thee as beseemeth the reality of Thy holy Being and no servant can ever worship Thee as is worthy of Thine unknowable Essence. Praise be unto Thee; too high is Thine exalted Self for any allusions proceeding from Thy creatures ever to gain access unto Thy presence.[113]

The elements of divine unity found in Islam which were emphasized by the Báb laid the foundation for Bahá'u'lláh's teachings on the subject of divine unity.

Thus when Bahá'u'lláh calls the 'believers in the Divine Unity to the court of the Presence of the Generous One', He appears to be addressing His call directly to the followers of Muḥammad and the Báb. In doing so, He is appealing to them to recognize the one who has been promised to them in their holy scriptures; that is, believers in the unity of God will appreciate and understand the singing of the Nightingale of Paradise.

# 16

# Divine Unity: Bahá'í Teachings

*calling the believers in the Divine Unity*
*to the court of the Presence of the Generous One*

According to the writings of Bahá'u'lláh, the meaning of divine unity embraces several fundamental concepts. As we have seen, one is the acceptance of the absolute, transcendent nature of God. Building on the foundation of Islamic and Bábí doctrines, the Bahá'í writings describe 'the one true God' as one who is genuinely capable of being the creator and undisputed ruler of the universe. Bahá'u'lláh advises:

> Regard thou the one true God as One Who is apart from, and immeasurably exalted above, all created things. The whole universe reflecteth His glory, while He is Himself independent of, and transcendeth His creatures. This is the true meaning of Divine unity.[114]

The transcendent nature of 'the one true God' should not, however, be understood to suggest that God in the Bahá'í concept is an impersonal or uncaring being. Quite the opposite.

'His reality transcendeth such limitations,' Bahá'u'lláh declares:

> . . . the one true God is in Himself exalted beyond and above proximity and remoteness. His reality transcendeth such limitations. His relationship to His creatures knoweth no degrees.[115]

He describes God as 'the Desire of every understanding heart',[116] 'the Most Trusted' and 'the Best Lover'.[117]

> Consider, moreover, how frequently doth man become forgetful of his own self, whilst God remaineth, through His all-encompassing knowledge, aware of His creature, and continueth to shed upon him the manifest radiance of His glory. It is evident, therefore, that, in such circumstances, He is closer to him than his own self. He will, indeed, so remain for ever . . .[118]

A second aspect of divine unity is the recognition of the essential unity of all the Messengers and Prophets of God. Bahá'u'lláh explains:

> Every one of them is the Way of God that connecteth this world with the realms above, and the Standard of His Truth unto every one in the kingdoms of earth and heaven.[119]

> Know thou assuredly that the essence of all the Prophets of God is one and the same. Their unity is absolute. God, the Creator, saith: There is no distinction whatsoever among the Bearers of My Message.[120]

Perhaps the most difficult aspect of divine unity to comprehend and appreciate is the unity between God and His chosen Manifestation. Historically, so many myths have been created to explain this relationship that the concept has become confused and distorted. Consider, for example, the arguments about the divinity of Christ that continue to trouble Christianity. The result has been that many people experience difficulty understanding the relationship between God and His Manifestation.

The Bahá'í writings explicitly and emphatically assert that the Manifestations are not God. God does not incarnate Himself in any form. Each Manifestation is a separate individual, with a soul and a reality which is inherently superior to every other human being. Every Manifestation possesses a divine, God-given station that connects Him with God in a unique relationship that is beyond our experience or capacity to comprehend. The Manifestations live, act and speak to us from this divine station.

The central concept is that the individuality of the Manifestation cannot be separated from the divine station He inherently possesses. Every Manifestation always represents God, not Himself. Paradoxically, there are passages in the writings of Bahá'u'lláh in which He refers to His human aspect, as the mouthpiece of God, the 'Pen'. For example:

> Glorified be God! The Pen is perplexed what to write and the Tongue wondereth what to utter.[121]

We see this also in the dialogue between Bahá'u'lláh and God in the Fire Tablet:

> Bahá is drowning in a sea of tribulation: Where is the Ark of Thy salvation, O Saviour of the worlds?[122]

Bahá'u'lláh explains that every Manifestation has been '*commissioned* [by God] to reveal Himself through specific acts.' 'It is for this reason', He adds, 'that they appear to vary in their greatness.'[123]

It is only that they *appear to us* to vary. In their relationship to God, however, there is no variation. Bahá'u'lláh likens the apparent variation of the Manifestations to the moon reflecting the light of the sun.[124] Although we observe a different phase of the moon every night and a differing amount of light, the inherent ability of the moon to reflect the sun's light does not change. Similarly, God's relationship with His Manifestations is constant and unchanging. Bahá'u'lláh further explains:

> Be ye assured, moreover, that the works and acts of each and every one of these Manifestations of God . . . are all ordained by God, and are a reflection of His Will and Purpose.[125]

The more carefully we study how the Bahá'í writings describe the intimate relationship between the Manifestation and God, the clearer it becomes that we cannot separate the actions of the Manifestation from His inherent, direct link with God. Bahá'u'lláh asserts that all the actions and words of every Manifestation are sanctioned by God and are a perfect reflection of His will and purpose:

> The essence of belief in Divine unity consisteth in regarding Him Who is the Manifestation of God and Him Who is the invisible, the inaccessible, the unknowable Essence as one and the same. By this is meant that whatever pertaineth to the former, all His acts and doings, whatever He ordaineth or forbiddeth, should be considered, in all their aspects, and under all circumstances, and without any reservation, as identical with the Will of God Himself.[126]

'Abdu'l-Bahá explains that the divine essence of God transcends our ability to understand or comprehend Him. The most we can strive to accomplish, He says, is the true recognition of God's chosen Manifestation. It is in this context that Christ declares, 'He that hath seen me hath seen the Father . . .'[127]

The phrase 'calling the believers in the Divine Unity to the court of the Presence of the Generous One' now takes on new meaning. In recognizing Bahá'u'lláh as the Promised One of God, we have recognized the source of all goodness, purity and love in the world of creation. The 'Presence of the Generous One' is the presence of Bahá'u'lláh.

# 17

# The Presence of the Generous One

*calling the believers in the Divine Unity*
*to the court of the Presence of the Generous One*

The 'Presence of the Generous One' may be understood as referring to Bahá'u'lláh Himself. In one of His Tablets Bahá'u'lláh calls Himself the 'most generous Lord':

> Bethlehem is astir with the Breeze of God.
>
> We hear her voice saying: 'O most generous Lord! Where is Thy great glory established? The sweet savours of Thy presence have quickened me, after I had melted in my separation from Thee. Praised be Thou in that Thou hast raised the veils, and come with power in evident glory.' [128]

In another Tablet He says:

> Turn with your hearts in the direction of your Lord, the Forgiving, the Generous.[129]

And in yet another passage, speaking of the steadfastness and devotion of the true believers, He affirms:

> The more grievous their woes, the greater waxed the love of the people of Bahá . . . So carried away have they been by the living waters of the love of the Most Merciful, that neither the arms of the world nor the swords of the nations have deterred them from setting their faces towards the ocean of the bounty of their Lord, the Giver, the Generous.[130]

The Báb also indicates that this name, 'the Generous', refers to Bahá'u'lláh:

> When the Day-Star of Bahá will shine resplendent above the horizon of eternity it is incumbent upon you to present yourselves before His Throne . . .
>
> Beg ye of Him the wondrous tokens of His favour that He may graciously reveal for you whatever He willeth and desireth, inasmuch as on that Day all the revelations of divine bounty shall circle around the Seat of His glory and emanate from His presence, could ye but understand it.
>
> . . . on that Day it is He Who is the All-Knowing, the Omniscient, the Source of all knowledge, far above such as are endued with learning; and it is He Who is the Potent, the All-Compelling, the Lord of power, in the face of those who wield power; and it is He Who is the Mighty, the Most August, the Most Glorious before such as display glory; and on that Day it is He Who is the Lofty, the All-Highest, the Source of exaltation, far above those who are elevated in rank; and it is He Who is the Almighty, the Source of glory and grandeur, far above the pomp of the mighty; and it is He Who is the Omnipotent, the Supreme Ruler, the Lord of judgement, transcending all such as are invested with authority; and *it is He Who is the Generous*, the Most Benevolent, the Essence of bounty, Who standeth supreme in the face of such as show benevolence; and it is He Who is the Ordainer and the Supreme Wielder of authority and power, inconceivably high above those who hold earthly dominion; and it is He Who is the Most Excellent, the Unsurpassed, the Pre-eminent in the face of every man of accomplishment.
>
> Ye have, one and all, been called into being to seek His presence and to attain that exalted and glorious station. Indeed, He will send down from the heaven of His mercy that which will benefit you, and whatever is graciously vouchsafed by Him shall enable you to dispense with all mankind.[131]

The 'Presence of the Generous One' may thus be seen as an affirmation that those who have recognized and accepted

Bahá'u'lláh have entered paradise and fulfilled the age-old promise of 'attaining the Presence of God'. This promise is enshrined in all the holy scriptures. For example, in the Book of Revelation, John shares his vision of that most holy day:

> And I heard a great voice out of heaven saying, Behold, the tabernacle of God is with men, and he will dwell with them, and they shall be his people, and God himself shall be with them, and be their God.[132]

In another sense, the 'Presence of the Generous One' may refer to nearness to God. The Arabic word translated here as 'Generous One' is *karím*. This is a typical Quranic attribute of God and is also the most frequent adjective modifying the word Qur'án, when it is translated as holy, as in 'the Holy Qur'án'. The word 'Presence' is translated from the Arabic *qurb*, which means nearness. The concept of nearness suggests a less intimate relationship than the word 'Presence' and it is worth pondering this when studying the Tablet of Aḥmad.

Bahá'u'lláh says that 'No theme hath been more emphatically asserted in the holy scriptures' [than] 'the reality of "attainment unto the divine Presence".'[133] He further explains:

> . . . the highest and most excelling grace bestowed upon men is the grace of 'attaining unto the Presence of God' and of His recognition, which has been promised unto all people.[134]

In the *Book of Certitude* Bahá'u'lláh explains that by attaining the Presence of God is meant the recognition and acceptance of God's promised Manifestation. He concludes:

> By attaining, therefore, to the presence of these holy Luminaries [the Manifestations of God], the 'Presence of God' Himself is attained . . . Therefore, whosoever, and in whatever Dispensation, hath recognized and attained unto the presence of these glorious, these resplendent and most excellent Luminaries, hath verily attained unto the 'Presence

> of God' Himself, and entered the city of eternal and immortal life.[135]

Bahá'u'lláh further explains that recognizing God's chosen Manifestation and choosing to live under the shelter of His care and protection is the essential purpose and ultimate meaning of human life:

> The purpose of God in creating man hath been, and will ever be, to enable him to know his Creator and to attain His Presence . . . Whoso hath recognized the Day Spring of Divine guidance and entered His holy court hath drawn nigh unto God and attained His Presence, a Presence which is the real Paradise, and of which the loftiest mansions of heaven are but a symbol.[136]

The Tablet of Aḥmad may be viewed as a proclamation by Bahá'u'lláh to the followers of the Báb, and to all the people of the world, that God has fulfilled His most sacred, divine promise, this 'highest and most excelling grace', through the Manifestation and Revelation of Bahá'u'lláh. 'The Presence of the Generous One' may thus be seen as an affirmation by Bahá'u'lláh that He is, indeed, 'the tabernacle of God' who will dwell with men and be their God.

# 18

# His Holy Court

*calling the believers in the Divine Unity*
*to the court of the Presence of the Generous One*

As we have seen, Bahá'u'lláh sets two conditions for attaining the Presence of God:

> Whoso hath recognized the Day Spring of Divine guidance and entered His holy court hath drawn nigh unto God and attained His Presence . . .[137]

We may infer that one must not only recognize the Manifestation but also 'enter His holy court'. What does it mean to enter the court of the Manifestation of God?

For the believers who lived during the lifetime of Bahá'u'lláh it had a literal meaning. If they received permission, they could undertake a pilgrimage to visit Him and be granted the immeasurable bounty of meeting Him in person. But, in fact, only a small handful of the early believers had the privilege of doing so. For the rest of the believers, and for all of us who have become Bahá'ís since the ascension of Bahá'u'lláh, attaining His physical presence is impossible. Surely God would not deprive us of 'this highest and most excelling grace'[138] simply because we do not live in the lifetime of Bahá'u'lláh. We must therefore look to the spiritual significance of the phrase.

It is obvious that entering His holy court is not a condition that can be achieved passively. 'To enter' is an active verb;

it requires action.[139] Bahá'u'lláh seems to be telling us that an action or change of behaviour on our part is required to enter His court. What kind of actions and behaviours are implied in this phrase?

We recall that Bahá'u'lláh is known as the King of Glory and that He refers to Himself as the King of Kings.[140] He tells us that earthly kingship is a sign of the majesty and sovereignty of God.[141] To better understand the significance of the phrase 'and entered His holy court', let us evoke the image of the majesty and grandeur of the royal court and consider the analogy of a subject appearing before his king.

How does a person approach his king? We can see a man walking into the royal court and humbly approaching the king's dais. As he nears the king, he kneels before him in a gesture of submission and obedience and swears his undying fealty.

In a similar manner, to enter the court of Bahá'u'lláh suggests that we approach Him with humility and reverence, that we offer Him our fidelity, acknowledge His divine authority in our lives and agree unconditionally to be submissive to Him and obey His commandments.

Thus it is through our acceptance of Bahá'u'lláh in our personal lives and through our acts of submission and obedience that we 'enter His holy court'. He counsels us:

> Thus God instructeth whosoever seeketh Him. He, verily, loveth the one that turneth towards Him. There is none other God but Him, the Forgiving, the Most Bountiful.[142]

The implication of this, and other similar verses, is that whenever we turn towards Bahá'u'lláh, He reciprocates by reaching out to us and accepting us in His court. Bahá'u'lláh assures us of this:

> No man that seeketh Us will We ever disappoint, neither shall he that hath set his face towards Us be denied access unto Our court.[143]

It is our obligation, as partners to the Covenant of Bahá'u'lláh, to strive to fulfil the requirements that our Lord asks of us. It is through the actions of our lives, our daily endeavours to fulfil His wishes, that we demonstrate our fealty to Him and are accepted in His holy court. Bahá'u'lláh declares:

> A twofold obligation resteth upon him who hath recognized the Day Spring of the Unity of God, and acknowledged the truth of Him Who is the Manifestation of His oneness. The first is steadfastness in His love . . . The second is strict observance of the laws He hath prescribed . . .[144]

In terms of the Covenant, entering His holy court implies our willingness and commitment to strive to fulfil this 'twofold obligation' in our lives. In return, Bahá'u'lláh assures us that God will most certainly reward us for all our efforts. He asserts, 'Whoso keepeth the commandments of God shall attain everlasting felicity.'[145] Simply recognizing Bahá'u'lláh is not sufficient to guarantee our attaining the presence of God. We must enter His court by accepting Him into our daily lives and by striving to fulfil the essential conditions of His Covenant, through our efforts to be steadfast in His love and to obey His commandments. In return, Bahá'u'lláh promises us the inestimable reward of His infinite love.

It is Bahá'u'lláh Himself who is 'calling the believers . . . to the court of the Presence of the Generous One'. In other words, He is the one who is urging us to reach out and approach Him. This is an essential message of the Tablet of Aḥmad. Bahá'u'lláh, the supreme Manifestation of God, is inviting us into the court of His Presence and is offering each one of us the bounties of His infinite love. In one of His prayers He assures us:

> Thou disappointest no one who hath sought Thee, nor dost Thou keep back from Thee any one who hath desired Thee. Ordain Thou for me what becometh the heaven of Thy generosity, and the ocean of Thy bounty. Thou art, verily, the Almighty, the Most Powerful.[146]

# 19

# Informing the Severed Ones

*informing the severed ones of the message which hath been revealed by God, the King, the Glorious, the Peerless*

Who are 'the severed ones'?

Several important categories of people appear to be suggested by this phrase. The lovers of God is one group that immediately comes to mind. Like mystic nightingales, they set their hearts so firmly on Him that they willingly detach themselves from everything else. Bahá'u'lláh describes them in these words:

> The essence of love is for man to turn his heart to the Beloved One, and sever himself from all else but Him, and desire naught save that which is the desire of his Lord.[147]

What does it mean to sever oneself from everything but God? Bahá'u'lláh explains that people's imaginations and superstitions have always prevented them from recognizing the new Manifestation of God when He appears. He says that we must stop relying on our own limited understanding and the misinformation we receive from others when judging the Cause of God. If we truly want to follow the path of God, He says, we must detach ourselves from our own conceptions and prejudices and learn to rely wholly on God. This is the meaning of severance and in the beginning of the *Book of Certitude* Bahá'u'lláh sets forth its essential requirements:

> No man shall attain the shores of the ocean of true understanding except he be detached from all that is in heaven and on earth. Sanctify your souls, O ye peoples of the world, that haply ye may attain that station which God hath destined for you . . .
>
> The essence of these words is this: they that tread the path of faith, they that thirst for the wine of certitude, must cleanse themselves of all that is earthly . . . They should put their trust in God, and, holding fast unto Him, follow in His way. Then will they be made worthy of the effulgent glories of the sun of divine knowledge and understanding . . . inasmuch as man can never hope to attain unto the knowledge of the All-Glorious . . . unless and until he ceases to regard the words and deeds of mortal men as a standard for the true understanding and recognition of God and His Prophets.[148]

Severance, as with other spiritual qualities, is not an 'all-or-nothing' proposition. Becoming detached from the world goes hand in hand with becoming attracted and attached to the divine kingdom. This is a dynamic process and Bahá'u'lláh seems to allude to this process of spiritual development in the opening paragraph of the Tablet of Aḥmad. In addressing those who are seeking Him, He calls them 'the sincere ones', 'the believers', 'the severed ones' and 'the lovers'. These attributes may be considered as signifying four different groups of people or they may also be understood as referring to a single group of people. In this latter sense, these qualities may represent a spiritual progression.

Bahá'u'lláh first proclaims His message to 'the sincere ones'. In order to recognize Bahá'u'lláh, we must become sincere in our devotion to God and our search for the truth. Then God can guide us to our heart's desire. Once we have accepted Bahá'u'lláh, we begin to learn more about His true station as God's promised Manifestation. As we become deepened in the fundamental verities of the Faith, we become 'believers in the Divine Unity'. As our understanding grows, we become attracted to the reality of Bahá'u'lláh and turn our hearts towards Him. This is a conscious choice on our part and to make this choice means that we must detach ourselves from notions and superstitions that prevent or inhibit us from loving Him. As we sever ourselves from these restraints, we become more aware of the significance of 'the message which hath been revealed by God'. This message, contained within His teachings and prayers, guides us to the love of Bahá'u'lláh. As we respond to His call of true love, we become His lovers. In the Seven Valleys He says:

> O My Brother! A pure heart is as a mirror; cleanse it with the burnish of love and severance from all save God, that the true sun may shine within it and the eternal morning dawn. Then wilt thou clearly see the meaning of 'Neither doth My earth nor My heaven contain Me, but the heart of My faithful servant containeth Me.'[149]

In another sense, 'the severed ones' may be the followers of the Báb. Aḥmad was sent to teach the Bábís that Bahá'u'lláh was indeed the one promised by the Báb. Thus the 'severed ones' may also refer to those Bábís who were willing to give up their own idle fancies and imaginations and listen to the claim of Bahá'u'lláh. In this sense, the phrase 'informing the severed ones of the message which hath been revealed by God' may be understood as referring simultaneously to the message of the Báb and to the Revelation of Bahá'u'lláh. On one hand, the Báb's message to His followers was to expect the advent of 'Him Whom God shall make manifest'. At the same time, Bahá'u'lláh's message was that He was 'Him Whom God shall make manifest'.

Yet another group of people to whom the term 'severed ones' may apply is suggested by the definition of the verb 'sever'. Sever means to separate or cut apart. The 'severed ones' may thus imply all those souls who have been separated from God. They are people from all religions and all parts of the world who have become disillusioned and alienated from God, who have left their churches or been forgotten or cast aside by the leaders of their faith. To all these souls Bahá'u'lláh reaches out with His message of divine love and the 'glad tidings of the nearness of God'.

## 20

# The Seat of Sanctity and This Resplendent Beauty

*guiding the lovers to the seat of sanctity and to this resplendent Beauty*

We can gain a deeper understanding of the prophetic allusions of this phrase when we consider the Arabic. In the Tablet of Aḥmad, the Arabic phrase Bahá'u'lláh uses to convey the expression 'guiding the lovers to the seat of sanctity and to this resplendent Beauty' is suggestive of two important, distinct verses in the Qur'án.

The first of these promises the righteous that they will dwell in paradise with the Promised One:

> Verily, amid gardens and rivers shall the pious dwell
> In the seat of truth, in the presence of the potent King.[150]

Notice the similarity between 'the seat of sanctity and to this resplendent Beauty' and 'in the seat of truth, in the presence of the potent King'. In these two expressions, the 'seat of sanctity' (*maq'ad al-quds*) and the 'seat of truth' (*maq'ad ṣidq*) appear to have the same connotations and implications. Both evoke an image of an exalted state of being, of saintly holiness, sanctified and purified from the things of this mundane world. A comparison of 'the presence of the potent King' and 'this resplendent Beauty' indicates that these phrases also have similar connotations and implications. Indeed, 'the omnipotent King' is another title of Bahá'u'lláh, 'this resplendent Beauty'. Thus it is possible that Bahá'u'lláh is alluding to this particular Islamic verse. In so doing, He is giving us yet another clear sign in the Tablet of Aḥmad that He is, indeed, the one who was promised by God in the Qur'án.

The second verse we will consider speaks of the twin trumpet blasts and is both a warning of the coming Day of Judgement and a promise of the glory of the advent of the Promised One. It is an important and very well-known Islamic literary theme related to the last days. The connection between it and this phrase from the Tablet of Aḥmad lies in the Arabic words Bahá'u'lláh chose for 'this resplendent Beauty' (*al-manẓar al-munír).* In Arabic, 'this resplendent Beauty' is related to a crucial term in this verse. The Qur'án says:

> And there shall be a blast on the trumpet, and all who are in the Heavens and all who are in the Earth shall expire, save those whom God shall vouchsafe to live. Then shall there be another blast on it, and lo! arising they shall gaze around them:
>
> And the earth shall shine with the light of her Lord, and the Book shall be set, and the prophets shall be brought up . . .[151]

The Arabic word for 'gazing around them' is *yanẓurúna. Yanẓurúna* comes from the Arabic roots meaning 'to look at', 'to gaze at' or 'to admire the beauty of'. In the above verse from the Qur'án, after the second trumpet blast, the people whom God has protected will be gazing around them, or admiring the beauty of (*yanẓurúna*), the wondrous sight before their eyes. What is it that will be so awe-inspiring and beautiful? The verse says that they will be admiring the breathtaking beauty of the earth shining 'with the glory of her Lord'.

To understand the relationship between this verse and the Tablet of Aḥmad, we must consider the grammatical implication, in Arabic, of *yanẓurúna*. The Quranic verse says that after the second trumpet blast, when the Promised One will have appeared, those who are saved by God will be *yanẓurún*, that is, they will be gazing at and admiring the beautiful scene before their eyes. In Arabic it would be said that what the people are gazing at (*yanẓurún*) is *manẓar*. *Manẓar*, which is constructed from the same three Arabic letters as *yanẓurúna*, literally means 'the object of all looking at', 'the object of all gazing at' or 'the object whose beauty is being admired'. In the Tablet of Aḥmad, 'this resplendent Beauty' is *al-manẓar al-munír*, which literally means 'the resplendent *manẓar*' or 'the resplendent Object Whose beauty is being admired and gazed at'. The connection between the verse from the Qur'án which says that the people will be gazing at (*yanẓurúna*) the earth shining with the glory of her Lord and the phrase from the Tablet of Aḥmad in which Bahá'u'lláh says that He is guiding the lovers to 'this resplendent Beauty' (*al-manẓar al-munír*) seems very strong. By using this Arabic phrase, Bahá'u'lláh seems to be very clearly indicating that He is the promised *manẓar*, the one who will appear after the second trumpet blast and illumine the whole earth with His light and glory.

In one of His Tablets Bahá'u'lláh asserts that He is the fulfilment of this particular verse of the Qur'án:

> The second blast hath been blown on the trumpet. On whom are ye gazing? This is your Lord, the God of Mercy.[152]

Through the Arabic words Bahá'u'lláh revealed He seems to be alluding to two significant verses of the Qur'án, both of which tell of the coming of the Promised One of God, and thus confirming our understanding that Bahá'u'lláh is the one whom God has promised in the Qur'án.

## 21

# The King, the Glorious, the Peerless

*the message which hath been revealed by God, the King, the Glorious, the Peerless*

A fundamental teaching of divine unity is that God is unknowable and that He can only be known through His Manifestations. Therefore, whenever any of the holy scriptures refer to a message from God, they must be referring to a message that God has given us through one of His Manifestations. Thus the phrase 'the message which hath been revealed by God' must refer to a revelation given by God to humanity through His Manifestations. This, in turn, suggests that the names of God in the phrase 'the King, the Glorious, the Peerless' may refer, on one level, to the Manifestations who have brought this message.

The Arabic phrase for 'the message which hath been revealed by God' is *bihatha'n-nabá' alathí fussila min nabá' alláh*. In one sense the *nabá' alláh* may refer to the Revelation of God which He gives to His Manifestations. Each Manifestation, in turn, reveals to the people of His time a pre-ordained measure of the Revelation of God. This pre-ordained measure (*nabá' fussila*) refers to the divine message which has been specifically designated for this time. This message becomes 'the message which hath been revealed by God' to the people of His age. It is the specific part of the larger message of God.

One aspect of this larger message has always been the promise of the great and holy Day of God, the Day which would witness the advent of the Promised One of all ages. In this sense 'the message which hath been revealed by God' in the Tablet of Aḥmad may refer to this promise which God had made a part of all previous Revelations. Thus we may say that the message which all the previous Manifestations have expounded to their people is this promise of the coming of this holy Day of God and that the message which is being expounded by both the Báb and Bahá'u'lláh is the fulfilment of this divine promise.

On another level we can look at the Tablet of Aḥmad in its historical context. We recall that it was revealed for Aḥmad to assist him in teaching the Bábís the truth of the claim of Bahá'u'lláh. In this sense 'the message which hath been revealed by God, the King, the Glorious, the Peerless' may be understood as referring to the Báb who told His followers to expect the coming of 'Him Whom God shall make manifest'.

On yet another level, the phrase 'the message which hath been revealed by God, the King, the Glorious, the Peerless' suggests a *sequence* of successive Manifestations. As an historical precedent for such a concept, consider this verse from the Book of Revelation:

> I am Alpha and Omega, the beginning and the ending, saith the Lord, *which is, and which was, and which is to come*, the Almighty.[153]

According to Bahá'u'lláh, the expression 'the beginning and the ending' applies to every Manifestation of God.[154] We now consider the specific phrase 'which is, and which was, and which is to come'. This verse was written soon after the martyrdom of Jesus Christ. In terms of a sequence of Manifestations, this suggests that it may refer to Christ ('which is'), to Moses ('which was') and to Muḥammad ('which is to come'), all of whom are the Manifestations of both 'the Beginning' and 'the End'.[155]

The phrase 'the message which hath been revealed by God, the King, the Glorious, the Peerless' may have a similar connotation. Bahá'u'lláh may here be alluding to the progressive unfoldment of the religion of God. In this sense, He may be referring to a sequence of the Báb ('the King'), Himself ('the Glorious') and He who in the future will follow Bahá'u-'lláh ('the Peerless'). Such a concept appears to be consistent with the following explanation from the writings of the Báb, which illustrates the divine progression and unfoldment of the religion of God through successive Manifestations:

> . . . the Revelation of God may be likened to the sun. No matter how innumerable its risings, there is but one sun, and upon it depends the life of all things. It is clear and evident that the object of all preceding Dispensations hath been to pave the way for the advent of Muḥammad, the Apostle of God. These, including the Muḥammadan Dispensation, have had, in their turn, as their objective the Revelation proclaimed by the Qá'im [the Báb]. The purpose underlying this Revelation, as well as those that preceded it, has, in like manner, been to announce the advent of the Faith of Him Whom God will make manifest. And this Faith – the Faith of Him Whom God will make manifest – in its turn, together with all the Revelations gone before it, have as their object the Manifestation destined to succeed it . . . The process of the rise and setting of the Sun of Truth will thus indefinitely continue – a process that hath had no beginning and will have no end.[156]

Returning to the Tablet of Aḥmad, it is possible that Bahá'u'lláh is conveying this same concept of a sequence of Manifestations. If this is so, it suggests that there may be yet another level of significance hidden in the opening invocation 'He is the King, the All-Knowing, the Wise', as well as in the phrase 'the King, the Glorious, the Peerless'. In this sense Bahá'u'lláh may be alluding to the continuous unfolding of the religion of God through the Manifestations.

In another sense we know that every Manifestation is the embodiment of all the names and attributes of God. Every

Manifestation, then, is 'the King, the All-Knowing, the Wise' and also 'the King, the Glorious, the Peerless'. This, too, appears to reinforce the idea of a sequence of Manifestations. For in this sense Bahá'u'lláh is testifying to all the Manifestations who have gone before Him and all who will appear in the future. Every one of them is the revealer of 'the message which hath been revealed by God'. All those who have gone before Bahá'u'lláh have promised His coming and all those who will be manifested in the future will be under His shadow and will testify to the greatness of His Revelation.

## 22

# The Lovers

*guiding the lovers to the seat of sanctity*
*and to this resplendent Beauty*

Love and sacrifice are inseparable. Becoming a lover of Bahá'u'lláh requires sacrifice. Sacrifice means to give up something of lesser value in order to gain something of greater value. The love of Bahá'u'lláh is the greatest treasure in the universe. Once our hearts have tasted the sweetness of His tender, unconditional love, we will settle for nothing else. As He says in one of His prayers:

> Armed with the power of Thy name nothing can ever hurt me, and with Thy love in my heart all the world's afflictions can in no wise alarm me.[157]

True lovers must sacrifice their own cares, their own desires and even their own opinions and understanding and embrace the teachings of Bahá'u'lláh. We must learn to let Bahá'u'lláh guide us in our daily lives. This is essential if we wish to become the individuals that the love of Bahá'u'lláh can enable us to become. We must become detached and sanctified from the limitations of this earthly life because these limitations prevent us from reaching our true home in the spiritual worlds of God. To gain the freedom of the heavenly kingdom and possess its treasures, we must become detached from the attitudes we have which tie us to this world. Bahá'u'lláh says:

> Pass beyond the narrow retreats of your evil and corrupt desires, and advance into the vast immensity of the realm of God, and abide ye in the meads of sanctity and of detachment . . .[158]

The Bahá'í writings tell us that this world, in spite of its physical vastness, is a dark and confining place. By its very nature it prevents us from seeing the reality of the spiritual worlds of God, our true home. Bahá'u'lláh asks us to give up the 'narrow retreats' of our fears and desires that bind us to this physical world. In return He offers us the 'vast immensity of the realm of God'. Should we choose to respond to His call ('let him choose the path to his Lord') we will find that the benefits of the spiritual realm are endless. Their value is immeasurable when compared with the apparent benefits of this material world. In another Tablet Bahá'u'lláh tells us that there is a sweetness in the spiritual worlds which cannot be found in materialistic pursuits:

> Sanctify your souls from whatsoever is not of God, and taste ye the sweetness of rest within the pale of His vast and mighty Revelation, and beneath the shadow of His supreme and infallible authority.[159]

Another implication of the phrase 'guiding the lovers' may be that we must learn to trust Bahá'u'lláh completely. We must learn to accept that whatever troubles we encounter in this life are for the best and will eventually lead us to 'the seat of sanctity'. We cannot become detached and be drawn closer to God unless we are willing to endure hardships. 'Abdu'l-Bahá says that troubles are the bounty and mercy of God. To understand why this is so, we need to remember that sacrifice also means to make sacred. Just as grapes must be pressed to yield the choice wine, so we, too, must experience the crucible of Bahá'u'lláh's love as we strive to purify our own hearts. It is through suffering and hardships in the path of the love of God that He sanctifies our lives and makes us worthy of His love and His infinite bounties and favours. Through trials and difficulties we are drawn closer to Him and become purified and detached from the things of this world. 'Abdu'l-Bahá says:

> Whatsoever may happen is for the best, because affliction is but the essence of bounty, and sorrow and toil are mercy unalloyed, and anguish is peace of mind, and to make a sacrifice is to receive a gift, and whatsoever may come to pass hath issued from God's grace.[160]

Bahá'u'lláh, in one of His prayers, affirms this:

> Glory to Thee, O my God! But for the tribulations which are sustained in Thy path, how could Thy true lovers be recognized; and were it not for the trials which are borne for love of Thee, how could the station of such as yearn for Thee be revealed?[161]

We see, then, that to become a lover of Bahá'u'lláh involves sacrifice. As we sacrifice in the path of Bahá'u'lláh we are giving up something of much lesser value for the love of Bahá'u'lláh. As we sacrifice in His path He makes us worthy of His love and we become His lovers. As we become His lovers and reach out to Him, He guides us to 'the seat of sanctity' and to the court of His love and infinite bounties.

# 23

# The Seat of Sanctity

*guiding the lovers*
*to the seat of sanctity*
*and to this resplendent Beauty*

Sanctity (*al-quds*) means saintliness, holiness of life and purity. It is also defined as the state of being consecrated to God. The term 'seat of sanctity' indicates the centre of sanctity, the source of all that is pure and holy.

In one sense the 'seat of sanctity' may signify the human heart. This may be seen by considering the following verses. In the Tablet of Aḥmad, Bahá'u'lláh describes the condition of those who 'are wandering in the paths of delusion' and who are thus veiled from recognizing Him. He says, 'Thus have their superstitions become veils between them and their own hearts . . .' Compare this statement with this one: 'O my Lord! Make . . . my dwelling-place the seat Thou hast sanctified from the limitations imposed upon them who are shut out as by a veil from Thee.'[162] Since He says that people's superstitions veil them 'from their own hearts', we may infer that 'the seat' mentioned in this phrase is the human heart.

Bahá'u'lláh describes the heart as 'the seat of the revelation of the inner mysteries of God'.[163] He also says that the heart is 'the throne, in which the Revelation of God the All-Merciful is centred'.[164] In the sense that 'the seat of sanctity' symbolizes the human heart, Bahá'u'lláh is 'guiding the lovers' of God to open their hearts to the outpourings of His grace so that

He may purify them and make them the sacred dwelling places of His love. He says:

> The things He hath reserved for Himself are the cities of men's hearts, that He may cleanse them from all earthly defilements, and enable them to draw nigh unto the hallowed Spot which the hands of the infidel can never profane.[165]

Elsewhere in His writings Bahá'u'lláh tells us that it is people's own thoughts, their vain imaginings, which prevent them from opening their hearts to God's new message. In one of His Tablets He says:

> Ponder a while. What is it that prompted, in every Dispensation, the peoples of the earth to shun the Manifestation of the All-Merciful? What could have impelled them to turn away from Him and to challenge His authority? . . . It is the veil of idle imaginations which . . . hath intervened, and will continue to intervene, between them and the rest of mankind.[166]

To be guided, therefore, to 'the seat of sanctity', we must not allow our hearts to become veiled by superstitions and vain imaginings. We must choose to turn to Bahá'u'lláh and open our hearts to Him. When we do so, we are rewarded with the outpouring of His love and grace. It is this grace of God, flowing through the Manifestation, that cleanses the human heart and sanctifies it from the things of this world. This is one of the fundamental teachings of the Bahá'í Faith. It is the *function* of the Manifestation of God to act as a vehicle for transmitting the grace of God to every human being. Bahá'u'lláh explains:

> . . . these resplendent Realities are the channels of God's all-pervasive grace . . . They are commissioned to use the inspiration of Their words, the effusions of Their infallible grace and the sanctifying breeze of Their Revelation for the

> cleansing of every longing heart and receptive spirit from the dross and dust of earthly cares and limitations. Then, and only then, will the Trust of God, latent in the reality of man, emerge, as resplendent as the rising Orb of Divine Revelation, from behind the veil of concealment, and implant the ensign of its revealed glory upon the summits of men's hearts.[167]

In this sense, when Bahá'u'lláh tells us that He is 'guiding the lovers to the seat of sanctity', He seems to be describing His God-given duty. This, too, in itself, is a sign that He is the Promised Manifestation of God.

The 'seat of sanctity' may also imply man's inmost true reality. This reality is his latent spiritual potential with which God has endowed his soul. In this connection, Bahá'u'lláh says:

> Through the Teachings of this Day Star of Truth every man will advance and develop until he attaineth the station at which he can manifest all the potential forces with which his inmost true self hath been endowed.[168]

Thus, in another sense, 'guiding the lovers to the seat of sanctity' suggests that Bahá'u'lláh is guiding us to the teachings of God which will enable us to unfold and develop all of the spiritual potential with which God has endowed our souls.

Elsewhere in His writings Bahá'u'lláh counsels us that if we desire to follow in His way and draw near to Him, we must cleanse and sanctify our hearts from the defilements of this world. For example, in the Hidden Words, He says:

> O Son of Being! Thy heart is My home; sanctify it for My descent. Thy spirit is My place of revelation; cleanse it for My manifestation.[169]

> O Son of Glory! Be swift in the path of holiness, and enter the heaven of communion with Me. Cleanse thy heart with the burnish of the spirit, and hasten to the court of the Most High.[170]

It is very interesting to reflect on the situation in which we find ourselves. We are exhorted to cleanse and sanctify our hearts so that we may experience the love and grace of God's Manifestation. But we cannot do this by ourselves; we need the help and assistance of the Manifestation. The key to solving this paradox, Bahá'u'lláh tells us, is that we must free ourselves from our own prejudices and vain imaginings. We must also free ourselves from the opinions and thoughts of others. We need to do this because all of these things cloud our thinking and prevent us from turning our hearts towards, and opening them to, Bahá'u'lláh's unconditional love. We must, as Christ said, become like little children and learn to trust Bahá'u'lláh. We must *choose to turn* to Bahá'u'lláh and invite Him into our hearts ('let him choose the path to his Lord'). When we do this we are guided to 'the seat of sanctity'. As we have seen, in the Seven Valleys, Bahá'u'lláh tells us:

> O My Brother! A pure heart is as a mirror; cleanse it with the burnish of love and severance from all save God, that the true sun may shine within it and the eternal morning dawn . . .
>
> Whensoever the Splendour of the King of Oneness settleth upon the throne of the heart and soul, His shining becometh visible in every limb and member . . . For thus the Master of the house hath appeared within His home, and all the pillars of the dwelling are ashine with His light. And the action and effect of the light are from the Light-Giver . . .[171]

And in the Hidden Words, He advises us:

> The candle of thine heart is lighted by the hand of My power, quench it not with the contrary winds of self and passion. The healer of all thine ills is remembrance of Me, forget it not. Make My love thy treasure and cherish it even as thy very sight and life.[172]

## 24

# The Seat of Sanctity: The Covenant

*guiding the lovers*
*to the seat of sanctity and*
*to this resplendent Beauty*

The phrase 'the seat of sanctity' may also be understood as symbolizing the protection and safety of the Covenant of God. The Covenant is God's sanctuary for all humankind and the word 'seat' as used in Bahá'u'lláh's writings suggests that 'the seat of sanctity' may allude to the security of this most holy institution. For example, in describing the mission of God's Messengers, He says:

> Unto the cities of all nations He hath sent His Messengers, Whom He hath commissioned to announce unto men tidings of the Paradise of His good pleasure, and to draw them nigh unto the Haven of abiding security, the Seat [*maq'ad al-amn*] of eternal holiness and transcendent glory.[173]

In one sense, the 'Seat of eternal holiness' and the 'Haven of abiding security' both symbolize the establishment of the Covenant of God in every dispensation.

Another example of this use of the word 'seat' is found in the Tablet of Carmel. In this Tablet Bahá'u'lláh speaks of the 'seat of His throne',[174] alluding to the future establishment of the Seat of the Universal House of Justice on Mount

Carmel. We note that the Universal House of Justice is the Centre of Bahá'u'lláh's inviolable Covenant and the central institution of the World Order of Bahá'u'lláh. Bahá'u'lláh declares:

> He, verily, loveth the spot which hath been made the seat of His throne, which His footsteps have trodden, which hath been honoured by His presence, from which He raised His call, and upon which He shed His tears.[175]

The 'seat of sanctity' may thus also be understood as alluding to the sacredness of this divine institution and the sanctity of the Covenant itself, the 'Haven of abiding security'.

On another level, 'guiding the lovers to the seat of sanctity and to this resplendent Beauty' may be seen as referring to the twin duties of obedience and recognition that Bahá'u'lláh sets out in the opening verses of the Kitáb-i-Aqdas, the Book of His laws:

> The first duty prescribed by God for His servants is the recognition of Him Who is the Dayspring of His Revelation and the Fountain of His laws . . . It behoveth every one who reacheth this most sublime station, this summit of transcendent glory, to observe every ordinance of Him Who is the Desire of the world. These twin duties are inseparable.[176]

And, as we have seen, in another Tablet He counsels us:

> O ye the beloved of the one true God! Pass beyond the narrow retreats of your evil and corrupt desires, and advance into the vast immensity of the realm of God, and abide ye in the meads of sanctity and of detachment . . . [177]

To reach the condition of abiding 'in the meads of sanctity' requires us to be obedient to the laws of God. Thus when Bahá'u'lláh says He is 'guiding the lovers to the seat of sanctity' this may indicate that He is guiding us to the sanctity of obedience to His laws and steadfastness in the Covenant. 'Guiding the lovers . . . to this resplendent Beauty' appears to indicate that Bahá'u'lláh is guiding us to recognize Him as God's Promised One. Thus when Bahá'u'lláh joins these two phrases together in the Tablet of Aḥmad, we may infer that He is alluding to the twin, inseparable duties of obedience to and recognition of God's Manifestation, the 'Dayspring of His Revelation'.

Thus we see that the expression 'the seat of sanctity' appears to have several important levels of meaning. At one level it may represent the haven of security and safety within the fortress of the Covenant of God; on another it may symbolize the sacredness and inviolable authority of the institutions of Bahá'u'lláh's World Order, especially the Universal House of Justice; and on yet another it may indicate the fundamental, inseparable duties of recognition of and obedience to God's promised Manifestation.

## 25

# The Most Great Beauty

*Verily, this is that Most Great Beauty foretold in the Books of the Messengers*

Bahá'u'lláh begins this paragraph by immediately unveiling His true station and asserting that He is 'that Most Great Beauty foretold in the Books of the Messengers'. There is no equivocation, no uncertainty. From this point on, there can be no further doubt as to whom He is referring nor to the true character of the station He claims for Himself.

Bahá'u'lláh is the Most Great Beauty. In Arabic the phrase 'Most Great Beauty' is *Manẓar-al-Akbar*, which literally means the Most Great *Manẓar*, the object of all gazing and looking at, the object whose beauty is being admired. That Shoghi Effendi translated the phrase *Manẓar-al-Akbar* as the 'Most Great Beauty' establishes a connection between this phrase and the Arabic word *jamál*, which means beauty. The early believers often referred to Bahá'u'lláh as 'Jamál-i-Mubárak', the 'Blessed Beauty'. This was one of His well-known titles. In His writings He also refers to Himself as the 'Ancient Beauty', as seen in such examples as:

> Consider these days in which He Who is the Ancient Beauty hath come in the Most Great Name, that He may quicken the world and unite its peoples.[178]

> The Most Great Law is come, and the Ancient Beauty ruleth upon the throne of David.[179]

We also find references and allusions to the beauty of Bahá'u-'lláh throughout the scriptures. For example, the Báb, glorifying the greatness of Bahá'u'lláh, extols His beauty in these terms:

> And when He intoneth the anthems of the greatness of God all Paradise waileth in its longing to gaze on His Beauty . . .[180]

> The glory of Him Whom God shall make manifest is immeasurably above every other glory, and His majesty is far above every other majesty. His beauty excelleth every other embodiment of beauty, and His grandeur immensely exceedeth every other manifestation of grandeur. Every light paleth before the radiance of His light . . .[181]

David, in his psalms, alludes to the beauty of Bahá'u'lláh:

> Out of Zion, the perfection of beauty, God hath shined. Our God shall come, and shall not keep silence . . .[182]

Bahá'u'lláh, 'the Blessed Beauty', the 'Ancient Beauty', the 'Beauty of God', proclaims the glory of His Manifestation and extols the radiance of this beauty in this well-known passage:

> Hear Me, ye mortal birds! In the Rose Garden of changeless splendour a Flower hath begun to bloom, compared to which every other flower is but a thorn, and before the brightness of Whose glory the very essence of beauty must pale and wither.[183]

Bahá'u'lláh identifies Himself by many different titles in the Tablet of Aḥmad. He begins by affirming that 'He is the King' and immediately declares that 'the Nightingale of Paradise singeth'. Proclaiming Himself to be God's promised Manifestation, Bahá'u'lláh calls Himself 'the nearness of God', 'the Presence of the Generous One', 'the King, the Glorious, the Peerless', and 'this resplendent Beauty'. He then asserts, 'this is that Most Great Beauty' and announces that 'He is the Tree of Life'.

Bahá'u'lláh then reveals the all-powerful affirmation 'He is God', which, in addition to its obvious meaning, may also refer to the greatness of Bahá'u'lláh's own Manifestation. He reinforces this truth by asserting that 'there is no God but Him, the King, the Protector, the Incomparable, the Omnipotent'. Two paragraphs later He again refers to Himself as 'the Nightingale' and, later in the Tablet, as 'this Beauty'. He concludes the Tablet by affirming that, 'Verily, He is the Merciful, the Compassionate.'

All these titles and names may, on one level, be understood as referring to Bahá'u'lláh Himself. It is an outpouring of divine proclamation, yet all done in the third person. Nowhere does Bahá'u'lláh assert, 'I am the Promised One of God.' Rather He says, 'He is the Tree of Life' or 'this is that Most Great Beauty'.

Why did Bahá'u'lláh choose to assert His claim in the third person rather than in the first?

It is not possible to give a definitive answer to this question. However, it may be an expression of Bahá'u'lláh's utter meekness and submissiveness before the will of God. In His writings He emphasizes that it is not He who advances these claims for Himself; rather it is God who claims them for Him:

> By My life! Not of Mine own volition have I revealed Myself, but God, of His own choosing, hath manifested Me.[184]

And in His Tablet to the Sháh of Persia Bahá'u'lláh affirms:

> This thing is not from Me, but from One Who is Almighty and All-Knowing. And He bade Me lift up My voice between earth and heaven . . .[185]

Thus in the Tablet of Aḥmad Bahá'u'lláh makes the unequivocal assertion that He is the 'Most Great Beauty' yet phrases this in language that suggests that God is speaking through His Manifestation.

# *Section 3: The Station of Bahá'u'lláh*

## 26

## The Promised One Foretold in the Books of the Messengers

*Verily, this is that Most Great Beauty foretold in the Books of the Messengers*

Bahá'u'lláh asserts, in unequivocal terms, that His advent fulfils innumerable prophecies found in all the holy scriptures of the world's religions. He emphasizes this fact in countless passages throughout His writings. For example, in a truly astounding passage He declares:

> This is the Day which the Pen of the Most High hath glorified in all the holy Scriptures. There is no verse in them that doth not declare the glory of His holy Name . . .[186]

'His holy Name' indicates Bahá'u'lláh's title 'the Glory of God'. Shoghi Effendi explains:

> He was formally designated Bahá'u'lláh, an appellation specifically recorded in the Persian Bayán, signifying at once the glory, the light and the splendour of God.[187]

Bahá'u'lláh's assertion that 'there is no verse in them [the holy scriptures] that doth not declare the glory of His holy Name' implies, for example, that many biblical references to 'the glory of the Lord', 'the glory of God' and 'the glory of the Father' are prophecies pointing to Bahá'u'lláh's advent. Bahá'u'lláh's statement tells us that it has always been God's intention to prepare humanity to accept Bahá'u'lláh at the time of His appearance. Further elaborating this point, 'Abdu'l-Bahá makes this astonishing declaration:

> Every proof and prophecy, every manner of evidence, whether based on reason or on the text of the scriptures and traditions, are to be regarded as centred in the persons of Bahá'u'lláh and the Báb. In them is to be found their complete fulfilment.[188]

How can we possibly review the numerous scriptural prophecies of the coming of Bahá'u'lláh? Shoghi Effendi tells us:

> To attempt an exhaustive survey of the prophetic references to Bahá'u'lláh's Revelation would indeed be an impossible task. To this the pen of Bahá'u'lláh Himself bears witness: 'All the Divine Books and Scriptures have predicted and announced unto men the advent of the Most Great Revelation. None can adequately recount the verses recorded in the Books of former ages which forecast this supreme Bounty, this most mighty Bestowal.'[189]

On a prophetic level, these statements by Bahá'u'lláh and 'Abdu'l-Bahá impel us to recognize that scriptural references are divine promises that have always alluded to the coming of Bahá'u'lláh. For example, Bahá'u'lláh asserts that He is the one

> . . . Who in the Old Testament hath been named Jehovah, Who in the Gospel hath been designated as the Spirit of Truth, and in the Qur'án acclaimed as the Great Announcement.[190]

Let us examine some of the particular references that Bahá'u'lláh mentions. In the Old Testament we find such references as these to the name Jehovah:

> And I appeared unto Abraham, unto Isaac, and unto Jacob, by the name of God Almighty, but by my name Jehovah was I not known to them.[191]

> That men may know that thou, whose name alone is Jehovah, art the most high over all the earth.[192]

> Trust ye in the Lord for ever: for in the Lord Jehovah is everlasting strength . . .[193]

The Jewish people have always considered the name 'Jehovah' too sacred and holy to read aloud. Even to this day, when it appears in prayers or scriptural readings, it is not read. The Hebrew word *Addonoi*, meaning 'our Lord', is recited instead.

Bahá'u'lláh also refers to Himself as 'the Spirit of Truth'. In the Gospels Christ prophesied the coming of the Spirit of Truth three times:

> If ye love me, keep my commandments. And I will pray the Father, and he shall give you another Comforter, that he may abide with you for ever; Even the Spirit of truth; whom the world cannot receive, because it seeth him not, neither knoweth him . . .[194]

> But when the Comforter is come, whom I will send unto you from the Father, even the Spirit of truth, which proceedeth from the Father, he shall testify of me . . .[195]

> I have yet many things to say unto you, but ye cannot bear them now. Howbeit when he, the Spirit of truth, is come, he will guide you into all truth . . .[196]

Bahá'u'lláh also asserts that He is the Great Announcement spoken of in the Qur'án. In a súrih entitled 'Nabá', meaning 'The Great Announcement' or 'The News',[197] Muḥammad reveals:

Of what ask they of one another?
Of the great News.[198]

These are but a few of the references to 'that Most Great Beauty foretold in the Books of the Messengers'. Bahá'u'lláh is the one who has been promised by all the Prophets of God. For this reason He is the 'Promised One of all ages'. It is very helpful, in this regard, to realize that this is His divine station, one that God has given to Him and commissioned Him to fulfil.

This may be one reason why this Tablet speaks in the third person. Bahá'u'lláh's claim is so great that it is God who makes the claim for Him. Later in the Tablet Bahá'u'lláh says, 'Nay, by the One in Whose hand is My soul, they are not, and never shall be able to do this,' apparently meaning, in one sense, that those who oppose Him cannot deny this truth nor will they ever be capable of denying it. The reason is simple. Numerous passages throughout the writings of each of the three Central Figures of the Faith, the Báb, Bahá'u'lláh and 'Abdu'l-Bahá, testify that it is God Himself who is asserting this claim and establishing its truth.

# 27

# Through Whom Truth Shall be Distinguished from Error

*Verily, this is that Most Great Beauty . . .*
*through Whom truth*
*shall be distinguished from error*

The significance of this verse appears to be based on the fact that the Manifestation of God is:

> . . . the Way of God that connecteth this world with the realms above, and the Standard of His Truth unto every one in the kingdoms of earth and heaven.[199]

What does it mean that Bahá'u'lláh is the 'standard' of God's truth? A standard is an object or quality against which other things are measured. It is used as a basis for comparison when the value or measure of anything is in question. The standard of God's truth implies that we use the Revelation of Bahá'u'lláh as the base against which to measure the validity and worth of all ideas, theories, decisions and modes of behaviour. In the Most Holy Book, Bahá'u'lláh declares:

> Weigh not the Book of God with such standards and sciences as are current amongst you, for the Book itself is the unerring balance established amongst men. In this most perfect balance whatsoever the peoples and kindreds of the earth possess must be weighed, while the measure of its weight

> should be tested according to its own standard, did ye but know it.[200]

In another sense, Bahá'u'lláh Himself is the standard of God's truth, implying that He is 'the Eternal Truth' and 'the true One from God'. It signifies that He has been manifested 'through the power of truth'. It also suggests that His Revelation, the Word of God, is the word of truth. And it implies that His laws and commandments, which are the commandments of God, are the commands of truth. On the most fundamental level, when we recognize Bahá'u'lláh, we have distinguished truth from error. By accepting Him as the representative of God and His intermediary on earth, we have found the source of all that is true in this world of existence.

Recall that Christ promised the coming of Bahá'u'lláh in these words:

> Howbeit when he, the Spirit of truth, is come, he will guide you into all truth.[201]

Bahá'u'lláh, in His Tablet to the Christians, declares:

> Verily, He Who is the Spirit of Truth is come to guide you unto all truth.[202]

That Bahá'u'lláh is the 'Spirit of Truth' suggests that He embodies the essence of all that is truthful and that from Him all truth is generated. The Báb refers to Bahá'u'lláh as 'the Sovereign Truth'.[203] He explains that by accepting or rejecting Bahá'u'lláh we distinguish ourselves as representing either 'the essence of truth' or 'the essence of error':

> If ye wish to distinguish truth from error, consider those who believe in Him Whom God shall make manifest and those who disbelieve Him at the time of His appearance. The former represent the essence of truth, as attested in the Book

> of God, while the latter the essence of error, as attested in that same Book.[204]

The Báb emphasizes that it is through the appearance of Bahá'u'lláh that truth will be distinguished from error:

> Say, verily, the criterion by which truth is distinguished from error shall not appear until the Day of Resurrection [the coming of Him Whom God shall make manifest]. This ye will know, if ye be of them that love the Truth.

In this sense we may infer that Bahá'u'lláh's assertion that He is the One 'through Whom truth shall be distinguished from error' is a reference to this particular statement by the Báb. It is, therefore, yet another sign from Bahá'u'lláh that He is the One who has fulfilled the promises of the Báb.

The Manifestation *defines* truth through His laws and teachings. It is this definition of truth that guides us through life and provides us with an anchor, a fixed standard, which we can always use to maintain our moorings and our balance amid life's ups and downs. This definition of truth, given to us by the Manifestation, is also a compass by which we can steer our way through the maze of life. It is this definition of truth that enables us to make moral and ethical decisions and enables us to distinguish between right and wrong. This definition of truth can only be found in the teachings and laws that are given to us by God's Manifestation. This is one of the essential reasons why God sends us His Manifestations. Bahá'u'lláh explains:

> Men at all times and under all conditions stand in need of one to exhort them, guide them and to instruct and teach them.[205]

Bahá'u'lláh and 'Abdu'l-Bahá explain the role and purpose of the divine laws in this process. Bahá'u'lláh tells us that such laws are necessary and that it is one of our fundamental duties to obey them:

> . . . laws which He hath always ordained, and will continue to ordain, unto men, and through which the truth may be distinguished and separated from falsehood.[206]

'Abdu'l-Bahá explains that the significance of divine law is that it is *spiritual truth*:

> . . . the Law of God is divided into two parts. One is the fundamental basis which comprises all spiritual things – that is to say, it refers to the spiritual virtues and divine qualities . . . it is spiritual and not material truth; it is faith, knowledge, certitude, justice, piety, righteousness, trustworthiness, love of God, benevolence, purity, detachment, humility, meekness, patience and constancy. It shows mercy to the poor, defends the oppressed, gives to the wretched and uplifts the fallen.
>
> These divine qualities, these eternal commandments, will never be abolished; nay, they will last and remain established for ever and ever.[207]

Considering the role of truth as an important element of this process, 'Abdu'l-Bahá tells us that:

> Truthfulness is the foundation of all human virtues. Without truthfulness, progress and success, in all the worlds of God, are impossible for any soul. When this holy attribute is established in man, all the divine qualities will also be acquired.[208]

Obviously if we are going to distinguish truth from error, we must develop the quality and virtue of truthfulness. What does truthfulness really mean?

In the above statement 'Abdu'l-Bahá indicates that truthfulness implies an attraction to divine virtues, a longing to do the will of God, a desire to transform and perfect our lives in a manner which is consistent with the teachings of Bahá'u-'lláh.

It is customary to think of truthfulness as meaning to 'tell the truth', to be honest, to be accurate and to be trustworthy. And these are essential and important elements of truthfulness.

But truthfulness has another level of significance. 'Truth-ful-ness' means to be full of truth. How can we become full of truth?

Bahá'u'lláh is 'the Spirit of Truth' who has been sent to guide us to all truth. His writings are the revealed Word of God. They are the word of truth, the 'Standard of Truth', and they give us the application of truth to our daily lives. In a very real sense, His teachings define reality. They distinguish what is true from what is false. They distinguish the path of true happiness from the many avenues that lead to unhappiness. The more we study Bahá'u'lláh's teachings and understand how they apply to our daily lives, the greater become our acceptance and belief in their validity and in their true worth. The result is that we become more willing to give up our own notions and opinions, our 'idle fancies and vain imaginings' as they are described in the writings of our Faith. Through this dynamic process we learn to evaluate our behaviour, our attitudes and our actions from the standards established in Bahá'u'lláh's teachings. We begin to adopt His perspective, a *Bahá'í* perspective. In short, the more we deepen in the Word of God, the more we become 'full of truth'. And the more in harmony we are with Bahá'u'lláh's teachings, the easier it becomes for us to 'distinguish truth from error' in our daily lives. This may be one of the reasons why it is part of Bahá'u'lláh's Covenant that we study the writings every day: God desires that we be nourished by truth and that our souls become full of truth.

# 28

# The Wisdom of Every Command Shall be Tested

*Verily, this is that Most Great Beauty*
*. . . through Whom . . .*
*the wisdom of every command*
*shall be tested*

The word wisdom is derived from two words meaning 'wise judgement'. Wisdom means making the best use of knowledge and understanding. Notice how accurately this describes the role of the Manifestation. Bahá'u'lláh explains:

> The Prophets of God should be regarded as physicians whose task is to foster the well-being of the world and its peoples, that, through the spirit of oneness, they may heal the sickness of a divided humanity. To none is given the right to question their words or disparage their conduct, for they are the only ones who can claim to have understood the patient and to have correctly diagnosed its ailments.[209]

In another Tablet He tells us:

> The All-Knowing Physician hath His finger on the pulse of mankind. He perceiveth the disease, and prescribeth, in His unerring wisdom, the remedy.[210]

And He counsels us:

> The whole of mankind is in the grip of manifold ills. Strive, therefore, to save its life through the wholesome medicine which the almighty hand of the unerring Physician hath prepared.[211]

The laws and teachings of Bahá'u'lláh are the divine remedy that He has, 'in His unerring wisdom', given to the world. As discussed in the previous chapter, Bahá'u'lláh is the standard of God's truth. His teachings are the very essence of truth and they define reality for all of us. We would, therefore, naturally expect it to be in our own best interest to strive to conform our lives to His teachings. If Bahá'u'lláh's laws and teachings form the best possible guidance for our lives, it seems most reasonable that our true happiness and well-being depend on how well we live our lives in accordance with these laws and teachings. The 'testing' enters the picture when any of us choose to do otherwise. We as individuals, as members of a community and as institutions of society, 'test' the validity and worth of Bahá'u'lláh's teachings whenever we choose to act or behave in a manner that is inconsistent with or contrary to His teachings. From a purely logical standpoint, if His laws and teachings are not the best expression of true happiness and well-being, then it follows that when individuals and institutions turn away from His teachings and take another path, they should find greater happiness and well-being. Even a casual observation of modern society clearly demonstrates that quite the opposite is true. We continue to find that the more people strive to live contrary to the teachings of Bahá'u-'lláh, the less happiness there is in the world and the greater is the disillusionment, alienation, pain and suffering, strife and turmoil. Individuals, groups, organizations and institutions are all discovering, in most cases without knowing the source, that the application of the principles and teachings of Bahá'u'lláh is very effective in solving problems, relieving chaos and suffering and in improving happiness and well-being. This fact is, of itself, the greatest proof of both the efficacy and value of Bahá'u'lláh's laws and teachings. It also demonstrates the truth of His assertion that 'the wisdom of every command shall be tested'.

The 'testing' of Bahá'u'lláh's laws and teachings occurs on an individual basis and for institutions and society as a whole. For individuals, 'the wisdom of every command shall be tested' may signify the life-giving, unifying power of the Covenant. In past religious dispensations, God blessed people regardless of the sects to which they belonged or the schisms they created within their religion. In the Revelation of Bahá'u'lláh, however, a fundamental principle is unity and oneness. This unity can be achieved only through obedience to the Covenant. God has unequivocally stated that He will not bless or nurture those who violate the Covenant and attempt to divide His Faith. A review of the history of the Bahá'í Faith shows that through the believers who have held fast to the Covenant and remained unified, the Cause of Bahá'u'lláh has continued to develop and advance and has grown throughout the world. It has gained in strength and diversity and its unifying, life-giving influence has spread and been increasingly recognized.

On the other hand, those individuals who have broken away from the Cause of Bahá'u'lláh and who have violated His Covenant have become like dead branches. All their efforts to establish separate denominations have failed, their members have become divided and their groups fragmented. Their influence has declined and died away and membership in their various groups has dwindled to insignificance. The history of the Bahá'í Faith shows that the wisdom of the divine institution of the Covenant has been thoroughly tested. The 'wholesome medicine' of the life-sustaining, life-producing power of Bahá'u'lláh's Covenant has been conclusively demonstrated.

For society and the world, the unifying principles and teachings of Bahá'u'lláh continue to be tested in the laboratory of world events. In one of His Tablets He voices this warning:

> The well-being of mankind, its peace and security, are unattainable unless and until its unity is firmly established. This unity can never be achieved so long as the counsels which the Pen of the Most High hath revealed are suffered to pass unheeded.[212]

The world continues to be rocked by crisis after crisis. Its people are bewildered and confused and seem unable to distinguish truth from error. This is yet another clear indication that the principles and laws given by Bahá'u'lláh are the only remedy that will enable the people of the world to save themselves. Were it otherwise, humankind certainly would have discovered the right path and found solutions to the serious problems threatening it. The continued decline in the fortunes of humanity demonstrates humanity's inability to find its own way out of the morass into which it is steadily sinking. This, too, is part of the divine testing process. Commenting on the problems currently facing the world Bahá'u'lláh notes:

> We can well perceive how the whole human race is encompassed with great, with incalculable afflictions. We see it languishing on its bed of sickness, sore-tried and disillusioned.[213]

> Its sickness is approaching the stage of utter hopelessness, inasmuch as the true Physician is debarred from administering the remedy, whilst unskilled practitioners are regarded with favour, and are accorded full freedom to act.[214]

Unfortunately, it seems that this 'testing' of the validity of Bahá'u'lláh's teachings will continue until, as Shoghi Effendi has noted, the wisdom of Bahá'u'lláh's divine guidance becomes clear and unmistakable to us all:

> What else, might we not confidently affirm, but the unreserved acceptance of the Divine Programme enunciated . . . by Bahá'u'lláh . . . is eventually capable of withstanding the

> forces of internal disintegration which, if unchecked, must needs continue to eat into the vitals of a despairing society.[215]

When we investigate the breakdown of modern society, we find that actions of individuals and institutions which are not based on the spiritual principles established by Bahá'u'lláh are destructive to society. Since these principles are based on unity and the oneness of humanity, decisions and actions which are not unifying, harmonizing and integrative eventually produce harmful results. This is part of the divine testing process occurring as a direct consequence of the spiritual forces released by the Revelation of Bahá'u'lláh. The expedient philosophy that says that ends justify the means is false. Such a view of life, and others like it, can have no place in the Kingdom of God. Ends can never justify the means. It is both a spiritual law and a law of the physical universe that the means *are* the ends. The consequences of this fact, for all human endeavours, are staggering. For the world, it must result in a complete, organic change in the life of society. This is thoroughly explained in the writings of Shoghi Effendi. In one of his letters he describes the organic changes that must take place as society conforms itself to these spiritual principles:

> Let there be no mistake. The principle of the Oneness of Mankind – the pivot round which all the teachings of Bahá'u'lláh revolve . . . implies an organic change in the structure of present-day society, a change such as the world has not yet experienced. It constitutes a challenge, at once bold and universal, to outworn shibboleths of national creeds – creeds that have had their day and which must, in the ordinary course of events as shaped and controlled by Providence, give way to a new gospel, fundamentally different from, and infinitely superior to, what the world has already conceived.[216]

Another consequence of this fact is that all decisions and actions must conform to the divine standard established by

Bahá'u'lláh in order to produce positive, constructive results. This is true whether we are considering an individual's development or personal relationships or considering institutional decisions and actions of governments. On a deeper level, the spiritual truth that means are the ends also suggests that decisions and actions which conform to the divine standard must be taken for the right reasons. The intention and motivation behind our individual and collective decisions and actions must be pure in order to produce the greatest possible benefit. Describing the condition of the world and its leaders, Bahá'u'lláh comments on the negative effects of unworthy motives:

> We behold it, in this day, at the mercy of rulers so drunk with pride that they cannot discern clearly their own best advantage . . . And whenever any one of them hath striven to improve its condition, his motive hath been his own gain, whether confessedly so or not; and the unworthiness of this motive hath limited his power to heal or cure.[217]

On the other hand, Bahá'u'lláh extols the beneficial effects of pure motives and virtue. It is this aspect of the means being the ends that holds the greatest promise for human advancement:

> O Children of Adam! Holy words and pure and goodly deeds ascend unto the heaven of celestial glory. Strive that your deeds may be cleansed from the dust of self and hypocrisy and find favour at the court of glory; for ere long the assayers of mankind shall, in the holy presence of the Adored One, accept naught but absolute virtue and deeds of stainless purity. This is the day-star of wisdom and of divine mystery that hath shone above the horizon of the divine will. Blessed are they that turn thereunto.[218]

Thus we see that the appearance of the Promised One and the establishment of the Kingdom of God on earth require fundamental changes in human affairs, both at the individual level and in all of the institutions of society. The revelation of the divine standard in this most holy Day of God has set in motion a testing process in which the actions of governments, institutions and individuals are constantly being weighed and measured. Actions and decisions which conform to the divine standard established by the Revelation of Bahá'u'lláh are confirmed and blessed. Those actions and decisions which are contrary to the principles and laws of Bahá'u'lláh produce harmful and destructive results in society and lead it down the path of disintegration. The contrast between these opposite patterns of human activity is very strong and clearly discernible. It is the practical result of this comparison that is the fruit of the divine testing process. The world is being led, slowly but surely and in spite of its preoccupation with behaviour contrary to Bahá'u'lláh's teachings, to recognize and accept that the divine guidance bequeathed to it by the divine physician is the one remedy that can save its life.

## 29

# The Wisdom of Every Command is Made Clear

*Verily, this is that Most Great Beauty*
*. . . through Whom . . .*
*the wisdom of every command*
*shall be tested*

As discussed previously, many of the Arabic phrases Bahá'u-'lláh uses in the Tablet of Aḥmad seem to allude to specific verses in the Qur'án. These verses often have prophetic allusions to the future advent of the Promised One. This is true of the phrase 'the wisdom of every command shall be tested'. It appears to refer to a nearly identical verse in the 44th súrih of the Qur'án. This súrih is entitled 'Smoke' and its opening verses are:

> By the Scripture that maketh plain;
> Lo! We revealed it on a blessed night
> Lo! We are ever warning –
> *Whereon every wise command is made clear*[219]
>
> By virtue of our behest. Lo! we have ever sent forth Apostles,
> A mercy from thy Lord: he truly heareth and knoweth all things . . .[220]

The opening lines of this súrih remind the reader that the Qur'án is a warning. This is a common theme throughout the book: the Qur'án repeatedly states that it has been sent down as a warning to prepare the believers for the Day of Judgement and the coming of the great Day of the Lord.

The above verses point out that God is continually sending His Apostle, or Messengers, to humankind as a mercy from His presence. In one sense this may be seen as an allusion to the advent of a future revelation that will succeed Muḥammad. This is explained in succeeding verses of this súrih, which specifically predict the coming of a future Messenger:

> But mark them on the day when the Heaven shall give out a palpable smoke.
>
> Which shall enshroud mankind: this will be an afflictive torment.
>
> They will cry, 'Our Lord! relieve us from this torment: see! we are believers.'
>
> But how did warning avail them, when an undoubted apostle had come to them;
>
> And they turned their backs on him . . .[221]

From these verses we may infer that when Bahá'u'lláh alludes to this súrih by using the phrase 'the wisdom of every command shall be tested', He is indicating that His coming was clearly foretold by Muḥammad in this chapter of the Qur'án.

In one of His Tablets Bahá'u'lláh comments on these verses and asserts that this is the day of their fulfilment:

> This is the Day whereon the earth shall tell out her tidings. The workers of iniquity are her burdens, could ye but perceive it. The moon of idle fancy hath been cleft, and the heaven hath given out a palpable smoke.[222]

In the *Book of Certitude* Bahá'u'lláh explains the symbolic meaning of the phrase 'the heaven will give out a palpable smoke':

> Likewise, He saith: 'On the day when the heaven shall give out a palpable smoke, which shall enshroud mankind: this

> will be an afflictive torment.' The All-Glorious hath decreed these very things, that are contrary to the desires of wicked men, to be the touchstone and standard whereby He proveth His servants, that the just may be known from the wicked, and the faithful distinguished from the infidel. The symbolic term 'smoke' denotes grave dissensions, the abrogation and demolition of recognized standards, and the utter destruction of their narrow-minded exponents.[223]

This is the standard of God. He issues His laws and commands and He sends His Prophets to humankind according to His wisdom and in a manner that only He can comprehend. Through this process He tests the hearts of all people. Those who respond to the call of His appointed Messenger and follow His laws and teachings are those who are truly sincere and have distinguished truth from error. These are the ones whom God has tested and found to be true believers in His Cause. This appears to be the meaning of the phrase 'the touchstone and standard whereby He proveth His servants'. Historically, touchstones were used to test the purity of gold. A touchstone is defined as any test or criterion for determining genuineness. The phrase 'the touchstone and standard whereby He proveth His servants' implies that God tests those who claim to be believers to see if they are sincere and genuine. By 'proving', Bahá'u'lláh seems to be indicating that through the divine testing process the true believers are distinguished by their faithfulness and obedience to God's new Messenger.

Those who turn away, who deny His Messenger or actively oppose Him are the people of negation whom no warning can awaken or help and who have failed the test of true faith. This, too, is the 'touchstone' of God whereby God separates the pretenders and the hypocrites from the true believers. Bahá'u'lláh explains that this is God's purpose in sending such tests to humanity. For example, He says:

> 'God verily will test them and sift them.' This is the divine standard, this is the Touchstone of God, wherewith He proveth His servants.[224]

In the *Book of Certitude* Bahá'u'lláh very clearly explains this:

> Meditate profoundly, that the secret of things unseen may be revealed unto you . . . that you may acknowledge the truth that from time immemorial even unto eternity the Almighty hath tried, and will continue to try, His servants, so that light may be distinguished from darkness, truth from falsehood, right from wrong, guidance from error, happiness from misery, and roses from thorns. Even as He hath revealed: 'Do men think when they say "We believe" they shall be let alone and not be put to proof?'[225]

From this explanation we see that one of the meanings of the phrase 'the wisdom of every command shall be tested' appears to be that God will separate the wicked and the infidels from the righteous. This also seems to be the message of the 44th súrih to which Bahá'u'lláh alludes. When the Qur'án says that the people will cry, 'See! we are believers',[226] it then points out that God will test them and prove the falseness of their claim when they turn away from His new Messenger. It says, 'But how did warning avail them, when an undoubted Messenger had come to them; And they turned their backs on him . . .'[227] It is this very test that Bahá'u'lláh appears to allude to when He declares that He is the One through whom 'the wisdom of every command shall be tested'.

The Arabic word for 'command' in the phrases 'the wisdom of every command' and 'every wise command' is *amr*. The word *amr* has many connotations in Arabic including 'dispensation', 'order', 'event', 'law', 'faith' and 'religion'. Let us consider Bahá'u'lláh's assertion that 'this is that Most Great Beauty . . . through Whom . . . the wisdom of every command shall be tested' in light of the various meanings of the word 'command' – *amr*.

At one level, we may infer that it is the wisdom of every religious dispensation and every religion that shall be tested through the appearance of the Most Great Beauty. In this sense Bahá'u'lláh seems to be suggesting that the divine wisdom underlying the appearance of every previous religion of God has been the coming of Bahá'u'lláh and His Revelation. It is His manifestation that tests the faith of the followers of all previous religions. If they turn to Bahá'u'lláh and accept Him, they have passed God's test. If they deny Bahá'u'lláh and turn away from Him, they have failed the test of the touchstone of God and have demonstrated the falseness of their belief in their own Messenger and His religion.

Similarly, let us look at the verse 'every wise command is made clear' from the viewpoint of the various connotations of the word *amr* – command. It seems that the Qur'án is telling us that the wisdom and purpose of every religion and dispensation will be made clear through the future advent of the 'undoubted Messenger', Bahá'u'lláh. In one of His Tablets the Báb affirms that the purpose of all previous faiths has been to prepare humankind for the coming of Bahá'u'lláh:

> Fear ye God and breathe not a word concerning His Most Great Remembrance other than what hath been ordained by God, inasmuch as We have established a separate covenant regarding Him with every Prophet and His followers. Indeed, We have not sent any Messenger without this binding covenant . . . Ere long the veil shall be lifted from your eyes at the appointed time. Ye shall then behold the sublime Remembrance of God, unclouded and vivid.[228]

Asserting that this is the Day in which God has fulfilled the prophecies in all previous religions, Bahá'u'lláh declares:

> The Revelation which, from time immemorial, hath been acclaimed as the Purpose and Promise of all the Prophets of God, and the most cherished Desire of His Messengers,

> hath now, by virtue of the pervasive Will of the Almighty and at His irresistible bidding, been revealed unto men. The advent of such a Revelation hath been heralded in all the sacred Scriptures.[229]

We see, then, that Bahá'u'lláh's use of the phrase 'the wisdom of every command shall be tested' and His apparent allusion to the Quranic phrase 'every wise command is made clear' suggests that the ultimate purpose of every previous religion has been made clear through Bahá'u'lláh's Revelation. This is further suggested by the construction of this particular paragraph of the Tablet of Aḥmad:

> Verily, this is that Most Great Beauty foretold in the Books of the Messengers, through Whom truth shall be distinguished from error and the wisdom of every command shall be tested. Verily, He is the Tree of Life that bringeth forth the fruits of God, the Exalted, the Powerful, the Great.

Notice that Bahá'u'lláh immediately establishes His claim to be 'that Most Great Beauty'. He then asserts that His coming has been 'foretold in the Books of the Messengers'. One way of looking at this paragraph is to see each phrase in it as a reference to a particular scripture, referring us to the book of each Messenger to substantiate Bahá'u'lláh's claim. From this point of view Bahá'u'lláh first refers us to the writings of the Báb in the phrase 'through Whom truth shall be distinguished from error'. He then directs us to the Qur'án with the phrase 'the wisdom of every command shall be tested'. With His declaration that 'He is the Tree of Life' He refers us to both the book of Genesis in the Torah and the Book of Revelation in the New Testament (see the discussion of the Tree of Life in the next chapter). With His affirmation that He is the one 'that bringeth forth the fruits of God', Bahá'u'lláh is directing our attention to the prophecies of Christ in the New Testament.

Thus we may conclude that it is we and all the peoples of the world who are being tested through the appearance of Bahá'u'lláh. Those of us who accept Him as the Promised One of God and who follow His laws and teachings have demonstrated what it means to have truly believed in the Báb, Muḥammad, Christ, Moses, Zoroaster, Buddha and Krishna. By our acceptance of Bahá'u'lláh and our obedience to Him we have demonstrated the wisdom of all previous religious dispensations and have been faithful to the Covenants of their divine Messengers.

# 30

# The Tree of Life

*Verily He is the Tree of Life*
*that bringeth forth the fruits of God*

The Tree of Life and similar concepts appear in many religions and there is a vast literature on the subject. The Tree of Life may, in one sense, be understood as another expression for the tree of divine revelation, the station of the Manifestation of God. 'Abdu'l-Bahá tells us the Tree of Life is also a specific reference to Bahá'u'lláh:

> The Tree of Life, of which mention is made in the Bible, is Bahá'u'lláh . . .[230]

The Tree of Life is found in the story of Adam and Eve, in the second and third chapters of the Book of Genesis in the Old Testament.[231] 'Abdu'l-Bahá's statement tells us that this particular reference, appearing in the very beginning of the Bible, is, on one level, a prophecy of the future advent of Bahá'u'lláh.

The Tree of Life is also mentioned in the Book of Revelation in the description of the holy city, the new Jerusalem.[232] This city, according to 'Abdu'l-Bahá, represents the Law of God.[233] The author of the Book of Revelation, in describing his vision of this city, seems to make a very clear reference to Bahá'u'lláh:

> And the city had no need of the sun, neither of the moon, to shine in it: *for the glory of God did lighten it* . . .[234]

The beginning of the next chapter of the Book of Revelation states that the Tree of Life is in this city:

> In the midst of the street of it, and on either side of the river, was there *the tree of life*, which bare twelve manner of fruits, and yielded her fruit every month: and the leaves of the tree were for the healing of the nations.[235]

In one sense, the fruits mentioned in this verse may be understood as the universal principles of the Revelation of Bahá'u'lláh. Similarly, the leaves of the Tree of Life may represent the teachings of Bahá'u'lláh that will heal the sicknesses of humankind and unite the nations and peoples of the earth in one human family. The fact that the Tree of Life 'yielded her fruit every month' may signify the unrivalled power and authority of Bahá'u'lláh's Revelation. The fact that there is no month or season that the Tree of Life does not yield fruit may also signify that in the dispensation of Bahá'u'lláh divine, infallible guidance has been guaranteed to humanity through the institution of the Centre of the Covenant. This institution is unique in religious history and through it Bahá'u'lláh has provided the necessary channel for continuous, uninterrupted divine guidance. He declares that this is:

> . . . the 'Day of God Himself', the 'Day which shall never be followed by night', the 'Springtime which autumn will never overtake' . . .[236]

The Tree of Life also has a special significance as a symbol of the Manifestation of God. It symbolizes the appearance of the *supreme* Manifestation.[237]

Since all the Manifestations of God possess the same divine station, what is the significance of the phrase 'supreme Manifestation of God?'

As we have seen, Bahá'u'lláh tells us that God has given each Manifestation a specific mission:

> The measure of the revelation of the Prophets of God in this world, however, must differ. Each and every one of them hath been the Bearer of a distinct Message, and hath been commissioned to reveal Himself through specific acts. It is for this reason that they appear to vary in their greatness. Their Revelation may be likened unto the light of the moon that sheddeth its radiance upon the earth.[238]

If the appearance of the Manifestations of God is symbolized by the moon reflecting the light of the sun, then the Revelation of Bahá'u'lláh can be compared to the appearance of the full moon. Muḥammad prophesied, 'Ye, verily, shall behold your Lord as ye behold the full moon on its fourteenth night.'[239] Similarly, if the Manifestations are symbolized by the rising of the sun itself, 'Abdu'l-Bahá tells us that Bahá'u'lláh's advent is the sun in its highest station of midsummer glory.[240] The full moon and the sun in its midsummer glory represent the highest and most perfect expression of the Manifestation of God. In one of His Tablets Bahá'u'lláh conveys this same concept:

> ... O Thou Who hast become manifest in the Greatest Name whereby ... the heavens of divine revelation have been adorned with the light of the appearance of the Sun of Thy countenance.[241]

According to 'Abdu'l-Bahá, this is one of the meanings of the phrase 'the supreme Manifestation of God'.[242]

The divine mission of Bahá'u'lláh is unique. He has been given the task of elevating humanity to its destined stage of maturity. In *Some Answered Questions*, 'Abdu'l-Bahá, in His discussion of universal cycles, explains:

> Briefly, we say a universal cycle in the world of existence signifies a long duration of time ... In such a cycle the Manifestations appear with splendour in the realm of the visible until a great and supreme Manifestation makes the world the

centre of His radiance. His appearance causes the world to attain to maturity, and the extension of His cycle is very great. Afterward, other Manifestations will arise under His shadow, Who according to the needs of the time will renew certain commandments relating to material questions and affairs, while remaining under His shadow.

We are in the cycle which began with Adam, and its supreme Manifestation is Bahá'u'lláh.[243]

Shoghi Effendi clarifies the station of Bahá'u'lláh's Revelation in lifting humankind to its promised stage of maturity. In doing so he gives us further insight into the true meaning of the term 'supreme Manifestation of God':

> After Bahá'u'lláh many Prophets will, no doubt, appear, but they will be all under His shadow. Although they may abrogate the laws of the Dispensation, in accordance with the needs and requirements of the age in which they appear, they nevertheless draw their spiritual force from this mighty Revelation. The Faith of Bahá'u'lláh constitutes, indeed, the stage of maturity in the development of mankind. His appearance has released such spiritual forces which will continue to animate, for many long years to come, the world in its development. Whatever progress may be achieved in the later ages, after the unification of the whole human race is achieved, will be but improvements in the machinery of the world. For the machinery itself has already been created by Bahá'u'lláh. The task of continually improving and perfecting this machinery is one which later Prophets will be called upon to achieve. They will move and work within the orbit of the Bahá'í cycle.[244]

This, then, is the significance of 'the supreme Manifestation of God' and Bahá'u'lláh's unequivocal assertion that 'He is the Tree of Life'.

# 31

# The Fruits of God

*Verily He is the Tree of Life*
*that bringeth forth the fruits of God,*
*the Exalted, the Powerful, the Great.*

The phrase 'that bringeth forth the fruits of God' has many levels of meaning and significance. In one sense, 'the fruits of God' may refer to the names and attributes of God which are revealed to humanity through God's chosen Manifestations. However, not every Manifestation has revealed all these names and attributes. Bahá'u'lláh explains that every Manifestation inherently possesses all the names and attributes of God.[245] But each Manifestation has been sent with a specific mission. Consequently, in each dispensation certain names and attributes may or may not have been revealed to humankind.[246] Since Bahá'u'lláh has been manifested in the station of the supreme Manifestation, He has revealed all the names and attributes of God to a greater degree than any previous Manifestation. This is one reason why Bahá'u'lláh's Revelation is likened to the light of the full moon and to the sun in its summer glory. In this sense, we may infer that when Bahá'u'lláh declares that 'He is the Tree of Life that bringeth forth the fruits of God', He is asserting that He has been empowered to reveal the names and attributes of God in a fuller measure than has occurred in the past.

In another sense 'the fruits of God' may signify the Manifestations themselves. In one of His Tablets Bahá'u'lláh says:

> Through His potency the Trees of Divine Revelation have yielded their fruits, every one of which hath been sent down in the form of a Prophet, bearing a Message to God's creatures . . .[247]

If the 'fruits of God' signify the other Manifestations, why then does Bahá'u'lláh assert that He is 'the Tree of Life that bringeth forth the fruits of God'?

Bahá'u'lláh is the Promised One of all ages, whose revelation will cause humanity to attain its destined stage of maturity. The purpose of all previous revelations and the appearance of the earlier Manifestations was to lay the foundation and pave the way for this most great revelation. For this reason it may be said that the previous Manifestations have all appeared under the umbrella of Bahá'u'lláh's Revelation. In the same vein, 'Abdu'l-Bahá tells us that future Manifestations who will arise during the Bahá'í cycle will all be under the shadow of Bahá'u'lláh's Revelation.[248] In the sense that Bahá'u-'lláh's Revelation is the culmination of all previous dispensations and the impetus for all future revelations within the Bahá'í cycle, it may be said that Bahá'u'lláh has brought forth all the other Manifestations, the 'fruits' of the Tree of Life. It appears to be in this respect that Bahá'u'lláh declares:

> But for Him no Divine Messenger would have been invested with the robe of prophethood, nor would any of the sacred scriptures have been revealed. To this bear witness all created things.[249]

And in another Tablet:

> He it is Who is the one Beloved of all things, whether of the past or of the future. Would that ye might set your hearts and hopes upon Him![250]

But it is not enough that the Manifestations of God have

appeared on earth and revealed His names and attributes. Humankind is an essential party to the Covenant of God and has an integral role to fulfil. Humanity must develop spiritual virtues, civilization must evolve and advance and individual human beings must reflect the attributes of God. Bahá'u'lláh explains:

> Having created the world and all that liveth and moveth therein, He . . . chose to confer upon man the unique distinction and capacity to know Him and to love Him – a capacity that must needs be regarded as the generating impulse and the primary purpose underlying the whole of creation . . . Upon the reality of man . . . He hath focused the radiance of all of His names and attributes, and made it a mirror of His own Self. Alone of all created things man hath been singled out for so great a favour, so enduring a bounty.[251]

It is for this reason that the Manifestations have been sent down and have revealed the names and attributes of God.[252] Through the influence of the divine Manifestations individuals develop spiritual virtues and reflect more fully these divine attributes. This spiritual development is the fruit of every divine revelation. The 'fruits of God' are, in this sense, the people who have turned their hearts to God's Manifestation and, through the light and love of His Revelation, have developed their latent spiritual potential.

In one of His Tablets Bahá'u'lláh says: 'All men have been created to carry forward an ever-advancing civilization.'[253] It is impossible for civilization to advance unless the individuals comprising it develop and mature. Thus, on one level, this verse seems to suggest that the purpose of God in creating humanity has been for people to reflect the names and attributes of God in an ever increasing measure and to an ever greater degree. In this promised Day of God, He has manifested Bahá'u'lláh, His supreme Manifestation, to uplift the whole human race to its spiritual maturity. This implies a tremendous growth in the spiritual character of humanity. This will be the fruit of Bahá'u'lláh's Revelation. Bahá'u'lláh affirms: 'The fruits of the tree of man have ever been and are goodly deeds and a praiseworthy character.'[254]

> Strain every nerve to acquire both inner and outer perfections, for the fruit of the human tree hath ever been and will ever be perfections both within and without.[255]

It is Bahá'u'lláh's station as the Manifestation of God to recreate every human being who turns to Him and seeks the shelter and care of His Revelation.[256] The believers who dedicate their lives to personal transformation, who choose to be recreated through the love and teachings of Bahá'u'lláh and the effusions of His infallible grace become the fruits of His Revelation. It is this transformation in the morals and character of humanity that is the essential purpose of every Prophet of God. In the *Book of Certitude*, Bahá'u'lláh sets forth this fundamental principle of the religion of God:

> . . . is not the object of every Revelation to effect a transformation in the whole character of mankind, a transformation that shall manifest itself both outwardly and inwardly, that shall affect both its inner life and external conditions? For if the character of mankind be not changed, the futility of God's universal Manifestations would be apparent.[257]

Bahá'u'lláh promises that the fruits of His Revelation will be the emergence of a new race of men, *khalq-i-jadíd*, a Quranic idea:

> A race of men, incomparable in character, shall be raised up which, with the feet of detachment, will tread under all who are in heaven and on earth, and will cast the sleeve of holiness over all that hath been created from water and clay.[258]

It is the destiny of each one of us to become the fulfilment of this prophecy. Our responsibility is to turn to Bahá'u'lláh and to allow Him to recreate us and thereby become the fruits of His Revelation.

The 'fruits of God' may also symbolize the spiritual transformation in the collective life of humanity. 'Abdu'l-Bahá explains that this will occur through the potency of the teachings of Bahá'u'lláh and the power of His Revelation:

> ... He will issue all the laws and teachings which are the spirit of the world of humanity and everlasting life. And *that universal Manifestation will subdue the world by spiritual power*, not by war and combat; He will do it with peace and tranquillity, not by the sword and arms; *He will establish this Heavenly Kingdom by true love*, and not by the power of war. *He will promote these divine teachings by kindness and righteousness*, and not by weapons and harshness. He will so educate the nations and people that, notwithstanding their various conditions, their different customs and characters, and their diverse religions and races, they will, as it is said in the Bible, like the wolf and the lamb, the leopard, the kid, the suckling child and the serpent, become comrades, friends and companions. The contentions of races, the differences of religions, and the barriers between nations will be completely removed, and all will attain perfect union and reconciliation under the shadow of the Blessed Tree.[259]

In another sense, we may conclude that it is this spiritual power released by Bahá'u'lláh's Revelation, the power of true love, kindness and righteousness, the spiritual power that is recreating the hearts of people, that is the divine fruit of the Tree of Life. In yet another sense, we may conclude that the laws and teachings of Bahá'u'lláh, which are transforming the personal lives of individuals and the collective life of society, are the priceless fruits of His Revelation. Bahá'u'lláh affirms that 'His ordinances constitute the fruits of the divine Tree'.[260]

An essential and vital feature of His teachings is the establishment of the Kingdom of God on earth, which is unfolding through the gradual evolution of the institutions of Bahá'u'lláh's World Order. Shoghi Effendi has described this World Order as the nucleus and pattern of the future, world-embracing civilization:

> . . . the World Order of Bahá'u'lláh . . . will give birth, in the fullness of time, to a world spiritual civilization, which posterity will hail as the fairest fruit of His Revelation.[261]

Thus 'the fruits of God' may be the names and attributes of God revealed to humanity through Bahá'u'lláh, whose divine mission is to build the Kingdom of God on earth and lead humankind into its next stage of maturity. The fruit of this most precious Tree of Life is, in one sense, the spiritual power He has released into the world to subdue the nations and revolutionize the life of humanity. In another sense, the 'fruits of God' are the laws and teachings of Bahá'u'lláh that are the life of the world. In yet another sense, the 'fruits of God' are the believers who have been recreated by the power of His Revelation. The 'fruits of God' may also be the institutions of Bahá'u'lláh's Administrative Order which are helping transform society and build the Kingdom of God on earth. And finally, the fruit of this sacred tree will be the future world civilization that will emerge as a result of the evolution and maturation of the World Order of Bahá'u'lláh.

# *Section 4: Twin Manifestations*

## 32

## Bear Thou Witness

*O Aḥmad! Bear thou witness*
*that verily He is God*
*and there is no God but Him*

To bear witness means to give evidence about the truth of an event, especially from direct, personal knowledge. It means 'to give testimony for the purpose of communicating to others a knowledge of something not known to them'.[262] It also means to testify publicly to the truth of one's belief. Bahá'u'lláh's exhortation to 'bear thou witness' may suggest: Be a teacher of the Cause of God. Believe with all your heart and soul and proclaim 'unto all who are in heaven and all who are on earth' the advent of the Promised One of God. Teach the people the truth of the new Revelation from God and let your life be an example of what it means to truly believe in Bahá'u'lláh.

It is also worthwhile pondering the connection between this verse and the historical origins of the word 'witness' meaning 'martyr'. Offering one's life in defence of and as a testimony to the truth that 'He is God and there is no God but Him' is perhaps the ultimate way to bear witness.

# 33

# There is No God but God

*O Aḥmad! Bear thou witness that*
*verily He is God*
*and there is no God but Him*

The significance of Bahá'u'lláh's affirmation 'verily He is God and there is no God but Him' cannot be overestimated. It has its roots in the Islamic verse 'There is no God but God'. Literally translated from Arabic, this verse is 'no god (or deity) but the God (Al-láh)'.[263] This verse and its variations appear many times throughout the Qur'án. It is at the very core of Islamic belief and is an essential element of the *shaháda*, the Islamic declaration of faith (which may also be translated as 'martyrdom'), which is recited daily by devout Muslims.[264]

In one sense 'no God but Alláh' epitomizes the victory of Muḥammad's doctrine of the oneness and unity of God over the idolatrous beliefs held by the Meccans and other Arabs at the time of Muḥammad's advent. The *shaháda* (the declaration of faith), which includes the phrase 'no god but Alláh', requires all faithful believers to affirm, numerous times each day, that idols are not God or, perhaps more precisely, that there is nothing deserving of worship and devotion except God. One implication of this statement is that there is only one Divine Being and He is supreme and transcendent over all of creation.[265]

Thus when Bahá'u'lláh asserts that 'verily He is God and there is no God but Him', on one level He is testifying to the truth of Muḥammad and His Revelation. In doing so,

Bahá'u'lláh is also confirming the fundamental Islamic concept of *tawhíd* (the affirmation of divine unity), that 'the one true God' transcends His creation and that God is one in His essence and one in His attributes.

Simultaneously, Bahá'u'lláh also affirms the Báb's teachings on divine unity. The Báb upheld the Islamic teachings of *tawhíd* and extended them by asserting that God in His essence is inherently unknowable. These fundamental teachings of divine unity are the foundation of the concept of monotheism. We may conclude that when Bahá'u'lláh told Aḥmad to 'Bear thou witness that verily He is God and there is no God but Him', on one level He was telling him to bear witness to the fundamental monotheistic truth of the religion of God.

# 34

# Verily He is God: The Historical Connection

*O Aḥmad! Bear thou witness*
*that verily He is God*
*and there is no God but Him*

Recall that while Aḥmad was in India in search of the Promised One, he was told that if he prostrated himself and repeated the verse 'there is no god but God'[266] from the Qur'án twelve thousand times, he would be guided to his heart's desire. It is reported that Aḥmad devoted himself to this task several times in his attempt to find the beloved of his heart. At the time he performed this arduous ritual, Aḥmad was not guided directly to the Promised One and found no result. He eventually returned to Persia, unfulfilled in his quest and quite disillusioned. It was much later that he was guided to the Bábí Faith and many years after that that he met Bahá'u'lláh in Baghdád and was guided by Him to recognize His true station.

Consider a possible connection between the story of Aḥmad's life and Bahá'u'lláh's call to Aḥmad, 'O Aḥmad! Bear thou witness that verily He is God and there is no God but Him.' This phrase is similar to the frequently recited verse from the Qur'án 'there is no god but God'. It seems that Bahá'u'lláh is clearly alluding to this particular verse from the Qur'án and assuring Aḥmad that God has heard his cry and answered his plea to find his promised beloved. We may infer that through this verse Bahá'u'lláh, the Promised One of God, is personally telling Aḥmad that his quest was not in vain, that God has indeed guided him to his goal and that he has attained his heart's most cherished desire by recognizing the true station of his Lord.

The fact that Bahá'u'lláh introduces this significant phrase with the admonition 'Bear thou witness' or 'testify' (even with your life, is one implication) suggests that Bahá'u'lláh is also requesting Aḥmad to testify to the truth of this most precious favour that God has bestowed upon him. We may conclude that not only is Bahá'u'lláh reminding and assuring Aḥmad of God's infinite bounties and love in guiding him to Bahá'u-'lláh, He is also pointing out to Aḥmad that because he knows and is assured of the truth of Bahá'u'lláh's claim to be the Promised One of the Báb, He is asking him to arise and teach his Cause.

# 35

# Verily He is God and There is No God but Him

*O Aḥmad! Bear thou witness*
*that verily He is God*
*and there is no God but Him*

Another possible meaning of the verse 'verily He is God and there is no God but Him' is the concept that there is no path to God except through His chosen Manifestation. In this sense the verse indicates that God is unknowable unless we turn to and recognize His chosen One.

Recall that *tawhíd*, the concept of divine unity introduced by Muḥammad, teaches that God transcends His creation. The Báb expanded this Islamic concept and explained that the divine essence of God is unknowable. Since God is unknowable, the fundamental question is, how do we human beings come to know God?

Both the Báb and Bahá'u'lláh teach that we can only know God through our recognition of His Manifestation. For example, the Báb says:

> Ye shall know God when the Manifestation of His Own Self is made known unto you, that perchance ye may not stray far from His Path.[267]

In a similar vein, Bahá'u'lláh declares:

> If it be your wish, O people, to know God and to discover the greatness of His might, look, then, upon Me with Mine own eyes, and not with the eyes of any one besides Me.[268]

This fundamental concept, that we must look to the Manifestation to know God, has been an essential element of the religion of God. In every dispensation God's chosen Messenger teaches His people that they must turn to Him to know God. For example, during the ministry of Jesus Christ, He declared:

> I am the way, the truth, and the life: no man cometh unto the Father, but by me. If ye had known me, ye should have known my Father also: and from henceforth ye know him, and have seen him.[269]

This pronouncement points to the fact that the true station of the Manifestations is that of divine intermediaries between God and humanity. The function of an intermediary is to provide a connection and means of communication between two separate parties. In this case, the separate parties are humankind and the infinite essence of God. Bahá'u'lláh explains that there can be no direct link between us and the infinite reality of the divine essence. So God has provided that link for us. The connection He has established between us and Himself is His Manifestation. Bahá'u'lláh further explains that one of the functions of the Manifestations of God is to convey the grace of God to humanity:

> Since there can be no tie of direct intercourse to bind the one true God with His creation, and no resemblance whatever can exist between the transient and the Eternal, the contingent and the Absolute, He hath ordained that in every age and dispensation a pure and stainless Soul be made manifest in the kingdoms of earth and heaven.[270]

> . . . it hath been made indubitably clear that in the kingdoms of earth and heaven there must needs be manifested a Being,

> an Essence Who shall act as a Manifestation and Vehicle for the transmission of the grace of the Divinity Itself, the Sovereign Lord of all.[271]

The Báb explains that the Manifestations function as the sole means of communication between God and humankind:

> Thy purpose in performing thy deeds is that God may graciously accept them; and divine acceptance can in no wise be achieved except through the acceptance of Him Who is the Exponent of His Revelation . . . Whatever is sent down cometh through the Exponent of His Revelation, and whatever ascendeth, ascendeth unto the Exponent of His Revelation.[272]

Now let us consider the teachings of Muḥammad. He, too, proclaimed an equivalent doctrine. This may be seen in the *shaháda*, the Islamic declaration of faith. It includes the pivotal verse:

> There is no God but God and Muḥammad is the Messenger (Prophet) of God.

This verse is the foundation of Islamic belief. In one sense it clearly affirms that idols are not God and that there are no other deities except the one true God. It also clearly states that Muḥammad is the Messenger of God. Since we know that God can only be known through His Manifestation, this verse implies that in the dispensation of Muḥammad God could only be known through His Prophet Muḥammad.

In this dispensation, Bahá'u'lláh makes the same claim as did the Báb, Muḥammad and Christ before Him. In this context, let us examine the significance of the phrase 'verily He is God and there is no God but Him'. As noted previously, this phrase is nearly identical to the verse 'there is no God but God and Muḥammad is the Messenger of God'. The only difference between them is that instead of declaring Muḥammad to be the Messenger of God, Bahá'u'lláh affirms that 'verily He is God'; the second half of the phrase is implied and a devout person such as Aḥmad would certainly have understood this. In another Tablet Bahá'u'lláh uses a similar phrase to explain His relationship to God and humanity:

> From His retreat of glory His voice is ever proclaiming: 'Verily, I am God; there is none other God besides Me, the All-Knowing, the All-Wise. I have manifested Myself unto men, and have sent down Him Who is the Day Spring of the signs of My Revelation. Through Him I have caused all creation to testify that *there is none other God except Him*, the Incomparable, the All-Informed, the All-Wise.'[273]

He adds:

> He Who is everlastingly hidden from the eyes of men can never be known except through His Manifestation, and His Manifestation can adduce no greater proof of the truth of His Mission than the proof of His own Person.[274]

Since God can only be known through the Manifestation for the age in which He appears, we may infer that 'verily He is God and there is no God but Him' implies that in this dispensation God can only be known through Bahá'u'lláh. In this sense, the 'He' and 'Him' in this verse appear to refer to Bahá'u'lláh, signifying that Bahá'u'lláh is God's representative on earth.

'Abdu'l-Bahá explains that it is impossible to imagine God.[275] He says that any attempt to envision or fashion a mental image of God is futile; it can only end in failure and frustration. The best we can do is to focus our thoughts on God's Manifestation. In a Tablet He explains that the specific phrase 'He is God' signifies the station of Bahá'u'lláh:

VERILY HE IS GOD AND THERE IS NO GOD BUT HIM

> Thou hast asked regarding the phrase, 'He is God!' written above the Tablets. By this Word is intended that no one hath any access to the Invisible Essence. The way is barred and the road is impassable. In this world all men must turn their faces toward 'Him whom God shall Manifest'. He is the 'Dawning-place of Divinity' and the 'Manifestation of Deity'. He is the 'Ultimate Goal', the 'Adored One' of all and the 'Worshipped One' of all. Otherwise, whatever flashes through the mind is not that Essence of essences and the Reality of realities; nay, rather it is pure imagination woven by man . . .[276]

From this discussion we see that the verse 'verily He is God and there is no God but Him' may signify the person of Bahá'u'lláh. In this sense this verse acknowledges the fact that God transcends His creation and that His essence is unknowable. To know God we must turn to His Manifestation for the age in which we live. In this day we must turn to Bahá'u'lláh and accept Him as the mouthpiece and representative of God.

In yet another sense the verse 'O Aḥmad! Bear thou witness that verily He is God and there is no God but Him' is significant because the Arabic word Aḥmad is a variation of the name Muḥammad. In the sense that Aḥmad alludes to Muḥammad, it is possible that Bahá'u'lláh is calling the followers of Muḥammad to recognize Him. Thus we may infer that this phrase is also directed to the Muslims and is calling them to witness that the promises in the Qur'án concerning the coming of the Promised One and the day of resurrection have been fulfilled.

# 36

# He is God: His Word of Affirmation

*O Aḥmad! Bear thou witness*
*that verily He is God*
*and there is no God but Him*

'He is God' may also be seen as a powerful affirmation. 'To affirm' stems from a word which means to present as fixed or to make firm. Affirmation means to assert as true. As an affirmation, 'He is God' is significant in several ways. In one sense 'He is God' may symbolize the pre-eminent character of Bahá'u'lláh's Revelation; in another it may signify the victory of the Cause of God in this day.

Referring to the greatness of Bahá'u'lláh's Revelation, 'He is God' may signify that this is the promised Day of God, the day 'in which God's most excellent favours have been poured out upon men, the Day in which His most mighty grace hath been infused into all created things'.[277] Throughout His writings Bahá'u'lláh extols, in superlative terms, the greatness of His Revelation. For example, He says:

> The excellence of this Day is immensely exalted above the comprehension of men, however extensive their knowledge, however profound their understanding.[278]

> The purpose underlying all creation is the revelation of this most sublime, this most holy Day, the Day known as the Day

> of God, in His Books and Scriptures – the Day which all the Prophets, and the Chosen Ones, and the holy ones, have wished to witness.[279]

In another sense 'He is God' may point to the ultimate triumph of the Faith of Bahá'u'lláh over all the forces of opposition and denial that have been leagued against it. From this perspective 'He is God' signifies that God has protected the Cause of Bahá'u'lláh from the attacks of its enemies. It may also signify that God has promised to secure the victory of His Faith over all the peoples and nations of the earth. From the dawn of His divine mission, when God spoke to Bahá'u'lláh as He lay chained in the Síyáh-Chál, God promised to ensure the victory of His Cause and protect His Messenger from the attacks of His enemies. Recalling His experience in the dungeon of Ṭihrán, Bahá'u'lláh says:

> One night in a dream, these exalted words were heard on every side: 'Verily, We shall render Thee victorious by Thyself and by Thy pen. Grieve Thou not for that which hath befallen Thee, neither be Thou afraid, for thou art in safety.'[280]

In another Tablet Bahá'u'lláh relates God's assurance of the victory of His Faith:

> We have pledged Ourselves to secure Thy triumph upon earth and to exalt Our Cause above all men, though no king be found who would turn his face towards Thee.[281]

Bahá'u'lláh explains that the power inherent in His Cause is so great that it is impossible for the forces of opposition to overcome or destroy it:

> The Daystar of His Cause shineth through every veil and *His Word of affirmation standeth beyond the reach of negation*. Neither the ascendancy of the oppressor nor the tyranny of the wicked hath been able to thwart His Purpose.[282]

What does it mean when Bahá'u'lláh says that His Cause stands 'beyond the reach of negation'?

In one of His as yet untranslated Tablets, the Tablet of Salmán, Bahá'u'lláh explains that in past religious dispensations God made allowances for humanity's weaknesses and frailties.[283] Because people's capacities were so limited, God permitted His Faith to become divided into different sects and denominations. He continued to shower His blessings upon all faithful believers, regardless of the sects they created or the particular groups to which they belonged.

But in this sacred dispensation, Bahá'u'lláh declares, no such process of corruption or division of the Bahá'í Faith can ever occur. God will not permit His religion to become divided nor will He allow it to be overrun by its enemies. Through an act of the divine will, God has protected His Cause from its attackers and He will forever prevent any of their schemes from succeeding. Bahá'u'lláh extols this outpouring of divine might in majestic terms:

> This Day is different from other days, and this Cause different from other causes.[284]
>
> This Day is God's Day, and this Cause His Cause.[285]
>
> All praise be to God Who hath adorned the world with an ornament, and arrayed it with a vesture, of which it can be despoiled by no earthly power, however mighty its battalions, however vast its wealth, however profound its influence.[286]

He adds:

> Such forces as have their origin in this world of dust are, by their very nature, unworthy of consideration.[287]

We must realize that in this most holy dispensation God has empowered His supreme Manifestation to act with invincible authority. Bahá'u'lláh, in the Tablet of Salmán, expresses this spiritual truth by declaring that He has removed the 'letter of negation' which stood in the way of affirmation. This expression has both a literal meaning and a symbolic significance. The literal meaning stems from Islam. As discussed previously, the Islamic declaration of faith includes the phrase 'there is no god but God'. In Arabic, it is literally 'no god but Alláh'. Bahá'u'lláh explains that because of the creative power of the Word of God, the 'no' positioned before the word 'Alláh' allowed the enemies of Muḥammad eventually to overcome His Faith and divide it. Bahá'u'lláh then explains that He has removed this letter of negation, this 'no' that was positioned before Alláh, and in place of the phrase 'no god but Alláh' Bahá'u'lláh has revealed the affirmation 'He is God'.

The expression 'letter(s) of negation' appears in the writings of both the Báb and Bahá'u'lláh. In these writings the 'letters of negation' signify the enemies of the religion of God and all those who either reject or oppose God's Messengers. When Bahá'u'lláh asserts that He has removed the 'letters of negation' that stood in the way of affirmation, He implies that He has released such spiritual forces that will prevent these people from ever succeeding in overthrowing His Faith. This appears to be the significance of His assertion that 'His Word of affirmation standeth beyond the reach of negation'. In the Tablet of Salmán, Bahá'u'lláh says that through the might of God He has seized the reins of authority and that no one is able to take them away from Him. Bahá'u'lláh goes on to explain that He has expressed these truths in His Tablets by His mighty affirmation 'He is God'.

On another level 'He is God' also gives hope and encouragement to the individual believer. It suggests that not only will the Faith itself be victorious but every believer who turns to Bahá'u'lláh, who puts his whole trust and confidence in Him and who is steadfast in His love will be empowered to succeed in his own spiritual struggle.

When Bahá'u'lláh declares that He has removed the letter

of negation that stood in the way of affirmation, we may have confidence that it operates not only on a worldwide scale but also at the level of the individual believer. For each one of us the 'letter of negation' may signify all those barriers and obstacles which, in the past, prevented people from becoming truly spiritual and developing angelic characters. By removing these 'letters of negation' Bahá'u'lláh has removed these impediments for the individual. As God has empowered the Cause of Bahá'u'lláh to succeed and triumph, so too has Bahá'u'lláh empowered us to succeed and triumph in our own spiritual growth and development. Bahá'u'lláh declares:

> By the righteousness of God, should a man, all alone, arise in the name of Bahá and put on the armour of His love, him will the Almighty cause to be victorious, though the forces of earth and heaven be arrayed against him.[288]

> By God besides Whom is none other God! Should any one arise for the triumph of our Cause, him will God render victorious though tens of thousands of enemies be leagued against him. And if his love for Me wax stronger, God will establish his ascendancy over all the powers of earth and heaven. Thus have We breathed the spirit of power into all regions.[289]

Thus the phrase 'verily He is God' is a powerful affirmation, one which Sufis, for example, have recited over many centuries. 'He is God' may be seen as a perfect expression of the spiritual significance of the phrase 'His Word of affirmation standeth beyond the reach of negation'. In this sense 'He is God' signifies the victory of the Cause of Bahá'u'lláh and the ultimate triumph of His Faith over all the obstacles and forces of opposition it has faced and will encounter in the future. 'He is God' also signifies that this is the promised Day of God and that this Cause is God's Cause. 'He is God' points to the greatness and exalted character of Bahá'u'lláh's

Revelation and may also be seen as a promise to the individual believer. In this sense, 'He is God' affirms that Bahá'u'lláh has empowered the believers to succeed in their personal struggles to become truly spiritual beings.

## 37

# He is God and There is No God but Him: Him Whom God Shall Make Manifest

*verily He is God*
*and there is no God but Him,*
*the King, the Protector,*
*the Incomparable, the Omnipotent*

'He is God and there is no God but Him' may also be seen as an assertion by Bahá'u'lláh that He is the One whose appearance fulfils the well-known prophecies of the Báb concerning the advent of 'Him Whom God shall make manifest'. Throughout His writings, especially in the Bayán, the Báb urges His followers to be prepared to accept 'Him Whom God shall make manifest' when He appears. He even addressed some of His Tablets to the one who was destined to succeed Him. We will examine two of these Tablets to see the relationship between the phrases 'Him Whom God shall make manifest' and 'He is God and there is no God but Him'.

In these Tablets the Báb uses the phrase 'He is God and there is no God but Him' to describe the loftiness and greatness of the Promised One. In one of them He says:

> This is an epistle from the letter 'Thá'[290] unto Him Who will be made manifest through the power of Truth – He Who is the All-Glorious, the Best Beloved – to affirm that all created things as well as myself bear witness for all time that

> *there is none other God but Thee*, the Omnipotent, the Self-Subsisting; *that Thou art God, there is no God besides Thee* and that all men shall be raised up to life through Thee.[291]

We note that the Báb first identifies 'Him Who will be made manifest' as 'He Who is the All-Glorious, the Best Beloved'. Let us consider these two names. In Arabic the All-Glorious is *Abhá*, a variation of the name Bahá, meaning glory, and is one of the many titles of Bahá'u'lláh. In the writings of both 'Abdu'l-Bahá and Shoghi Effendi, Bahá'u'lláh is often referred to as the 'Abhá Beauty', which can be translated as either 'the Most Glorious Beauty' or 'the All Glorious Beauty'. Concerning the name 'the Best Beloved', another of the many phrases referring to Bahá'u'lláh is 'the Beloved of the worlds'. In one of His Tablets Bahá'u'lláh refers to the Báb and declares, 'I am His Well-Beloved.'[292] We see, then, that the Báb seems to be referring specifically to Bahá'u'lláh when He calls Him 'He Who is the All-Glorious, the Best Beloved'. It is possible, therefore, that the Báb is extolling and glorifying the station of Bahá'u'lláh when He declares that 'there is none other God but Thee' and that 'Thou art God, there is no God besides Thee'.

In a second Tablet addressed to 'Him Who will be made manifest', the Báb declares:

> He is the Most Glorious. *He is God, no God is there but Him*, the Almighty, the Best Beloved. All that are in the heavens and on the earth and whatever lieth between them are His. Verily He is the Help in Peril, the Self-Subsisting.[293]

At first glance we might conclude that this passage is directed to God and is extolling and glorifying the divine essence of God. In one sense it most certainly is; however, there are always numerous levels of meaning and significance to the Word of God. When we examine the next passage of this Tablet, the first paragraph acquires another significance entirely. The Báb continues:

> This is a letter from God, the Help in Peril, the Self-Subsisting, unto God, the Almighty, the Best Beloved, to affirm that the Bayán and such as bear allegiance to it are but a present from me unto Thee and to express my undoubting faith that *there is no God but Thee*, that the kingdoms of Creation and Revelation are Thine, that no one can attain anything save by Thy power and that He Whom Thou hast raised up is but Thy servant and Thy Testimony . . .[294]

From the context of this passage we see that its opening phrase, 'a letter from God', appears to signify the Báb Himself. Since the Báb declares that His letter is 'a present from me unto Thee', we may conclude that the 'Thee' He is referring to is Bahá'u'lláh. This suggests that the significance of the specific phrase 'a letter from God . . . unto God' implies that this Tablet has been revealed by the Báb for Bahá'u'lláh, His Best Beloved. In this sense, the specific titles 'God, the Help in Peril, the Self-Subsisting' may refer to the Manifestation of the Báb. Similarly, the titles 'God, the Almighty, the Best Beloved' may refer to the Manifestation of Bahá'u'lláh.

Now let us re-examine the first paragraph of this Tablet. In the context of the Báb's glorification of the station of Bahá'u'lláh, it appears that the opening verses of this Tablet

> He is the Most Glorious. He is God, no God is there but Him, the Almighty, the Best Beloved

also signify the station of Bahá'u'lláh. In this sense, the Báb's phrase 'He is God, no God is there but Him' may be understood as yet another sign of the greatness of the station and mission of the one who is to succeed Him, 'Him Whom God shall make manifest', Bahá'u'lláh.

Returning to the Tablet of Aḥmad, we see that Bahá'u'lláh's affirmation 'He is God and there is no God but Him' is essentially identical to the phrases used by the Báb in His Tablets addressed to 'Him Who will be made manifest'. In this context we may conclude that Bahá'u'lláh's use of the specific phrase 'verily He is God and there is no God but Him' is an assertion by Him that He, and He alone, is the Promised One of the Báb, His Well-Beloved.

## 38

# The True One from God

*And that the One Whom He hath sent forth*
*by the name of 'Alí*
*was the true one from God,*
*to Whose commands we are all conforming.*

This verse of the Tablet of Aḥmad, as well as the following paragraph, appear to be Bahá'u'lláh's testimony to and glorification of the Manifestation of the Báb. Testifying that the Báb was the 'True One from God', Bahá'u'lláh asserts His own belief that the Báb was the promised Manifestation of God. This indicates the respect and reverence that one Manifestation of God holds for another. Through this verse Bahá'u'lláh also seems to be telling us that there is a divine connection between His own Revelation and that of the Báb.

This Tablet was Bahá'u'lláh's call to Aḥmad to teach the Bábís the truth of Bahá'u'lláh's claim to be the one promised by the Báb. We should therefore expect the Tablet of Aḥmad to include Bahá'u'lláh's personal testimony to His own belief in the Báb. Since one of the objectives of this Tablet is to teach the followers of the Báb, we would also expect to find references to the indissoluble link between the Báb's Revelation and that of Bahá'u'lláh. It is in this verse that Bahá'u'lláh establishes this connection.

After exhorting Aḥmad to 'Bear . . . witness that verily He is God', Bahá'u'lláh says, 'And that the One Whom He hath sent forth by the name of 'Alí was the true One from God'. The Báb's given name was 'Alí-Muḥammad. The 'and' which connects the previous sentence with this one suggests that Bahá'u'lláh is telling Aḥmad to bear witness to two fundamental truths: that 'He is God' and that the Báb 'was the true One from God'. In the sense that 'verily He is God' refers to the station of Bahá'u'lláh Himself (see the discussion in the previous chapter), Bahá'u'lláh is telling us that we must recognize both Himself and the Báb as Manifestations of God. The implications of Bahá'u'lláh's assertion are profound. In this promised Day of God, as attested by Shoghi Effendi, God has sent humankind twin Manifestations.[295] This tells us that we cannot separate the Manifestation of the Báb from the Manifestation of Bahá'u-'lláh, that to accept the Báb is to accept Bahá'u'lláh and to accept Bahá'u'lláh is to accept the Báb. It also means that to reject one is to reject them both.

Let us look more closely at the verse 'And that the One Whom He hath sent forth by the name of 'Alí'. To whom does the 'He' refer? In one sense it obviously refers to God. God is the one by whose command all the Manifestations have appeared.

Yet there appears to be another level of significance to the phrase. In the sense that the preceding verse, 'verily He is God', alludes to the Manifestation of Bahá'u'lláh, then the 'He' in the phrase 'the One Whom He hath sent forth' may also refer to Bahá'u'lláh. That Bahá'u'lláh appears to be saying that He, Bahá'u'lláh, is the one who 'sent forth' the Báb seems to be upheld by the Báb Himself. For example, as we saw in the last chapter, in His glorification of Him who will be made manifest, the Báb asserts that it is Bahá'u'lláh who has 'raised [Him] up' and that He, the Báb, is 'but Thy servant and Thy Testimony'.[296]

Thus we may infer that when Bahá'u'lláh says 'And that the One Whom He hath sent forth by the name of 'Alí', He is alluding to this particular Tablet and verse from the Báb. Taken together, the verse from the Báb 'He Whom Thou hast raised up' and the phrase by Bahá'u'lláh in the Tablet of Aḥmad, 'the One Whom He hath sent forth', appear to contain a divine mystery. Both the Báb and Bahá'u'lláh seem to be saying that it was Bahá'u'lláh who 'sent forth' and 'raised up' the Báb. How can we understand these statements? We know that both the Báb and Bahá'u'lláh are Manifestations of God. We also know that as Manifestations they both have the same station. Exactly what these statements mean is not evident and must remain a mystery. However, we know that the Báb, describing the purpose of His own Revelation, declares:

> I have revealed Myself for His Manifestation, and have caused My Book, the Bayán, to descend upon you for no other purpose except to establish the truth of His Cause.[297]

In this sense the significance of these statements that Bahá'u'lláh 'raised up' and 'sent forth' the Báb may be that no one can truly accept the Báb without also accepting Bahá'u'lláh. True recognition of God in this day is not complete without recognizing both the Báb and Bahá'u'lláh. These statements may also indicate that the purpose of all previous revelations has been to lay the foundation and to prepare the way for the Revelation of Bahá'u'lláh. In this sense we may say that Bahá'u'lláh is the one who 'sent forth' the Báb and all the previous Manifestations; similarly, we may also say that as the Báb's book is the Mother Book, the Báb 'sent forth' Bahá'u'lláh.

It is also significant that in the very next sentence Bahá'u'lláh, still speaking about the Báb, says, 'to Whose commands we are all conforming'. In one sense, by including Himself in the 'we', Bahá'u'lláh seems to be reciprocating the homage that the Báb had paid to Him. In the sense that the Báb asserts that it was Bahá'u'lláh who raised Him up, now it is Bahá'u'lláh who asserts that He, Bahá'u'lláh, is conforming to the commands of the Báb. What we see in all the mystical interplay between the Báb and Bahá'u'lláh is the unfathomable love that each one has for the other and the divine humility that each demonstrates towards the other. It is a supreme example to us of what divine humility, devotion and unconditional love are between the Manifestations of God. We may also say that these statements suggest an attitude of reverence and humility that we human beings need to develop towards all the Manifestations of God and each other.

## 39

# To Whose Commands We are All Conforming

*And that the One Whom He hath sent forth*
*by the name of 'Alí*
*was the true One from God,*
*to Whose commands we are all conforming.*

Testifying to the truth of the Báb's station and divine mission, Bahá'u'lláh declares that the Báb 'was the true One from God to Whose commands we are all conforming'. This assertion appears to be Bahá'u'lláh's glorification of the true station of the Báb's Revelation and a testimony to the supreme authority exercised by the Báb. On another level, 'to Whose commands we are all conforming' appears to indicate Bahá'u'lláh's own dependence on the Báb. In this sense the verse is yet another sign of the twin Revelations of the Báb and Bahá'u'lláh.

To understand the significance of the phrase 'to Whose commands we are all conforming' we need to consider the character of the station of the Manifestations of God. Recall that the writings of the Báb and Bahá'u'lláh emphasize that the Manifestations are divinely appointed intermediaries between God and humanity. This implies that the Manifestations exercise supreme authority over all the people of the earth. This is confirmed by Bahá'u'lláh. He asserts that human beings 'live by the operation of Their Will' and the 'outpourings of Their grace'.[298] He says that we cannot escape the operation of their will. This seems to imply that we are bound by the decrees of the Manifestations. Bahá'u'lláh also tells us that if we choose, we can reflect the light and glory of the divine Manifestation. In other passages Bahá'u'lláh explains that to reflect the attributes of the Manifestation of God is our true glory and the purpose of God for each one of us:

> Every one of them is a mirror of God, reflecting naught else but His Self, His Beauty, His Might and Glory, if ye will understand. All else besides them are to be regarded as mirrors capable of reflecting the glory of these Manifestations Who are themselves the Primary Mirrors of the Divine Being, if ye be not devoid of understanding. No one hath ever escaped them, neither are they to be hindered from achieving their purpose.[299]

In the *Book of Certitude*, Bahá'u'lláh adds:

> . . . all else besides these Manifestations, live by the operation of their Will, and move and have their being through the outpourings of their grace.[300]

In another passage from the *Book of Certitude* similar to those above Bahá'u'lláh speaks specifically about the station of the Báb, declaring that people 'move and have their being through His law':

> No understanding can grasp the nature of His Revelation, nor can any knowledge comprehend the full measure of His Faith. All sayings are dependent upon His sanction, and all things stand in need of His Cause. All else save Him are created by His command, and move and have their being through His law.[301]

From these statements we see that we live through the operation of the Báb's will and that we cannot escape Him. It follows logically that we must all be conforming to the Báb's commands. In this context, it is important to note that Bahá'u-'lláh revealed the *Book of Certitude* several years before He revealed the Tablet of Aḥmad. This means that He had already established a solid foundation for our understanding of the station of the Manifestations and particularly the station of the Báb prior to His revelation of the Tablet of Aḥmad. From this we see that when Bahá'u'lláh, in the Tablet of Aḥmad, asserts that the Báb is the One 'to Whose commands we are all conforming', He is testifying, in a manner that no human being can, that the Báb is a true Manifestation of God.

There are passages in the writings of the Báb and Bahá'u-'lláh which seem to indicate that it is the Báb who, by His command, ordained Bahá'u'lláh's Revelation. For example, in the Persian Bayán, the Báb declares:

> Well is it with him who fixeth his gaze upon the Order of Bahá'u'lláh, and rendereth thanks unto his Lord. For He will assuredly be made manifest. God hath indeed irrevocably ordained it in the Bayán.[302]

Echoing this statement, Bahá'u'lláh appears to say that He is fulfilling the will of the Báb by manifesting Himself and revealing the Cause of God. In one of His Tablets Bahá'u'lláh states that if the destiny of the Cause of God had been in His hands, He would never have consented to reveal Himself.[303] In another Tablet Bahá'u'lláh says that it is because of what the Báb had written that He revealed Himself:

> By the righteousness of God! But for the anthem of praise voiced by Him Who heralded the divine Revelation, this Wronged One would never have breathed a word which might have struck terror into the hearts of the ignorant and caused them to perish.[304]

We see, then, that it is the Báb who asserts that He has irrevocably ordained Bahá'u'lláh's Revelation in His book, the

Bayán. In this context we may infer that Bahá'u'lláh is conforming to the commandments of the Báb by revealing Himself.

In the previous chapter it was explained that the beginning of this verse, 'And that the One Whom He hath sent forth by the name of 'Alí', appeared, on one level, to indicate the Báb's dependence upon Bahá'u'lláh. In this chapter we see that the last part of this same verse, 'to Whose commands we are all conforming', appears, on another level, to indicate Bahá'u-'lláh's dependence upon the Báb. Taken together, these two verses suggest how completely interdependent are the Revelations of the Báb and Bahá'u'lláh and how impossible it is to separate their dispensations.

# 40

# O People be Obedient

*Say: O people be obedient to the ordinances of God,
which have been enjoined in the Bayán
by the Glorious, the Wise One.*

At first glance this verse, telling us to 'be obedient to the ordinances of God which have been enjoined in the Bayán', may appear to be a contradiction. The Bayán was the central book of the Báb's Revelation and contained all the laws of God for His dispensation. Shoghi Effendi tells us that the Bayán was 'designedly severe in the rules and regulations it imposed'.[305] He also explains that

> The Báb states that His laws are provisional and depend upon the acceptance of the future Manifestation. This is why in the Book of Aqdas Bahá'u'lláh sanctions some of the laws found in the Bayán, modifies others and sets aside many.[306]

Why, then, we may ask, would Bahá'u'lláh direct us to obey the laws found in the Bayán?

Although the Bayán was the book containing the Báb's laws, these laws were not its central purpose. Shoghi Effendi states that the Bayán 'should be regarded primarily as a eulogy of the Promised One rather than a code of laws and ordinances'.[307] The main purpose of the Bayán was to guide the Bábís to the recognition of Bahá'u'lláh. The Báb affirms that the Bayán is a testimony to the greatness of Bahá'u'lláh's Revelation and that it extols, in unmistakable terms, His superlative virtues. The Báb explains:

> The Bayán is, from beginning to end, the repository of all of His attributes, and the treasury of both His fire and His light.[308]

As to the Bayán's significance, the Báb declares:

> . . . those who will bear allegiance unto Him Whom God shall make manifest are the ones who have grasped the meaning of that which hath been revealed in the Bayán.[309]

Expressing His devotion to the Cause of Bahá'u'lláh and wishing to emphasize the supreme importance of recognizing and accepting Bahá'u'lláh, the Báb says:

> I have not wished that this Tree should ever bear any branch, leaf, or fruit that would fail to bow down before Him, on the day of His Revelation . . .[310]

So that no doubt may be left in anyone's mind as to His intention, the Báb adds this solemn request:

> And shouldst Thou behold, O my God, any branch, leaf, or fruit upon Me that hath failed to bow down before Him, on the day of His Revelation, cut it off, O My God, from that Tree, for it is not of Me, nor shall it return unto Me.[311]

We see, then, that 'the ordinances of God which have been enjoined in the Bayán' by the Báb may refer to His repeated exhortations to His followers to recognize and accept Bahá'u'lláh as soon as He appeared. Bahá'u'lláh confirms this in His writings. He clearly testifies that the Báb was the divinely appointed herald of His own Revelation. Bahá'u'lláh calls the Báb 'My Previous Manifestation' and says that the whole purpose of the Báb's Revelation was to prepare the way for humanity to accept Bahá'u'lláh:

> . . . the sole object of whatsoever My Previous Manifestation and Harbinger of My Beauty hath revealed hath been My Revelation and the proclamation of My Cause.[312]

The Báb also testifies to this:

> I swear by God, the Peerless, the Incomparable, the True One: for no other reason hath He – the Supreme Testimony of God – invested Me with clear signs and tokens than that all men may be enabled to submit to His Cause.[313]

We see, then, that the verse in the Tablet of Aḥmad urging obedience to the laws of the Bayán appears to be yet another indication of how closely interwoven the Revelations of Bahá'u-'lláh and the Báb are. It also appears that through this verse Bahá'u'lláh is exhorting the followers of the Báb to obey the Báb's explicit, unequivocal and repeated command for them to recognize Bahá'u'lláh and to arise and serve His Cause. In this sense 'be obedient to the ordinances of God' is an emphatic assertion that the Bábís cannot fulfil the commandments of the Báb unless they recognize and accept Bahá'u'lláh.

41

# O People be Obedient: The Covenant

*. . . to Whose commands we are all conforming.*
*Say: O people be obedient to the ordinances of God,*
*which have been enjoined in the Bayán*
*by the Glorious, the Wise One.*

On another level, the verse 'O people be obedient to the ordinances of God' may signify man's obligation to be obedient to the Covenant of God. In commanding us to be obedient, Bahá'u'lláh is reminding us that it is our duty, as believers and partners to God's Covenant, to obey whatever laws the Manifestation of God has given us.

The requirement to 'be obedient' is an affirmation of the fundamental spiritual truth that all of us are bound by the law of God. The universe is His creation. Whatever He decrees is law and we, as part of His creation, are bound by what He ordains. This may be one of the significances of the verse 'to Whose commands we are all conforming': that no one is exempt from the operation of His law.

The Covenant of God imposes a twin, twofold obligation on each one of us as believers and parties to the Covenant. These duties, as explained by Bahá'u'lláh, are to recognize and obey the Manifestation of God and to be obedient to His laws and steadfast in His Cause.

As vitally important as it is to recognize the Manifestation of God, recognition alone is not enough. In order for our recognition to be of value to us and lead us along the path of spiritual development and nearness to God, it must be accompanied by obedience. This is the core and foundation of the religion of God and the essence of His Covenant. As we have seen, in the opening paragraph of the Kitáb-i-Aqdas, Bahá'u'lláh declares:

> The first duty prescribed by God for His servants is the recognition of Him Who is the Dayspring of His Revelation and the Fountain of His laws . . . It behoveth every one who reacheth this most sublime station. . . to observe every ordinance of Him Who is the Desire of the world. These twin duties are inseparable. Neither is acceptable without the other.[314]

God's purpose in establishing His Covenant with humankind is to provide the means and establish the spiritual connection through which we can know God and draw ever closer to Him. It is for this reason that He sets forth our obligation to recognize His Manifestation and obey His laws. In one of His Tablets Bahá'u'lláh explains this fundamental truth:

> The supreme cause for creating the world and all that is therein is for man to know God.[315] In this Day whosoever is guided . . . [to] the station of recognizing the Source of divine commandments and the Dayspring of His Revelation, hath everlastingly attained unto all good. Having reached this lofty station a twofold obligation resteth upon every soul. One is to be steadfast in the Cause . . . The other is observance of the divine ordinances which have streamed forth from the wellspring of His heavenly-propelled Pen. For man's knowledge of God cannot develop fully and adequately save by observing whatsoever hath been ordained by Him and is set forth in His heavenly Book.[316]

We see, then, that God imposes the requirement on us to 'be obedient to the ordinances of God' for our own good. We have been given this obligation so that we may truly know God and be drawn near to Him, so that we may experience His Love in our lives and may be enabled to develop to our fullest and highest potential.

## 42

# The King of the Messengers

*Say, O people be obedient to the ordinances of God*
*which have been enjoined in the Bayán*
*by the Glorious, the Wise One.*
*Verily He is the King of the Messengers*

In one sense 'the King of the Messengers' may refer to God Himself. God is, without question, the King through whose commands all the Messengers have been sent down. Yet, on another level, 'the King of the Messengers' may signify the Báb. Notice that in the previous sentence of the Tablet of Aḥmad, Bahá'u'lláh says, 'be obedient to the ordinances of God which have been enjoined in the Bayán by the Glorious, the Wise One'. Bahá'u'lláh then asserts, 'Verily He is the King of the Messengers.' Since the author of the Bayán is the Báb, it is possible that Bahá'u'lláh is telling us that the Báb is 'the King of the Messengers'.

We know that it is an essential tenet of the Bahá'í Faith, a teaching emphasized by Bahá'u'lláh, that all the Manifestations of God have the same station. On this subject, Bahá'u'lláh says:

> God, the Creator, saith: There is no distinction whatsoever among the Bearers of My Message.[317]

In another Tablet He warns:

> Beware, O believers in the Unity of God, lest ye be tempted to make any distinction between any of the Manifestations

> of His Cause, or to discriminate against the signs that have accompanied and proclaimed their Revelation.[318]

In light of these emphatic statements regarding the oneness of the station of all the Manifestations, we may ask what the significance is of Bahá'u'lláh's designation of the Báb as 'the King of the Messengers'.

In one of His Tablets Bahá'u'lláh explains that the revelation of each of the Messengers in this world must differ. He points out that every Manifestation has been commissioned by God to reveal a specific message that is designed to meet the needs and capacities of the people to whom His message is given:

> The measure of the revelation of the Prophets of God in this world, however, must differ. Each and every one of them hath been the Bearer of a distinct Message, and hath been commissioned to reveal Himself through specific acts. It is for this reason that they appear to vary in their greatness . . . Every Prophet Whom the Almighty and Peerless Creator hath purposed to send to the peoples of the earth hath been entrusted with a Message, and charged to act in a manner that would best meet the requirements of the age in which He appeared.[319]

In this passage Bahá'u'lláh points out that the Manifestations only *appear* to 'vary in their greatness'. The implication of this statement is that the inherent station of all the Manifestations is the same, a fact which Bahá'u'lláh affirms in His writings.[320]

Regarding the differences between the revelations of the Manifestations, the Guardian explains the implications of the principle of progressive revelation:

> . . . in accordance with the principle of progressive revelation every Manifestation of God must needs vouchsafe to the peoples of His day a measure of divine guidance ampler than any which a preceding and less receptive age could have received or appreciated.[321]

Returning to the question of the Báb's station, we know that the Báb occupies a unique position in the line of successive Manifestations. His Revelation links two great cycles in the progressive unfoldment of the religion of God. On the one hand, the Báb's Revelation is the culmination of the age of prophecy which began with Adam. From this point of view the Báb is the completion of the cycle of all the earlier Prophets. In this sense the Báb is the King of all the previous Messengers.

On the other hand, the Báb's Revelation marks the beginning of the age of fulfilment of the prophecies made in all the earlier scriptures. These prophecies concern the appearance of the promised Day of God and the building of the Kingdom of God on earth. From this perspective, the Báb is the first in the new cycle of Manifestations who will lead humanity into its promised stage of spiritual maturity.

The fact that the Báb is the link between two cycles is significant. His title 'the Báb' means 'the Gate'. In one sense the Báb is the gate between the age of prophecy and the age of fulfilment. The uniqueness of this position among all the Prophets of God may be one reason why Bahá'u'lláh calls Him 'the King of the Messengers'.

Shoghi Effendi explains that the greatness of the Báb is due to the fact that He was empowered by God to exercise greater authority than any previous Manifestation had been allowed to do:

> Indeed the greatness of the Báb consists primarily, not in His being the divinely-appointed Forerunner of so transcendent a Revelation, but rather in His having been invested with the powers inherent in the inaugurator of a separate religious Dispensation, and in His wielding, to a degree unrivalled by the Messengers gone before Him, the sceptre of independent Prophethood.[322]

In this same vein, Bahá'u'lláh explains that the Báb was

commissioned to reveal a much greater measure of divine revelation than any which the preceding Messengers had been given:

> No eye hath beheld so great an outpouring of bounty, nor hath any ear heard of such a Revelation of loving-kindness . . . The Prophets 'endowed with constancy', whose loftiness and glory shine as the sun, were each honoured with a Book which all have seen, and the verses of which have been duly ascertained. Whereas the verses which have rained from this Cloud of divine mercy have been so abundant that none hath yet been able to estimate their number.[323]

In one of His Tablets 'Abdu'l-Bahá defines for us the true station of the Báb:

> The Báb, the Exalted One, is the Morn of Truth, the splendour of Whose light shineth throughout all regions. He is also the Harbinger of the Most Great Light, the Abhá Luminary.[324]

In His Will and Testament, 'Abdu'l-Bahá again delineates what our understanding of the Báb's station should be:

> His Holiness the exalted One (the Báb) is the Manifestation of the unity and oneness of God and the Forerunner of the Ancient Beauty (Bahá'u'lláh).[325]

Bahá'u'lláh, in the *Book of Certitude*, gives further testimony to the greatness of the Báb's Revelation. Affirming our understanding of the position of the Báb in the line of Messengers, Bahá'u'lláh asserts:

> No understanding can grasp the nature of His Revelation, nor can any knowledge comprehend the full measure of His Faith. All sayings are dependent upon His sanction, and all things stand in need of His Cause. All else save Him are

> created by His command, and move and have their being through His law. He is the Revealer of the divine mysteries, and the Expounder of the hidden and ancient wisdom. Thus it is related . . . of Ṣádiq, son of Muḥammad, that he spoke these words: 'Knowledge is twenty and seven letters. All that the Prophets have revealed are two letters thereof. No man thus far hath known more than these two letters. But when the Qá'im shall arise, He will cause the remaining twenty and five letters to be made manifest.' . . . Behold from this utterance how great and lofty is His station! His rank excelleth that of all the Prophets, and His Revelation transcendeth the comprehension and understanding of all their chosen ones.[326]

Notice that Bahá'u'lláh does not say that the *station* of the Báb is different than the station of the other Manifestations. Rather He asserts that the Báb's '*rank* excelleth that of all the Prophets'. The term *rank* denotes a functional position of responsibility and authority within a designated group. The fact that Bahá'u'lláh says that the Báb's rank excels that of the other Prophets seems to imply that the Báb was given a greater mission to accomplish. This is consistent with the Guardian's explanation that the greatness of the Báb lies in His 'wielding, to a degree unrivalled by the Messengers gone before Him, the sceptre of independent Prophethood'.[327] That the Báb holds a superior rank among the previous Messengers may be yet another reason why Bahá'u'lláh identifies the Báb as 'the King of the Messengers'.

# 43

# The Mother Book

*Verily He is the King of the Messengers*
*and His Book is the Mother Book*
*did ye but know.*

In the Qur'án, the term 'Mother Book' refers to the book which is in heaven with God and through whose creative power all the holy scriptures have been generated.[328] We may say that the 'Mother Book' is the essence and the pure, original form, pattern or archetype of all holy books and scriptures. The Qur'án uses the term 'Mother of the Book', apparently symbolizing its spiritual function as the source and creator of all divine revelation. We recall that the concept of divine unity, which is a fundamental teaching of both the Báb and Bahá'u'lláh, states that the essence of God is unknowable and that God can only be known through His Manifestations. In the *Book of Certitude* Bahá'u'lláh explains that the divine reality of all the Manifestations of God is one. It follows that if their reality is one then their revelation must also be one. This means that in the realm of divine revelation there is only one revelation, a fact which Bahá'u'lláh affirms:

> These Countenances are the recipients of the Divine Command, and the day-springs of His Revelation. This Revelation is exalted above the veils of plurality and the exigencies of number.[329]

In another Tablet He says:

> Every true Prophet hath regarded His Message as fundamentally the same as the Revelation of every other Prophet gone before Him.[330]

We see, then, that all the revelations which the different Manifestations of God have revealed to humanity are aspects of this one revelation, this archetype of all revelation, known as the 'Mother Book'. Prior to the appearance of the Báb and Bahá'u'lláh, the Prophets of God revealed only a portion of the Mother Book, in accordance with the limited capacity of the people living in their day. The revelations of the Báb and Bahá'u'lláh, however, are different from all previous ones in that they provide the whole revelation.

Thus when Bahá'u'lláh in the Tablet of Aḥmad describes the Báb's writings as the 'Mother Book', He is on one level glorifying and exalting the Báb's station. On yet another level He is telling us that the Báb is the possessor of the Mother Book. The implication of this is that it is through the Báb that all the divine revelations have been generated. Bahá'u'lláh also alludes to the Báb's greatness as the one who 'will cause the remaining twenty and five letters [of all knowledge] to be made manifest'.[331] The Báb, testifying to the truth of His own station, declares:

> I am one of the sustaining pillars of the Primal Word of God.[332]

Again He says:

> I am the Primal Point from which have been generated all created things.[333]

A significant verse in the Qur'án provides yet another level of meaning of the term 'Mother Book' and seems to allude prophetically to the Báb:

> By the Book that makes things clear, –
> We have made it a Qur'án in Arabic,
> that ye may be able to understand (and learn wisdom).
> And verily, it is in the Mother of the Book, in Our Presence,
> high (in dignity), full of wisdom.[334]

In Arabic the phrase 'high in dignity' is the word 'Alí. In one sense this word may be understood as the name 'Alí and thus the verse is about the name 'Alí and not the phrase 'high in dignity'. From this point of view, this verse in the Qur'án translates as:

> Verily He is the One mentioned in the Mother Book as 'Alí, full of wisdom.

When the Báb revealed the Qayyúmu'l-Asmá', His first book, He referred to this particular verse from the Qur'án and declared that the 'Alí mentioned referred to Himself. From this we may infer that when Bahá'u'lláh in the Tablet of Aḥmad says that the Báb's book is the 'Mother Book', He may, on yet another level, be alluding to both this assertion of the Báb and to this reference in the Qur'án. In this sense we may infer that Bahá'u'lláh, by asserting that 'His Book is the Mother Book', is testifying that the Báb had been prophesied in the Qur'án by Muḥammad.

In various passages Bahá'u'lláh uses the term 'Mother Book' to denote the Word of God, the revelation of the Word of God and the Manifestation Himself.[335] He extols the divine creative power of the Word of God in such exalted and majestic terms that it is impossible to exaggerate its all-pervasive influence. In one sense it is this all-embracing influence of the Word of God that leads to its characterization as 'the Mother Book'. In one of His Tablets Bahá'u'lláh asserts, 'Every thing which can be perceived is but an emanation therefrom.'[336] In another Tablet He likens the creative power of the Word of God to that of a mother who gives birth to advances in human society and to new spiritual life within individuals:

> Every word that proceedeth out of the mouth of God is endowed with such potency as can instil new life into every human frame.[337]

He goes on to describe the effects of the revelation of the names of God. Giving as an example the name 'the Fashioner', He explains:

> No sooner is this resplendent word uttered, than its animating energies, stirring within all created things, give birth to the means and instruments whereby such arts can be produced and perfected . . . Know thou of a certainty that the Revelation of every other Name is accompanied by a similar manifestation of Divine power. Every single letter proceeding out of the mouth of God is indeed a mother letter, and every word uttered by Him Who is the Well Spring of Divine Revelation is a mother word, and His Tablet a Mother Tablet.[338]

From this we see that when Bahá'u'lláh asserts that the writings of the Báb are the 'Mother Book', He is giving His personal testimony that the verses of the Báb are the divine, creative Word of God.

Speaking about cause and effect in the physical world, Bahá'u'lláh asserts that the Word of God is the cause underlying all of creation:

> Every thing must needs have an origin and every building a builder. Verily, the Word of God is the Cause which hath preceded the contingent world . . .[339]

From these passages we see that Bahá'u'lláh, in proclaiming the Báb to be the King of the Messengers and His writings to be the Mother Book, is offering the strongest possible testimony, in a manner which no ordinary human being can do, that the Báb is the promised Qá'im and that, paradoxically, His Book is the source of all previous books.

## 44

# The Call and the Clear Message

*Thus doth the Nightingale utter His call unto you*
*from this prison.*
*He hath but to deliver this clear message.*

What is Bahá'u'lláh's call to us in the Tablet of Aḥmad and what is the clear message He conveys? Does Bahá'u'lláh issue only one call to us or are there more? Is there only one clear message or are there many clear messages to be found?

Let us examine the definitions of the words 'call' and 'message'. In English, the word 'call' has many meanings, several of which may help us gain a better understanding of Bahá'u'lláh's statement. The word 'call' means a loud utterance or to say something in a loud voice. 'To call' means to select or appoint for a specific duty. It also means to appeal to; to arouse or awaken, as from sleep. 'Call' also means a summons or an invitation, a signalling or a signal. 'Call' can also mean a religious duty regarded as divinely inspired.

The word 'message' in English can mean an inspired or important communication, as of a prophet.

With these definitions in mind, we see that the Tablet of Aḥmad may be viewed as an appeal by Bahá'u'lláh to awaken us and arouse us to action. It may be understood as Bahá'u'lláh's invitation to us to arise and serve Him and to fulfil our sacred duty to God. The clear message it conveys is obviously divinely inspired and very important. It is a personal communication to us through Aḥmad from Bahá'u'lláh, giving us very clear guidance on what He wants us to do.[340]

In one sense we may say that these two sentences are the pivotal verses of the Tablet of Aḥmad and that all the other verses revolve around them. Seen in this way, these two sentences take on new meaning. Every paragraph of the Tablet of Aḥmad may be characterized as 'His call' to us. At the same time, we see that all the exhortations, such as 'Bear thou witness' and 'be thou so steadfast in My love', may be considered as integral parts of the 'clear message' conveyed by Bahá'u'lláh. In fact, every phrase and verse of this Tablet may be understood as an essential part of His clear message.

To discover the many allusions and significances concealed in this Tablet requires persistent study. Bahá'u'lláh seems to indicate this near the end of the English translation of the Tablet when He says, 'Learn well this Tablet . . . and withhold not thyself therefrom'. It appears that Bahá'u'lláh wants us to understand the fundamental spiritual truths He has placed within this special Tablet and to meditate on them so that they will become clear to us. As we reflect on the significance of its verses, doors open and previously hidden meanings become evident. Every time an insight crystallizes in our mind, it becomes part of the 'clear message' put there by Bahá'u'lláh for us to find. Each new insight may be regarded as a confirmation of the spiritual potency with which Bahá'u'lláh has invested this particular Tablet.

An essential aspect of the Tablet's spiritual potency is its personal appeal. Bahá'u'lláh has fashioned it in such a way that it becomes extremely personal to every individual who reads it and takes it to heart. For instance, He declares, 'Thus doth the Nightingale utter His call *unto you*.' Who can read this and not feel that this Tablet was written, in part, to himself? In a similar vein, near the end of the Tablet Bahá'u'lláh assures us, 'By God! Should one who is in affliction or grief read this Tablet with absolute sincerity, God will dispel his sadness, solve his difficulties and remove his afflictions.' Many people have been comforted and given hope by this promise of Bahá'u'lláh. Surely we may say it was Bahá'u'lláh's intention to comfort us and to make us feel that He was writing to us personally. This, too, may be His call to us and the clear message He wishes to convey.

These two sentences may be viewed as Bahá'u'lláh's assurance that He has personalized a 'clear message' for every one of us who believes in Him and reads this Tablet. All the exhortations in the Tablet of Aḥmad, such as 'be not of those who doubt' and 'be thou assured in thyself', are the personal counsels of Bahá'u'lláh. They are His directions guiding each one of us who sincerely wants to reach out to Him and serve Him. To everyone who desires to receive His assistance, the Tablet of Aḥmad peals out its promise of unfailing help and guidance. This, in itself, is one of its clear messages.

The Tablet of Aḥmad encourages us to turn our hearts to Bahá'u'lláh and beseech His aid, His grace and His favours in our daily lives. This may be regarded as Bahá'u'lláh's call to us in this Tablet. The clear message He has delivered to every devoted follower may be understood as His loving counsels to cherish the bounties of His love which He unceasingly offers us.

We must never underestimate the importance of these messages and the value of such an immeasurable bounty. It is truly awe-inspiring to contemplate that Bahá'u'lláh has revealed a Tablet, the Tablet of Aḥmad, through which He addresses each one of us personally. In the Kitáb-i-Aqdas Bahá'u'lláh explains that the bounty of having our Lord, the supreme Manifestation of God, direct even one word of His writings to us personally is worth more than all the treasures of the earth:

> The peoples of the world are fast asleep. Were they to wake from their slumber, they would hasten with eagerness unto God, the All-Knowing, the All-Wise. They would cast away everything they possess, be it all the treasures of the earth, that their Lord may remember them to the extent of addressing to them but one word. Such is the instruction

given you by Him Who holdeth the knowledge of things hidden . . .[341]

Obviously we are not able to ask Bahá'u'lláh to reveal a Tablet for us personally. However, He has given us the Tablet of Aḥmad and we may feel that it is a personal gift to us from Him. He promises every one of us who sincerely reads this Tablet that He will assist us, guide us to our own understanding and grant us unlimited bounties *if* we simply follow the guidance He has offered us. In one sense, this may be seen as the promise enshrined within the first paragraph of the Tablet of Aḥmad. The Nightingale of Paradise, with its sweet melody, cries out to all the lovers of God, calling us to the presence of our Lord, the Generous One. The 'glad tidings' He proclaims may be understood as the infinite bounties of His love, which He promises He will pour out upon us if we but choose to arise and serve Him. To experience these bounties is to become aware of the real 'nearness of God'. One of the clear messages of the Tablet of Aḥmad thus appears to be that Bahá'u'lláh wants us to know that His love and bounties encompass every human being who reaches out to Him.

The holy scriptures promise that, in the Day of God, the chosen ones of God will be gathered before the throne of their Lord and will receive His blessings and His grace. In the Tablet of Aḥmad, Bahá'u'lláh, the Promised One of God, the Lord of Hosts, offers this promised grace to each and every one of us. All He asks of us is that we turn our hearts to Him, that we arise to serve Him and that we accept the gifts He offers.

The focus of human existence in this holy day is the recognition of the Promised One of God. This is the purpose for which we have been created. We have been given life upon this earth to be with our Lord, to feel His love and to be His lovers. This is the aim of our existence. The whole purpose for which creation has been called into being is that we might recognize Bahá'u'lláh and arise to serve Him. In the Tablet of Aḥmad, Bahá'u'lláh offers this most precious favour to each one of us and does so with simple clarity. He invites us to walk in His way, to feel close to Him and to bask in the sunshine of His love. This appears to be the essence of this sacred Tablet and one of its very clear messages.

In summary, we see that there is more than one call in the Tablet of Aḥmad and many messages. When we reflect on the perfection of this Tablet, we are led to the conclusion that the whole Tablet is, in a very real sense, Bahá'u'lláh's call to us. We see that within these few verses Bahá'u'lláh has conveyed so many ideas, in such clear, precise language, that we may say that every phrase in the Tablet of Aḥmad is a clear message. We also see that His call is a personal one to each one of us to arise and serve Him and to feel close to Him.

# 45

# The Call and the Clear Message: Historical Perspective

*Thus doth the Nightingale utter His call unto you*
*from this prison.*
*He hath but to deliver this clear message.*

The Tablet of Aḥmad was revealed by Bahá'u'lláh specifically for Aḥmad. In its historical context, then, when Bahá'u'lláh says, 'Thus doth the Nightingale utter His call unto you', we may infer that He is directing His call to Aḥmad. After reading this Tablet Aḥmad realized that Bahá'u'lláh desired him to teach His Cause. With this in mind, let us examine the significance of these two sentences.

One of the first things we may take note of is that Bahá'u-'lláh twice tells Aḥmad that He is in prison: 'Thus doth the Nightingale utter His call unto you from this prison'; 'Remember . . . My distress and banishment in this remote prison.' Why does Bahá'u'lláh emphasize His imprisonment to Aḥmad?

It seems that Bahá'u'lláh may have had at least two reasons for focusing Aḥmad's attention on this fact. The first may have been to help Aḥmad realize that Bahá'u'lláh did not want Aḥmad to become a prisoner with Him. Recall that when Bahá'u'lláh was exiled from Bag͟hdád to Constantinople Aḥmad was one of His close companions who was not invited to accompany Him. Along with some others, Aḥmad was asked by Bahá'u'lláh to remain behind in Bag͟hdád. Notice also that in the Tablet of Aḥmad Bahá'u'lláh does not invite Aḥmad to join Him in His exile and imprisonment; rather, Bahá'u'lláh indicated to Aḥmad that it was not Aḥmad's mission to share His exile.

Another reason why Bahá'u'lláh emphasized His imprisonment may have been to help Aḥmad understand why He wanted him to teach His Cause. The relentless attacks and never-ending persecution by the enemies of His Faith prevented Bahá'u'lláh from personally travelling and teaching His Cause. During the entire 40 years of His earthly ministry He was a prisoner and an exile. Only during the latter years of His stay in Bag͟hdád, prior to His declaration and further banishment, did Bahá'u'lláh have relative freedom to move about the city. In those days He was accessible to all the people and openly taught the Cause of God Himself. Following His exile to Constantinople and His further banishment to Adrianople, however, Bahá'u'lláh was no longer as free to openly teach His Cause. In Adrianople Bahá'u'lláh faced the additional problem of being so far away from Persia that access to and communication with the Bábí community in His native land was extremely difficult and time-consuming.

With this in mind, it is significant that Bahá'u'lláh tells Aḥmad, 'Thus doth the Nightingale utter His call unto you from this prison. He hath but to deliver this clear message.' On one level it seems that Bahá'u'lláh is telling Aḥmad that in spite of His imprisonment He has been commissioned by God to deliver a message. It may be that Bahá'u'lláh wanted Aḥmad to realize that His enemies were striving to prevent Him from carrying out His God-given mission. If Aḥmad did realize this, its implication is very clear. From this perspective, Bahá'u'lláh is telling Aḥmad that it is up to Aḥmad to deliver His message, on His behalf, to the peoples of the world. This appears to be the call of the caged nightingale to His devoted and trusted disciple Aḥmad and the 'clear message' He wants Aḥmad to comprehend.

We also know that when Aḥmad realized that Bahá'u'lláh wanted him to teach, he immediately returned to Persia and began teaching the Bábís the truth of Bahá'u'lláh's claim to be the one promised by the Báb. In the preceding paragraph of the Tablet of Aḥmad Bahá'u'lláh says, 'Say: O people be obedient to the ordinances of God which have been enjoined in the Bayán by the Glorious, the Wise One.' As has been discussed, this exhortation may have been directed to the followers of the Báb. It may be understood as a warning and a reminder to them that their belief in and loyalty to the Báb required that they now recognize Bahá'u'lláh. In the sense that this is the 'clear message' Bahá'u'lláh had been commissioned to deliver to the Bábís, we may say that His call to Aḥmad was that Bahá'u'lláh was being prevented from personally delivering this message and so it was up to Aḥmad to deliver it for Him.

Another important characteristic of the Tablet of Aḥmad is Bahá'u'lláh's personal guidance to Aḥmad. On one level it appears that Bahá'u'lláh may be telling Aḥmad how to teach His Cause and the attitude he must have in order to teach successfully. In reviewing this Tablet we note that Bahá'u'lláh tells Aḥmad to 'Bear . . . witness' to the truth of both Bahá'u'lláh's Revelation and the Revelation of the Báb. He intimates to Aḥmad that he should point out to the followers of the Báb that the Báb had repeatedly advised them in His writings to expect the advent of the Promised One. Bahá'u'lláh also tells Aḥmad 'Forget not My bounties' and exhorts him to be 'so steadfast in My love' that his 'heart shall not waver'. Bahá'u'lláh then gives Aḥmad this specific instruction:

> Be thou as a flame of fire to My enemies and a river of life eternal to My loved ones, and be not of those who doubt.

This exhortation may be viewed as Bahá'u'lláh's guidance to Aḥmad on the intention and attitude he should have when teaching the Cause of God. Bahá'u'lláh then counsels Aḥmad that if he is 'overtaken by affliction' or degradation in the path of service to the Cause of God he is, in all circumstances, to 'rely upon God' and not be troubled by such adversities. Bahá'u'lláh also assures Aḥmad that if people turn away from Him they have also 'turned away' from all the previous Messengers of God. He points out that such behaviour is unacceptable before God. And finally, Bahá'u'lláh promises Aḥmad God's unfailing aid and assistance any time he is in need of it. These exhortations, this guidance and this promise of divine assistance may be understood as essential parts of Bahá'u'lláh's 'clear message' to Aḥmad.

Another significant feature of this Tablet is that Bahá'u'lláh also seems to have indicated to Aḥmad that He did not want Aḥmad to become a martyr for His Faith. Near the end of the English translation of the Tablet Bahá'u'lláh promises Aḥmad 'the reward of a hundred martyrs' if he will simply 'chant' the Tablet and not withhold himself therefrom. If Bahá'u'lláh wanted Aḥmad to offer up his life in sacrifice to His Cause, why would He promise Aḥmad the reward of not only a single martyr but a hundred in return for Aḥmad's chanting this Tablet? With hindsight it seems clear that Bahá'u'lláh was letting Aḥmad know that the path of martyrdom (that is, *s͟hahāda*, testimony of faith) was not the mission he was being given.

In conclusion, it appears that Bahá'u'lláh has given Aḥmad very specific guidance in the Tablet and that it was this personal guidance, Bahá'u'lláh's promise to Aḥmad of His bounties and His love and the promise of divine assistance which uplifted and empowered Aḥmad and enabled him to carry out his arduous and difficult teaching assignment. The paradox for Aḥmad was that by going away from Bahá'u'lláh back to Bag͟hdád, he was, according to the clear text of the Tablet, 'choosing the path to his Lord'.

# 46

# Deliver This Clear Message

*Thus doth the Nightingale utter His call unto you*
*from this prison.*
*He hath but to deliver this clear message.*

In Arabic the verse 'He hath but to deliver this clear message' is similar to several verses in the Qur'án. Each of these verses declares that it is the duty of God's Messengers to proclaim His message clearly. For example, the Qur'án says:

> Obey God, and obey the Messenger,
> And beware (of evil): if ye do turn back, know ye that it is Our Messenger's duty to proclaim (the message) in the clearest manner.[342]

In another passage we read:

> The worshippers of false gods say: 'If God had so willed, we should not have worshipped aught but Him – neither we nor our fathers.' So did those who went before them. But what is the mission of messengers but to preach the Clear Message?[343]

And in yet another verse the Qur'án says:

> The Messenger's duty is only to preach the clear Message.[344]

And again:

> And if they argue with thee, (O Muhammad), say: I have surrendered my purpose to Allah and (so have) those who follow me. And say unto those who have received the Scripture and those who read not: Have ye (too) surrendered?
>
> If they surrender, then truly they are rightly guided, and if they turn away, then it is thy duty only to convey the message (unto them). Allah is Seer of (His) bondmen.[345]

We see, then, that the verse in the Tablet of Aḥmad 'Thus doth the Nightingale utter His call unto you from this prison. He hath but to deliver this clear message' is likely to have been quoted from the Qur'án.[346] Bahá'u'lláh seems to be suggesting that God has given Him a duty identical to that which God had given to Muḥammad and His other Messengers. The clear implication of this is that Bahá'u'lláh is most certainly a divinely-appointed Messenger of God. In this sense Bahá'u-'lláh is giving us yet another proof of His claim to be the Promised One of the Báb.

Recall that the Tablet of Aḥmad was revealed around 1864–5. This was the early period of Bahá'u'lláh's banishment to Adrianople, a year or two after the public declaration of His mission to His family and close followers in the garden of Riḍván. The Tablets revealed by Bahá'u'lláh during this period of His ministry generally extol and glorify the station of the Báb. At the same time, these Tablets also glorify the station and mission of Bahá'u'lláh and establish the connection between Himself and the Báb. Notice how clearly and powerfully the Tablet of Aḥmad does this. We find many bold, unequivocal assertions by Bahá'u'lláh concerning His station and mission in this Tablet. We also note how many references and allusions to the Qur'án and the writings of the Báb He has included in this relatively short Tablet. Bahá'u'lláh is giving His reader, who, historically, was most likely either a Bábí or a Muslim, many Quranic references to substantiate Bahá'u'lláh's claim to be the Promised One of God. The verse 'He hath but to deliver this clear message' is a prime example of this.

These two sentences from the Tablet of Aḥmad also seem to indicate that Bahá'u'lláh is asserting that the 'call' which He has spelled out in this Tablet is the fulfilment of His God-given duty to deliver the message as clearly as possible. The implication of these two sentences, together with the subsequent verse 'O people, if ye deny these verses, by what proof have ye believed in God' seems to be that it is not possible for Bahá'u'lláh to be any more clear than He has already been. A further implication of this is that those who deny these verses will be subjected to the punishment prescribed by the Qur'án for those who reject God's Messengers.

The Arabic word for 'message' in this verse from the Tablet of Aḥmad is *balágh*. *Balágh* is derived from the three Arabic letters b, l and gh. In Arabic these letters taken together can also signify teaching and proclamation (and maturity). One inference of this Arabic word is that once we have accepted Bahá'u'lláh as the one who has been commissioned to deliver this clear message from God, then it is our duty, as those who have accepted Him, to follow in His way and also deliver this clear message to the people.

Finally, the very word 'Bayán', usually translated as 'explanation', also means 'clear message' or 'proof'. Indeed, the adjective 'clear' in the Tablet of Aḥmad is derived from the same root as bayán, *mubín*, a term frequently used in the Qur'án; the term bayán itself occurs three times in the Qur'án.[347] Thus the connection between Bahá'u'lláh's use of the phrase 'clear message' and the Revelations of both Muḥammad and the Báb is again confirmed and Bahá'u'lláh's claim to be the Promised One of both dispensations further strengthened.

# 47

# Choose the Path to Your Lord

*Whosoever desireth,*
*let him turn aside from this counsel*
*and whosoever desireth*
*let him choose the path to his Lord.*

Bahá'u'lláh is the divine Counsellor whose coming was promised by Isaiah[348] in his memorable passage:

> . . . and his name shall be called Wonderful, Counsellor, The mighty God, The everlasting Father, The Prince of Peace.[349]

In one of His Tablets Bahá'u'lláh urges us to 'Give ear unto the Voice of this trustworthy Counsellor'.[350] In other Tablets He refers to Himself as the 'All-Knowing Counsellor',[351] 'the True Counsellor',[352] 'this benevolent Counsellor'[353] and 'the faithful Counsellor'.[354] In this latter passage He appeals to us to:

> Abandon the things current amongst you and adopt that which the faithful Counsellor biddeth you. Deprive not yourselves of the bounties which have been created for your sake.[355]

The bounties of God which are being showered from the heaven of Bahá'u'lláh's Revelation are one of the major themes of the Tablet of Aḥmad. If we choose to follow the teachings of 'this benevolent Counsellor', we open ourselves to the outpourings of His inestimable favours and blessings. 'How high the reward of him that hath not deprived himself of so great a bounty,' Bahá'u'lláh tells us.[356] Should we choose not to follow His teachings, however, we will shut ourselves out from this promised grace.

We may regard the Tablet of Aḥmad as a guide to the bounties of God. It is a set of instructions which we can choose to follow in order to win the good pleasure of our Lord. In this sense, the verses of this paragraph summarize everything Bahá'u'lláh has revealed in the Tablet.

Consider the first paragraph. He begins by announcing 'the glad tidings of the nearness of God'. Whoever responds to this announcement is invited to 'the court of the Presence of the Generous One'. Those who accept this invitation are enlightened by 'the message which hath been revealed by God'. For those of us who respond to His message He becomes our guide, 'guiding the lovers to the seat of sanctity and to this resplendent Beauty'. In the next paragraph He informs us that His teachings are the divine standard through which 'truth shall be distinguished from error' and He warns us that we will be tested to determine if we are truly sincere and willing to follow His teachings. He promises us that if we follow in His way, He will make us 'the fruits of God'. He then informs us that our mission in life is to 'Bear thou witness that verily He is God'. He reminds us that we are all bound by the commandments of God and admonishes us to 'be obedient' to His ordinances. Assuming the role of a patient teacher, He calls our attention to the fact that this is His 'clear message' to us and reminds us that it is up to each individual to decide for himself how he will respond to His call.

'Whosoever desireth, let him turn aside from this counsel and whosoever desireth let him choose the path to his Lord' may be understood simply as a statement that God does not demand from us more than we are prepared to offer Him. It is our responsibility to make our own choices; God will never impose His will on us. Should we choose to respond to His call, Bahá'u'lláh assures us, it is for our own well-being and benefit.[357]

'Whosoever desireth' is also both a warning and a promise. The reader is warned that every choice has its own consequences. For instance, to those who rejected His message and actively opposed Him, Bahá'u'lláh wrote, 'If ye believe, to your own behoof will ye believe; and if ye believe not, ye yourselves will suffer.'[358] At the same time the phrase is a promise that should we decide to respond to His call, we can win the good pleasure of our merciful Lord by our own choices and actions. In one of His Tablets Bahá'u'lláh explains:

> For every act performed there shall be a recompense according to the estimate of God, and unto this the very ordinances and prohibitions prescribed by the Almighty amply bear witness . . . However, unto them that are rid of all attachments a deed is, verily, its own reward.[359]

Here Bahá'u'lláh emphasizes a fundamental principle of human existence: that virtue is its own reward. This principle is the foundation of all Bahá'í teachings and is implicit in Bahá'u'lláh's advice to the individual to 'choose the path to his Lord'.

In one of His Tablets Bahá'u'lláh asserts that the purpose of God in manifesting Himself to humanity is 'to array every man with the mantle of a saintly character, and to adorn him with the ornament of holy and goodly deeds'.[360]

In another Tablet He declares:

> We, verily, have decreed in Our Book a goodly and bountiful reward to whosoever will turn away from wickedness and lead a chaste and godly life. He, in truth, is the Great Giver, the All-Bountiful.[361]

The Bahá'í writings assure us that God rewards everyone who

arises to serve Him. The only requisite is that we arise and act. If we do not take action, we cannot be assisted. This is the crux of the matter; this is the essence of Bahá'u'lláh's advice to every human being to 'choose the path to his Lord'. It is up to each individual to arise and take the first step. In one of His Tablets Bahá'u'lláh points out:

> All that which ye potentially possess can, however, be manifested only as a result of your own volition. Your own acts testify to this truth.[362]

For those who truly desire to serve Bahá'u'lláh, 'Whosoever desireth' is also an appeal to teach His Cause. This appeal is echoed throughout His writings. In one of His Tablets He urges us:

> Centre your energies in the propagation of the Faith of God. Whoso is worthy of so high a calling, let him arise and promote it. Whoso is unable, it is his duty to appoint him who will, in his stead, proclaim this Revelation . . .[363]

The Arabic for the word 'path' in the verse 'let him choose the path to his Lord' is *sabíl*, which connotes sacrifice in the way of God.[364] When we study the life of Aḥmad, we find that he offered his whole life as a sacrifice to his beloved and in the path of service he endured many hardships and sufferings. Thus this verse may also be understood as an invitation to the station of sacrifice. From this perspective, Bahá'u'lláh does not require anyone to offer this kind of sacrifice if he is unwilling to do so. He specifically counsels us that we may turn aside from this path of service and choose another. But for those who hold an overwhelming love for Him and a burning desire to sacrifice in His path, Bahá'u'lláh offers this advice:

> If thine aim be to cherish thy life, approach not Our court; but if sacrifice be thy heart's desire, come and let others come

> with thee. For such is the way of Faith, if in thy heart thou seekest reunion with Bahá . . .[365]

In another Tablet He says:

> Know ye that trials and tribulations have, from time immemorial, been the lot of the chosen Ones of God and His beloved, and such of His servants as are detached from all else but Him . . . Blessed are the steadfastly enduring, they that are patient under ills and hardships, who lament not over anything that befalleth them, and who tread the path of resignation . . .[366]

If a believer sincerely wishes to transform himself and serve the Cause of God, he must be willing to bear at least some tests and ordeals because, as 'Abdu'l-Bahá has pointed out, it is impossible for any individual to grow and change without experiencing pain and difficulties. Commenting on what it means to serve the Cause of God in this day, 'Abdu'l-Bahá writes:

> It is inevitable that, walking the pathway of Bahá'u'lláh, they too [the friends in the West] will become targets for persecution by the oppressors . . . Now ye, as well, must certainly become my partners to some slight degree, and accept your share of tests and sorrows.[367]

# 48

# If Ye Deny These Verses

*O people, if ye deny these verses,*
*by what proof have ye believed in God?*

Throughout His writings Bahá'u'lláh asserts that His verses are the clearest proof of His claim to be the Promised One of God. For example, He says:

> Let him that doubteth the words which the Spirit of God hath spoken seek the court of Our presence and hear Our divinely-revealed verses, and be an eye-witness of the clear proof of Our claim.[368]

He emphatically asserts that He is not dependent upon anyone or anything else to establish the truth of His claim. He unequivocally declares that His revealed verses are superior to all other proofs and testimonies:

> Truly this Wronged One desireth not to demonstrate His Own Cause with proofs produced by others.[369]

> To demonstrate the truth of His Revelation He hath not been, nor is He, dependent upon any one. Well nigh a hundred volumes of luminous verses and perspicuous words have already been sent down . . . and are available unto all. It is for thee to direct thyself towards the Ultimate Goal . . . that thou mayest hear and behold what hath been revealed by God, the Lord of the worlds.[370]

From Bahá'u'lláh's own statements we see that the phrase 'these verses' does not merely refer to the Tablet of Aḥmad itself but alludes to His entire Revelation.

In every age the Prophet's Revelation of divine verses is the essential proof of His claim to be God's appointed Messenger. Bahá'u'lláh emphatically asserts, 'He hath established the words He hath revealed as proof of His reality and truth.'[371] The standard of true belief in God's Messenger that is specified in the New Testament, in the Qur'án, in the writings of the Báb and once again in the writings of Bahá'u-'lláh is man's response to the Word of God. To truly believe in God is to accept and believe in the Word of God revealed by His chosen mouthpiece. For example, in one of His Tablets the Báb, emphasizing the significance of the divine verses, asks a Muslim why he has embraced the Faith of Muḥammad. He points out that if his belief is based on superstition, it is not acceptable before God. But, He says, if the Muslim believes in Muḥammad because his heart responded to the Word of God, this is the sign of true belief and is acceptable in the sight of God:

> By what proof hast thou embraced the Religion of Islám? Is it the Prophet on whom thou hast never set eyes? Is it the miracles which thou hast never witnessed? If thou hast accepted Islám unwittingly, wherefore hast thou done so? But if thou hast embraced the Faith by recognizing the Qur'án as the testimony . . . or if thou hast, upon hearing the divine verses and by virtue of thy spontaneous love for the True Word of God, responded in a spirit of utter humility and lowliness – a spirit which is one of the mightiest signs of true love and understanding – then such proofs have been and will ever be regarded as sound.[372]

Notice how clearly this principle applies not only to Muslims but to anyone who claims to believe in a religion. The statement applies equally to Jews, Christians, Bábís and

Bahá'ís. God's standard is different from that which is commonly accepted among people. The proof of a person's belief in his own religion, the Báb points out, is that individual's love of and belief in the Word of God revealed by the Prophet.

The supremacy of the revealed Word of God above other proofs and testimonies is a fundamental principle of the religion of God. Bahá'u'lláh declares:

> He verily establisheth the truth through His verses, and confirmeth His Revelation by His words.[373]

In many of His writings Bahá'u'lláh describes the power and exalted character of the divinely revealed verses. For example, He says:

> . . . the Word which is uttered by God shineth and flasheth as the sun amidst the books of men.[374]

In the *Book of Certitude* He explains:

> For compared with all other proofs and tokens, the divinely-revealed verses shine as the sun, whilst all others are as stars.[375]

> . . . nothing greater than these verses hath ever appeared, nor will ever be made manifest in the world![376]

> This is the testimony which He, Himself, hath ordained; greater proof than this there is none, nor ever will be.[377]

> . . . no manifestation greater than the Prophets of God hath ever been revealed, and no testimony mightier than the testimony of their revealed verses hath ever appeared upon the earth.[378]

It is beyond the capability of human beings to imitate the

Word of God. The Word of God emanates from the exalted spiritual realms of the divine Being, far beyond the reach and understanding of mortal men. Its essential nature is creative. It acts in the world by transforming human existence and bringing into being new human realities and a new social order. No matter how inspired or beautiful human speech or prose may be, it does not possess this creative power. As mentioned earlier, Bahá'u'lláh explains that 'the gift of Divine Revelation' 'pertaineth to God Himself'. 'It is God's supreme testimony, the clearest evidence of His truth . . .' [379]

To deny the divine origin of the words revealed by the Manifestation of God is to deny God's supreme testimony.

'O people, if ye deny these verses' may also be a warning to the Bábís that if they reject Bahá'u'lláh's verses, they have denied the proof promised them by the Báb. The Báb testified to the supremacy of the verses that Bahá'u'lláh would reveal and warned His followers not to turn aside from them:

> Recognize Him by His verses. The greater your neglect in seeking to know Him, the more grievously will ye be veiled in fire.[380]

The Báb explained to His followers that if they rejected Bahá'u'lláh's verses, all the writings of the Báb and all the sacred scriptures of the past would be of no value to them:

> . . . in the Day of the appearance of Him Whom God shall make manifest a thousand perusals of the Bayán cannot equal the perusal of a single verse to be revealed by Him Whom God shall make manifest.[381]

> Better is it for a person to write down but one of His verses than to transcribe the whole of the Bayán and all the books which have been written in the Dispensation of the Bayán. For everything shall be set aside except His Writings, which will endure until the following Revelation.[382]

# 49

## O Assemblage of False Ones

*Produce it, O assemblage of false ones.*
*Nay, by the One in Whose hand is my soul,*
*they are not, and never shall be able to do this,*
*even should they combine to assist one another.*

These verses indicate the real authority and divine sovereignty of God's supreme Manifestation. The Báb calls Bahá'u'lláh the 'Sovereign Truth' and says that His explanations are like pure light. If anyone opposes them and offers a conflicting explanation, such arguments are false and empty. The Báb asserts that such an attitude would be like darkness trying to overcome the light of the sun:

> . . . His testimony would be like unto the sun, while theirs would be even as a false image produced in a mirror which is not facing the sun. For had it been otherwise their testimony would have proved a faithful reflection of His testimony.[383]

Bahá'u'lláh, in the Kitáb-i-Aqdas, emphatically asserts His God-given station and proclaims the supremacy of His divinely revealed verses in clear, unmistakable terms:

> Say: O leaders of religion! Weigh not the Book of God with such standards and sciences as are current amongst you, for the Book itself is the unerring balance established amongst men . . .

> O ye leaders of religion! Who is the man amongst you that can rival Me in vision or insight? Where is he to be found that dareth to claim to be My equal in utterance or wisdom? No, by My Lord, the All-Merciful! All on the earth shall pass away; and this is the face of your Lord, the Almighty, the Well-Beloved.[384]

Bahá'u'lláh challenges the deniers of the Faith of God to produce a testimony comparable to the testimony of the divine verses that God has revealed in support of His supreme Manifestation.[385] Historically, God has always upheld the sovereignty of His appointed Messenger. For example, the stories of Moses in the Old Testament and the Qur'án demonstrate that when Moses was challenged by Pharaoh and later by some of the Jews, it was God Himself who established the authority of His chosen one.

Christ, who was repeatedly challenged to substantiate His claim to be the Messiah, established His divine authority with these now famous words:

> I am the way, the truth and the life: no man cometh unto the Father, but by me.[386]

A few verses later He significantly asserts:

> The words that I speak unto you I speak not of myself: but the Father that dwelleth in me, he doeth the works.[387]

Muḥammad was also challenged by the leaders of the people, who claimed that the verses of the Qur'án He revealed were mere poetry. They ridiculed Him and asserted that anyone could write similar poetry. In response, God revealed the following verses of the Qur'án:

> And if ye be in doubt as to that which we have sent down to our servant [Muḥammad], then produce a Sura like it, and

> summon your witnesses, beside God, if ye are men of truth:
>
> But if ye do it not, and never shall ye do it, then fear the fire prepared for the infidels . . .[388]

The Báb was attacked by the religious leaders of Persia, who challenged the divine origin of His revealed verses. He responded:

> Say, O peoples of the earth! Were ye to assemble together in order to produce the like of a single letter of My Works, ye would never be able to do so, and verily God is cognizant of all things . . .[389]

Compare the above statements of Muḥammad and the Báb to the words of Bahá'u'lláh in the Tablet of Aḥmad:

> Nay, by the One in Whose hand is my soul, they are not and never shall be able to do this, even should they combine to assist one another.

In these verses Bahá'u'lláh, the supreme Manifestation of God, clearly sets forth His God-given authority, as did Moses, Christ, Muḥammad and the Báb before Him. He leaves no doubt as to who He represents or by whose authority He speaks. It is as if He says: I have been sent to you by the same one who sent you the Messengers of the past; My testimony is the same testimony that they brought you. It is not Me you challenge if you deny My verses; it is God. And it is God Himself who declares the falsity of your complaints against Me.

# *Section 7: The Bounties of Bahá'u'lláh's Love*

## 50

## Counsels

*O Aḥmad!*
*Forget not My bounties while I am absent.*
*Remember My days during thy days,*
*and My distress and banishment in this remote prison.*
*And be thou so steadfast in My love*
*that thy heart shall not waver,*
*even if the swords of the enemies rain blows upon thee*
*and all the heavens and the earth arise against thee.*

With this appeal the tone and style of the Tablet changes. Now Bahá'u'lláh addresses Himself with tenderness and love to the personal guidance of the individual. Having given each person the choice to accept or reject His message – 'Whosoever desireth, let him turn aside from this counsel, and whosoever desireth let him choose the path to his Lord' – He now sets forth loving and detailed counsels for those who sincerely desire to follow in His way. 'This clear message' becomes specific instructions from the 'Friend', the 'True Counsellor' and 'Best Lover' to His faithful followers. It includes the following exhortations:

Forget not My bounties

Remember My days

Remember . . . My distress and banishment

. . . be thou so steadfast in My love that thy heart shall not waver

Be thou as a flame of fire . . . and a river of life eternal

. . . be not of those who doubt

. . . be not thou troubled

Rely upon God, thy God

Be thou assured in thyself

Learn well this Tablet

Chant it during thy days and withhold not thyself therefrom

. . . be of those who are grateful

. . . read this Tablet with absolute sincerity

The Tablet which began as a mighty proclamation has been transformed by the pen of Bahá'u'lláh into an ocean of tender love for the nourishment of His devoted servants. We begin our study of this half of the Tablet by examining the significance of this opening paragraph.

# 51

# Forget Not My Bounties (I)

*O Aḥmad! Forget not My bounties*

The mission of Bahá'u'lláh is to bestow the love, the grace and the bounties of God on all humanity. He declares:

> By the righteousness of the Almighty! The measure of the favours of God hath been filled up . . . the glory of His Revelation hath been made manifest, and His bounties have rained upon all mankind.[390]

In another Tablet He says:

> This Day a door is open wider than both heaven and earth. The eye of the mercy of Him Who is the Desire of the worlds is turned towards all men.[391]

In yet another Tablet He declares:

> Shouldst thou rend asunder the grievous veil that blindeth thy vision, thou wouldst behold such a bounty as naught, from the beginning that hath no beginning till the end that hath no end, can either resemble or equal.[392]

Throughout His writings Bahá'u'lláh reiterates this fundamental truth of His Revelation. He appeals to every soul in these stirring words:

> The whole duty of man in this Day is to attain that share of the flood of grace which God poureth forth for him.[393]

Bahá'u'lláh, the redeemer of all humankind, desires to bestow on every human being the gift of everlasting life. In a Tablet addressed to the 'nightingales of God', He expresses His abiding love for us:

> Behold how the manifold grace of God, which is being showered from the clouds of Divine glory, hath, in this day, encompassed the world. For whereas in days past every lover besought and searched after his Beloved, it is the Beloved Himself Who now is calling His lovers and is inviting them to attain His presence. Take heed lest ye forfeit so precious a favour; beware lest ye belittle so remarkable a token of His grace.[394]

Again and again Bahá'u'lláh appeals to every sincere seeker. In another Tablet He counsels us:

> The Hand of Divine bounty proffereth unto you the Water of Life. Hasten and drink your fill.[395]

In yet another Tablet He appeals to us in these terms:

> Withhold not yourselves from that which hath been revealed through His grace. Seize ye the living waters of immortality in the name of your Lord, the Lord of all names . . .[396]

These are the bounties of God which His Promised One reminds the faithful never to forget. So lavish are outpourings of these bounties that they have not, from time immemorial, previously been seen on earth. To His devoted followers He also offers the inestimable gift of the paradise of His nearness and presence.[397] 'The glad tidings of the nearness of God' and 'the Presence of the Generous One', promised in the opening paragraph of the Tablet of Aḥmad, may be understood as closeness to Bahá'u'lláh. His writings indicate that it is not necessary to be in His physical presence to experience this closeness. In one of His Tablets He promises:

> Haste ye to enter into Paradise, as a token of Our mercy unto you, and drink ye from the hands of the All-Merciful the Wine that is life indeed.
>
> Drink with healthy relish, O people of Bahá. Ye are indeed they with whom it shall be well. *This is what they who have near access to God have attained.*[398]

In several Tablets Bahá'u'lláh defines paradise as reunion with Him and indicates that the 'Wine that is life indeed' is the bounty of His presence. For example, He says:

> This is the Day whereon He Who is the Revealer of the names of God hath stepped out of the Tabernacle of glory, and proclaimed unto all who are in the heavens and all who are on the earth: 'Put away the cups of Paradise and all the life-giving waters they contain, for lo, the people of Bahá have entered the blissful abode of the Divine Presence, and quaffed the wine of reunion . . .'[399]

In another Tablet He offers the gift of the 'wine of His Presence' to every devoted believer. He says:

> This is the Day whereon the true servants of God partake of the life-giving waters of reunion, the Day whereon those that are nigh unto Him are able to drink of the soft-flowing river of immortality, *and they who believe in His unity, the wine of His Presence*, through their recognition of Him Who is the Highest and Last End of all . . .[400]

The word 'wine' in these passages invokes the mystical tradition, that is Sufism.[401] One association of 'wine' in this tradition is with love, as in being 'intoxicated with the wine of the love of God'.[402] Aḥmad spent many years in Ba<u>gh</u>dád living in close proximity to Bahá'u'lláh, enjoying 'the wine of His Presence' on a regular basis and being intoxicated with Bahá'u'lláh's love. In this passage of the Tablet of Aḥmad, Bahá'u'lláh reminds Aḥmad of His deep and abiding love for him, urges him never to forget the bounties he received from Him and admonishes him to cherish His love in his heart. Bahá'u'lláh's advice to Aḥmad appears to apply equally to each one of us.

In one of His prayers Bahá'u'lláh makes it clear that it is possible to realize the bounty of His Presence even though we cannot attain His physical presence:

> Write down, then, for me the recompense decreed for such as have gazed on Thy face, and have, by Thy leave, gained admittance into the court of Thy throne, and have, at Thy bidding, met Thee face to face.[403]

We see, then, that when Bahá'u'lláh counsels us to 'Forget not My bounties while I am absent', He is reminding us of the infinite bounties of His love, which in this promised Day of God He is pouring forth on all humanity and which encompass each one of us. He is also indicating that we can reap the bounty of His presence through our communion with His spirit. It is this bounty, the bounty of His presence, which makes the Tablet of Aḥmad so significant. Indeed, this may be one of the most profound messages of the Tablet.

## 52

# Forget Not My Bounties (II)

*Forget not My bounties*
*while I am absent*

The verse 'Forget not My bounties while I am absent' may indicate that Bahá'u'lláh's bounties are so numerous that they envelop our entire lives. On one level this phrase may be intended to remind us that it is only through the bounties of His love that we truly have our being.

In one sense this verse may be understood as Bahá'u'lláh's reminder to us not to forget all the bounties He has bestowed on us in the past. One of the implications of this is that He is assuring us of His continuing bounties in the present and in the future. In one of His Tablets He states that 'His bounties and bestowals are ever present and manifest'.[404]

In effect Bahá'u'lláh seems to be telling us that if we become cognizant of how much He has helped us in the past, then we may be confident that He will always help us, now and in the future. In one of His Tablets He says:

> It is incumbent in this Day, upon every man to place his whole trust in the manifold bounties of God . . .[405]

In another Tablet He unequivocally assures us:

> The friends of God, one and all, are remembered by the Supreme Pen: The bounties of the Source of Bounty are at every moment visibly descending.[406]

The bounties of God are favours and gifts. They are freely given to us through the loving-kindness, mercy and generosity of our Lord. Because they are favours and gifts, we cannot earn them. Our duty is to graciously accept them from the hand of Bahá'u'lláh. He points this out near the end of the Tablet of Aḥmad:

> These favours have We bestowed upon thee as a bounty on Our part and a mercy from Our Presence, that thou mayest be of those who are grateful.

To 'be of those who are grateful' suggests that we thank Bahá'u'lláh for all His bounties to us. Even more importantly, we can demonstrate how grateful we are by accepting His gifts and favours. Often we may feel that we are too unworthy to ask Him for any special bounties. We may even seek not to accept the gifts He offers us because we feel inadequate or undeserving. In our Western culture we may have been trained to refuse favours and kindnesses offered to us by others. We may consider this to be humility on our part. However, if we evince such an attitude in our relationship with Bahá'u'lláh because we do not feel we are worthy of His favours, we are not demonstrating humbleness. True humility before Bahá'u'lláh is for us to thankfully and graciously accept all that He offers us.

If we feel that we are too undeserving to turn to Bahá'u'lláh and ask Him for special consideration, then we might ask ourselves two questions. If we do not feel worthy at the present time, then when in the future will we feel worthy? If we are not worthy now, what is it that we can do in the future that will make us worthy? The more we study the Bahá'í writings on this subject, the more apparent it becomes that we live through the bounties and favours of God and not by what we may earn by our own actions. This can be seen clearly in the Bahá'í prayers. For example we read:

> O Divine Providence! All existence is begotten by Thy bounty . . .[407]

In another prayer we say:

> Thou seest me, O Lord, detached from all things but Thee, clinging to the cord of Thy bounty and craving the wonders of Thy grace . . . My tongue, my pen, my whole being, testify to Thy power, Thy might, Thy grace and Thy bounty, that Thou art God and there is none other God but Thee, the Powerful, the Mighty.[408]

This prayer says we cling to 'the cord of Thy bounty'. The prayer also says that we crave 'the wonders of Thy grace'. These phrases help us define our true relationship with our Lord. In reading Bahá'í prayers we beseech God for His bounty, His grace and mercy. Nowhere do we beseech God to bestow upon us what we have earned by our own deserving. Why is this so?

None of us can stand before the justice seat of God. We are simply unworthy to claim such a station for ourselves and nothing we can do in this earthly life can ever make us deserving of such a station. The Bahá'í writings make this very clear. For example, one of the prayers of the Báb says:

> No deed have I done, O my God, to merit beholding Thy face, and I know of a certainty that were I to live as long as the world lasts I would fail to accomplish any deed such as to deserve this favour, inasmuch as the station of a servant shall ever fall short of access to Thy holy precincts, unless Thy bounty should reach me and Thy tender mercy pervade me and Thy loving-kindness encompass me.[409]

Here the Báb reminds us that it is not through our deeds that we are enabled to behold the face of God. He points out that our station is that of servants. Because we are God's servants, there is nothing we can ever do to become equal with our Lord. However, through God's bounty, His mercy and His loving-kindness He lifts us up and enables us to attain His holy precincts. This leads us to ask: if we can never 'earn' the privilege of being in the presence of God but can only be given this priceless favour through His bounty, then what can we do that He may choose to bestow this grace on us?

As we reflect on what the scriptures have to say about this, the clearer it becomes that all God asks of us is to love Him. For example, the Hebrew Bible tells us:

> Thou shalt love the Lord thy God with all thine heart, and with all thy soul, and with all thy might. And these words, which I command thee this day, shall be in thine heart.[410]

In the New Testament Christ says that the commandment to love God with all our heart is the greatest commandment.[411] Similarly, the Báb explains that it is our love for God which draws His gifts and bounties to us in great abundance. In one of His prayers He says:

> Thy goodly gifts are unceasingly showered upon such as cherish Thy love and the wondrous tokens of Thy heavenly bounties are amply bestowed on those who recognize Thy divine Unity.[412]

In this passage the Báb sets forth two conditions. The first is that He asks us to cherish God's love. As we practise cherishing His love in our daily lives, we fulfil the essential condition God has given us and His 'goodly gifts' are 'unceasingly showered' upon us.

The second condition He gives us is to 'recognize' His 'divine Unity'. As has been discussed in earlier chapters, to 'recognize' His 'divine Unity' implies that we recognize the unknowability of the divine essence. The true meaning of divine unity, Bahá'u-'lláh tells us, is that God can only be known through His Manifestation. We see, then, that when we accept Bahá'u'lláh as the Promised One of God and turn our hearts to Him, we fulfil the second condition God has given us. As we turn our hearts to Bahá'u'lláh the 'wondrous tokens' of His 'heavenly bounties' are 'amply bestowed' on us. This, the Bahá'í writings tell us, is how we can 'earn' the love of God.

When Bahá'u'lláh counsels us in the Tablet of Aḥmad to 'Forget not My bounties while I am absent', He seems to be telling us not to forget the 'goodly gifts' and 'wondrous tokens' of the 'heavenly bounties' He is offering us. All He asks of us is that we simply turn our hearts to Him and cherish His love, as He urges us to do in this well-known Hidden Word:

> O Son of Being! Love Me, that I may love thee.[413]

Elsewhere Bahá'u'lláh counsels us:

> Deprive not yourselves of the bounties which have been created for your sake.[414]

Thus to 'be of those who are grateful' implies that we recognize that we live through the bounty, grace and mercy of our Lord. When Bahá'u'lláh tells us not to forget His bounties He seems, on one level, to be encouraging us to turn our hearts to Him and to beseech His bounties and favours in our daily lives. This verse also implies that we should cherish His love in our hearts. This appears to be one of the essential, clear messages of the Tablet of Aḥmad.

# 53

# The Wonders of My Munificence and Bounty

*O Aḥmad! Forget not My bounties*

'Forget not My bounties' may also signify the spiritual bounties with which we have been endowed by our Creator. Consider the following passage:

> O My servants! Could ye apprehend with what wonders of My munificence and bounty I have willed to entrust your souls, ye would, of a truth, rid yourselves of attachment to all created things, and would gain a true knowledge of your own selves . . . Ye would find yourselves independent of all else but Me, and would perceive, with your inner and outer eye, and as manifest as the revelation of My effulgent Name, the seas of My loving-kindness and bounty moving within you.[415]

Bahá'u'lláh states that the soul of *every* human being has been endowed with the 'munificence and bounty' of God and that 'the seas of [His] loving-kindness and bounty [are] moving' within each one of us. 'Forget not' these bounties, He counsels us in the Tablet of Aḥmad. When we feel them in our heart and know that these bounties are within *us*, we will find ourselves, Bahá'u'lláh promises us, 'independent of all else' but Him.

In another passage Bahá'u'lláh says, 'It is the waywardness of the heart that *removeth it* far from God'.[416] It is not God who separates Himself from us; on the contrary, it is we who separate ourselves from Him. God is faithful, constant, ever-abiding and unchanging in His love and concern for each one of us; He 'continueth to shed upon [each individual] the manifest radiance of His glory'.[417] 'Forget not My bounties while I am absent' implies that in the natural course of our daily lives, when we stray from our focus on God and find ourselves distant and removed from Him, we should never forget that He is ever-present and close to us. We can always return to Him by simply choosing to do so, reaching out to Him and communing with Him.

# 54

# While I am Absent

*Forget not My bounties*
*while I am absent*

'While I am absent'[418] appears to have several significant implications. At the most basic level, Bahá'u'lláh is referring to His physical separation from Aḥmad, who was not among the companions chosen by Bahá'u'lláh to accompany Him on His exile from Baghdád. In this verse Bahá'u'lláh seems to be saying: Don't forget the bounties you received from Me when you were My close companion. I am confined in this distant prison and can no longer be with you physically. But I haven't forgotten you. Don't forget Me. Remember what I have chosen to go through for the sake of God and you will realize how much I love you and will always love you.

This is the outward message. From another point of view, Bahá'u'lláh is referring to the closeness of hearts and souls which cannot be separated by physical distance. Recall that the Tablet of Aḥmad begins with the proclamation to the sincere ones of 'the *nearness* of God'.[419] The purpose of our lives is to walk with our Lord, to feel His love in our daily lives, to draw ever closer to Him and commune intimately with His spirit. In the Hidden Words Bahá'u'lláh says:

> O Son of Light! Forget all save Me and commune with My spirit. This is of the essence of My command, therefore turn unto it.[420]

Notice that Bahá'u'lláh says that *communing* with Him is the *essence* of His command. If we take all the laws and teachings and reduce them to their essence, this is it: commune intimately with Him and be one of His true lovers. This is not dependent on physical nearness. It is a spiritual state, a condition of the heart. In one of His Tablets Bahá'u'lláh explains:

> 'Earth and heaven cannot contain Me; what can alone contain Me is the heart of him who believeth in Me, and is faithful to My Cause.'. . . *Those hearts, however, that are aware of His Presence, are close to Him,* and are to be regarded as having drawn nigh unto His throne.[421]

Our own emotional–spiritual state and the condition of our hearts can bring each one of us close to Bahá'u'lláh. When our hearts are 'aware of His Presence' we are close to Him. In the Hidden Words He affirms:

> Thy Paradise is My love; *thy heavenly home, reunion with Me.* Enter therein and tarry not. *This is that which hath been destined for thee* in Our kingdom above and Our exalted dominion.[422]

Each one of us can achieve this nearness. In moments of prayer or meditation, in the exhilaration of the inner joy of serving and loving others, in receiving love or a special kindness from someone else we may experience loving feelings in our hearts which we might attempt to describe by words such as tenderness, warmth, joy, happiness, exaltation and sweetness. It is in such precious moments as these that we become 'aware of His Presence'. 'Rejoice in the gladness of thine heart, that thou mayest be worthy to meet Me,' He advises us in the Hidden Words.[423] It is our essential, God-given nature to experience such wonderful feelings in our hearts. He *wants* us to be aware of these feelings, to strive to achieve this state of being and to appreciate the joy and happiness it brings us.

If we contrast the feelings of these treasured experiences with the times when we find ourselves distant and apparently remote from Bahá'u'lláh, we realize that the difference is not a physical condition. It is only the change in our own spiritual state that makes the difference.

'Forget not My bounties while I am absent' emphasizes the truth that physical separation does not matter. Bahá'u'lláh points out to Aḥmad, and through Aḥmad to each of us, that the inner joy of feeling close to Him in our hearts can be just as wonderful, just as powerful, as being physically in His presence. It is the condition of our hearts, our yearning and attraction to Him that matter. Bahá'u'lláh reiterates and emphasizes this truth when He exhorts us to 'be thou so steadfast in My love that thy heart shall not waver', 'be not of those who doubt', 'be thou assured in thyself' and 'be of those who are grateful'. 'Forget not My bounties while I am absent' implies that His bounties are always with us, even though He is physically absent. The message of this paragraph and of the entire second half of the Tablet seems simply to be that each one of us is to turn our hearts to Him, to commune with His spirit, to be assured of His love and not to doubt that this is why we have been created. Bahá'u'lláh admonishes us not to allow the misfortunes of the world – which are bound to occur – to turn us away from Him but rather to be so steadfast in our love for Him and in our belief and assurance of His love for us that this bond of love will never be broken by anything that happens to us in this life.

Another possible significance of the verse 'Forget not My bounties *while* I am absent' is the implication that Bahá'u'lláh's absence is only for a while. From this point of view, Bahá'u'lláh is assuring Aḥmad – and everyone else who sincerely believes in Him – that he, and we, will once again attain His presence, even if this is in the world to come. Bahá'u'lláh goes on to say, 'And be thou so steadfast in My love that thy heart shall not waver' *even if* all the misfortunes of the world fall upon you. This implies that if we keep our inner life focused on

Bahá'u'lláh, outward misfortunes and circumstances cannot affect our long term destiny, which is to be with Him in the next world.

'Abdu'l-Bahá offers us the same assurance in His memorable words to the first group of Western pilgrims to visit Him in the Holy Land in 1898, at the time when He was still a prisoner in 'Akká:

> Now I give you a commandment which shall be for a covenant between you and Me – that ye have faith; that your faith be steadfast as a rock that no storms can move, that nothing can disturb, and that it endure through all things even to the end; even should ye hear that your Lord has been crucified, be not shaken in your faith; for I am with you always, whether living or dead, I am with you to the end.[424]

# 55

## My Distress and Banishment

*Remember My days during thy days,*
*and My distress and banishment*
*in this remote prison.*

Does Bahá'u'lláh's promise of His bounties in this Tablet, which was revealed specifically for Aḥmad, apply to us? Since we are unable to be in Bahá'u'lláh's physical presence, can we, like Aḥmad, be assured of the constancy and ever-present bounty of His love?

Consider the meaning of Bahá'u'lláh's statement, 'Remember . . . My distress and banishment in this remote prison.' Every day of Bahá'u'lláh's life He took on the sufferings of the world. He never wavered, He never succumbed to the attacks of His enemies. He was always steadfast and forbearing in the face of the constant assaults and persecutions which rained down upon Him. He writes of His sufferings in poignant terms:

> Ponder a while on the woes and afflictions which this Prisoner hath sustained. I have, all the days of My life, been at the mercy of Mine enemies, and have suffered each day, in the path of the love of God, a fresh tribulation.[425]

> By the righteousness of God! Every morning I arose from My bed, I discovered the hosts of countless afflictions massed behind My door; and every night when I lay down, lo! My heart was torn with agony at what it had suffered from the

> fiendish cruelty of its foes. With every piece of bread the Ancient Beauty breaketh is coupled the assault of a fresh affliction, and with every drop He drinketh is mixed the bitterness of the most woeful of trials. He is preceded in every step He taketh by an army of unforeseen calamities, while in His rear follow legions of agonizing sorrows.[426]

What greater love and faithfulness can one person show for another than the constancy Bahá'u'lláh demonstrated every day of His 40 years' exile and imprisonment? This is the divine standard of fidelity and true love from the 'Most Trusted' and the 'Best Lover'. 'Greater love hath no man than this, that a man lay down his life for his friends,' Christ said, commenting on His own sacrifice.[427] In a similar vein Bahá'u'lláh describes His own imprisonment and sufferings:

> Behold Him, an exile, a victim of tyranny, in this Most Great Prison. His enemies have assailed Him on every side, and will continue to do so till the end of His life. Whatever, therefore, He saith unto you is wholly for the sake of God . . .[428]

This is the sign of His fidelity to us and the assurance of His unrestrained love for each and every human being who turns his heart to Him. Every day for more than 40 years He took on the sufferings of the world for our sake. Every day He endured what no other human being could bear to endure. In the face of such an overwhelming testimony of unwavering devotion, super-human fortitude and divine acquiescence, can anyone imagine that Bahá'u'lláh would withhold His love from any soul who is seeking Him? In a Tablet He promises, 'He, verily, will aid everyone that aideth Him, and will remember everyone that remembereth Him.'[429]

Why, we may well ask, did He, the supreme Manifestation of God, agree to endure such cruelties and intense suffering? One might wonder why He did not use His God-given power to change the conditions He was forced to endure. We must look to His own statements for an explanation:

> The Ancient Beauty hath consented to be bound with chains that mankind may be released from its bondage, and hath accepted to be made a prisoner within this most mighty stronghold that the whole world may attain unto true liberty. He hath drained to its dregs the cup of sorrow, that all the peoples of the earth may attain unto abiding joy, and be filled with gladness. This is of the mercy of your Lord, the Compassionate, the Most Merciful. We have accepted to be abased, O believers in the Unity of God, that ye may be exalted, and have suffered manifold afflictions, that ye might prosper and flourish.[430]

This passage gives us a great insight into why Bahá'u'lláh allowed Himself to suffer so much. It may also shed light on why in the Tablet of Aḥmad He tells us to remember His distress and banishment. We note that none of His suffering was in isolation from the human affairs of the world around Him. Everything He suffered was for the purpose of transforming humanity. We see that He contrasts each one of His afflictions with the benefits it will bring to humankind.

In light of these profound assurances, how can we ever doubt the promises Bahá'u'lláh gives us in the Tablet of Aḥmad? Notice that His admonition to remember His distress and banishment is followed by His command to be steadfast in His love. We may infer that, in one sense, Bahá'u'lláh is telling us to remember His distress and banishment so that we will have absolute assurance of the promise of His love and bounties.

In another sense Bahá'u'lláh may be telling us to remember His distress and banishment so that we will realize that He has a very serious purpose in mind in revealing this Tablet. He may be reminding us to recognize how much He has suffered so that we will listen to His appeal and respond to His call.

In still another sense Bahá'u'lláh has taken on all these sufferings so that we may be filled with gladness, attain unto abiding joy and may prosper and flourish. This is a profound expression of the will of God for humanity in this promised day. It suggests that our attitude in life must be founded on a positive outlook, one of happiness and appreciation of the joy and gladness in our lives. As we strive to attain this state of being, in spite of outward circumstances, we will be fulfilling Bahá'u'lláh's wish for us. As we reflect these qualities of divine joy and happiness in our own lives, we will demonstrate that Bahá'u'lláh's sufferings were not in vain. It is this personal transformation He seeks to establish in the hearts of all people.

The more we study the Bahá'í writings on this subject, the clearer it becomes that events are not what they seem by their outward appearance. It is an essential, spiritual truth that there is always an inner significance to life's occurrences. Nowhere is this more true than in the earthly life of the Manifestation of God. Everything He does, every action He takes, every situation He creates, every ordeal He allows Himself to be a victim of – all are pregnant with the divine, creative energies that transform civilization and the personal lives of all the people of the earth. In the life of the Manifestation of God there is another reality, hidden from the sight of men. It is this inner reality, mysterious and wonderful, that is the real cause of all outward events. Bahá'u'lláh gives us a glimpse of its existence in this passage:

> . . . We have been cast into an afflictive Prison, and are encompassed with the hosts of tyranny . . . Such is the gladness, however, which the Youth hath tasted that no earthly joy can compare unto it. By God! The harm He suffereth at the hands of the oppressor can never grieve His heart, nor can He be saddened by the ascendancy of such as have repudiated His truth.[431]

It is apparent from His words that events cannot be what they seem on the surface. In spite of suffering agonizing afflictions and enduring endless cruelties and hardships, Bahá'u'lláh was able to speak of the gladness He experienced and asserted that 'no earthly joy can compare unto it'. What a profound contrast between the outward torment and the inward joy He describes. Despite this contrast, let no one doubt the severity of the ordeals He endured. He cautions us:

> Couldst thou be told what hath befallen the Ancient Beauty, thou wouldst flee into the wilderness, and weep with a great weeping. In thy grief, thou wouldst smite thyself on the head, and cry out as one stung by the sting of the adder.[432]

These outward events, no matter how cruel they are – or perhaps because of their extreme oppressiveness and injustice – give birth to this inner reality, as Bahá'u'lláh indicates:

> Say: Tribulation is a horizon unto My Revelation. The day star of grace shineth above it, and sheddeth a light which neither the clouds of men's idle fancy nor the vain imaginations of the aggressor can obscure.[433]

In one of His prayers He explains:

> Had not every tribulation been made the bearer of Thy wisdom, and every ordeal the vehicle of Thy providence, no one would have dared oppose us . . .[434]

In the Fire Tablet Bahá'u'lláh affirms that it is the divine, creative energies that transform these outward injustices into an infinite grace, a grace which is transforming the world and building the Kingdom of God on earth:

> Give Thou ear unto what the Tongue of Grandeur uttereth, O Wronged One of the worlds! . . .
>
> Were it not for calamity, how would the sun of Thy patience shine, O Light of the worlds?

> Lament not because of the wicked. Thou wert created to bear and endure, O Patience of the worlds . . .
>
> By Thee the banner of independence was planted on the highest peaks, and the sea of bounty surged, O Rapture of the worlds.
>
> By Thine aloneness the Sun of Oneness shone, and by Thy banishment the land of Unity was adorned. Be patient, O Thou Exile of the worlds.[435]

Since every Manifestation 'hath been commissioned to reveal Himself through specific acts',[436] it seems especially significant that Bahá'u'lláh allowed Himself to be a prisoner and an exile during His entire 40–year ministry. On a global level we may infer that He ensured the victory of the Cause of God by virtue of the suffering He chose to endure.

Bahá'u'lláh emphasizes the extreme injustice of the treatment He received at the hands of His enemies by calling Himself the 'Wronged One of the worlds'. How, may we ask, does this relate to personal suffering?

It implies that no suffering is ever in vain. Bahá'u'lláh's own life is a supreme testimony to the fact that whatever happens outwardly has a profound inner significance. 'My calamity is My providence, outwardly it is fire and vengeance, but inwardly it is light and mercy,' He assures us in the Hidden Words.[437] To endure pain, suffering or the injustice of others is very difficult. Although it does not lessen the pain, it can be reassuring to know that what we experience is ultimately for our own benefit. In moments of agony and despair it is also comforting to realize that we are not the first to suffer what life deals us. Bahá'u'lláh's words to 'Remember . . . My distress and banishment' are a poignant reminder that He has been there before us. He may be reminding us in our moments of grief and hardship that we are not alone. He knows what real suffering is and He assures us that He is always there to comfort and sustain us.

# 56

# This Remote Prison and the Nearness of God

*O Aḥmad!*
*Forget not My bounties while I am absent.*
*Remember My days during thy days,*
*and My distress and banishment*
*in this remote prison.*

Aḥmad was longing to be with Bahá'u'lláh and was on his way to visit Him when he received this Tablet. As he himself testifies, after reading the Tablet many times he changed his mind and, without visiting Bahá'u'lláh, returned to Persia to teach His Cause. Throughout the remainder of his long life, Aḥmad never again visited Bahá'u'lláh.

Aḥmad understood this Tablet to be Bahá'u'lláh's instruction to him to teach His Cause and not to visit Him. We might wonder if this message was a devastating setback to Aḥmad, who so wanted to be with Bahá'u'lláh. But it was obviously not. His whole life changed when he received this Tablet. He faithfully and devotedly carried out the instructions of Bahá'u'lláh and became the embodiment of his own Tablet. Why did Aḥmad change his mind and give up his one remaining chance to be with Bahá'u'lláh? What did he find within these verses that enabled him to forego the bounty of the presence of his Lord and spend the rest of his life serving the Faith with such devotion and happiness?

The whole paragraph that begins with the phrase 'Forget not My bounties' has the quality of an intimate letter from one very dear friend to another. Looked at in this way each phrase of this paragraph takes on new meaning. For example, 'Remember My days during thy days' suggests that Bahá'u'lláh is reminding Aḥmad to recall the wonderful times Aḥmad shared with Bahá'u'lláh in Baghdád, the joys and happiness he felt and all the favours and bounties he received when he was with Bahá'u'lláh. Never forget these, Bahá'u'lláh seems to say. 'Remember . . . My distress and banishment in this remote prison' appears to be a poignant reminder that God has given Bahá'u'lláh a most arduous mission to fulfil. He must endure all the sufferings of the world. He must remain a captive of His enemies, a prisoner and an exile. This is what God has commissioned Him to do. The subtle implication for Aḥmad seems to be that being a prisoner and an exile is not what Bahá'u'lláh wants Aḥmad to be. If this is correct then Bahá'u'lláh is indicating to Aḥmad that He has given him a different mission. 'And be thou so steadfast in My love that thy heart shall not waver even if . . .' may imply that wherever Aḥmad went and whatever he did, there was one thing Bahá'u'lláh wanted him never to forget and always to count on: His love. One of the implications of this verse is that Bahá'u'lláh will never forget Aḥmad and that He will never leave him alone and unaided.

This paragraph may be understood as Bahá'u'lláh's most tender, loving farewell message and reassurance to His trusted and devoted servant Aḥmad. In this paragraph Bahá'u'lláh seems to be telling Aḥmad that He has given him a mission which is different from His own. Because of this, Bahá'u'lláh may be indicating to Aḥmad that he will no longer be with Bahá'u'lláh physically in this earthly life and so He assures him of His unfailing love. Before Aḥmad received this Tablet, he could no longer bear being separated from Bahá'u'lláh yet he willingly gave up the opportunity to visit Him after reading it. No doubt the promises Bahá'u'lláh gives Aḥmad in this Tablet comforted his heart and gave him the strength and reassurance he needed to return to Persia and carry out the teaching mission Bahá'u'lláh had entrusted to him.

To help us gain a better understanding of Bahá'u'lláh's assurances to Aḥmad, let us consider the implications of His verse 'Remember My days during thy days, and My distress and banishment in this remote prison.' In Arabic the word for 'remote' is *bu'd*. 'Remote' is contrasted with the word 'near' or 'nearness', which in Arabic is *qurb*.[438] The implication is that what is thought to be remote may actually be very near at hand. In Arabic this inference is derived from a verse in the Qur'án concerning the advent of the Day of God:

> Be thou patient therefore with becoming patience;
> They forsooth regard that day as distant,
> But we see it nigh . . .[439]

Were we reading the Tablet of Aḥmad in Arabic, we would associate the phrase 'this remote prison' with the contrasting *qurb*, 'nearness', translated by Shoghi Effendi as 'presence', both of which are found in the opening paragraph of the Tablet. The implication appears to be that while Bahá'u'lláh is telling Aḥmad that He is physically in 'this remote prison', He is in fact spiritually near to him, reminding him of 'the nearness of God'. Since Aḥmad had known for a long time that Bahá'u'lláh was the promised Manifestation of God whose presence is the presence of God Himself ('the Presence of the Generous One'), it seems clear that he understood this reference as meaning the nearness of his Lord. The Qur'án too assures us of the nearness of God:

> We created man: and we know what his soul whispereth to him, and we are closer to him than his neck-vein.[440]

Thus this Quranic verse together with these particular phrases of the Tablet of Aḥmad suggest that Bahá'u'lláh was counselling Aḥmad not to be concerned with Bahá'u'lláh's physical absence because He was spiritually close to him: Aḥmad has chosen the 'path to His Lord'.

## 57

# Be Thou So Steadfast in My Love

*And be thou so steadfast in My love*
*that thy heart shall not waver*

In what does Bahá'u'lláh ask us to be steadfast?

'My love (*ḥubbí*),' He says.

Bahá'u'lláh emphasizes that His divine love is not dependent on how we are faring in the world or how we are being treated by others, whoever they may be. He makes it abundantly clear that above all else we can *always* count on His love. His love is constant and continuous, like the rays of the sun. He does not bestow His love conditionally or capriciously. His love for each individual is never withdrawn, nor does it wane when the forces of this world – 'all the heavens and the earth' – are arrayed against a person.

Notice how all-encompassing is the phrase '*even if* the swords of the enemies rain blows upon thee, *and all* the heavens and the earth arise against thee' (emphasis added). He is telling us that if enemies of His Cause or those who personally oppose us attack and harm us in any way, whether it be physically or verbally, mere gossip or malicious slander, we can always count on His love. We must never consider such attacks or personal difficulties, whatever form they may take, to mean that we have been abandoned by Bahá'u'lláh or that He loves us less than others.

If we are maligned or attacked in the service of the Cause of God, we should always turn to Bahá'u'lláh and seek His love. He is our constant comfort and refuge. Never should we allow such attacks to shake our faith. These are His reassuring words:

> Whatever hath befallen you, hath been for the sake of God. This is the truth, and in this there is no doubt. You should, therefore, leave all your affairs in His Hands, place your trust in Him, and rely upon Him. He will assuredly not forsake you. In this, likewise, there is no doubt . . .
>
> If, however, for a few days, in compliance with God's all-encompassing wisdom, outward affairs should run their course contrary to one's cherished desire, this is of no consequence and should not matter.[441]

Throughout His writings Bahá'u'lláh assures us of His unfailing love. He points out that it is the *duty* of every believer to seek His love and cleave wholeheartedly to Him. He asserts that no person, no force on earth has the power to interfere with the flow of His love to an individual:

> For every one of you his paramount duty is to choose for himself that on which no other may infringe and none usurp from him. Such a thing – and to this the Almighty is My witness – is the love of God [*ḥubb Alláh*], could ye but perceive it.[442]

# 58

# Even If

*even if*
*the swords of the enemies rain blows upon thee*
*and all the heavens and the earth arise against thee*

The meaning of 'the swords of the enemies' seems obvious but what of 'all the heavens and the earth'?

This phrase is a frequent Quranic trope. Shoghi Effendi pointed out that its meaning is symbolic. In a letter to an individual he wrote:

> Concerning . . . the meaning of passages in the Tablet of Aḥmad: The figure of speech, 'heavens' and 'earth' arising against one is not to be taken literally. It means in spite of every opposition.[443]

In the *Book of Certitude* Bahá'u'lláh states that the terms 'heaven' and 'earth' as used in the scriptures have a variety of meanings. The term 'heavens' can refer to the religious leaders, while 'earth' is related to the human heart.[444] The implication of this verse for those who teach His Cause seems to be that if all the religious leaders and their followers arise to oppose and persecute us, we must not be shaken or troubled by such attacks and should rely wholly on the love and protection of Bahá'u'lláh.

In another sense, the term 'heavens' can apply to those in authority. From this point of view, Bahá'u'lláh is telling us that if while serving the Cause of God we are attacked by the government or by others in positions of authority, we should not be grieved but should continue steadfastly in His love. In one of His Tablets Bahá'u'lláh cautions us:

> Beware, O people of Bahá, lest the strong ones of the earth rob you of your strength, or they who rule the world fill you with fear. Put your trust in God, and commit your affairs to His keeping. He, verily, will, through the power of truth, render you victorious . . .[445]

Because 'enemies' are specifically mentioned, 'all the heavens and the earth' also implies persons other than one's enemies. It suggests that even if our family and friends rise up to oppose and persecute us, we must not let their attacks prevent us from serving the Cause of God. If one's closest friends or members of the Bahá'í community were to arise against an individual, Bahá'u'lláh counsels him to remain steadfast in His love. The love of Bahá'u'lláh for every human being has never been, nor will it ever be, dependent upon the approval of others. He admonishes us never to doubt His love and assistance. The focus of our lives, He tells us, is to learn to put our whole trust and reliance in Him. This is a gradual learning process. The more we practise turning to Bahá'u'lláh, the more detached we become from the happenstance of daily events. And the more detached we become, the more impervious we will be to the attacks of others.

There seems to be yet another, more subtle meaning to the phrase 'even if . . . all the heavens and the earth arise against thee'. There are times in our lives when we become our own worst enemy. For example, in spite of the advice and encouragement of those closest to us, we sometimes fail to make decisions and take actions which will help us progress and develop. At other times we may even act in a manner which we know is not in our own best interest. One example of this is when we do not pray or deepen in the writings regularly.

Further, there are instances in everyone's life when one knowingly fails to live up to Bahá'í standards of conduct or violates a Bahá'í law. At such times our behaviour and the choices we make are not helpful to our own happiness and personal development. We may even fall into a downward spiral, when one bad choice leads to another bad action. Such actions may harm us physically, emotionally, psychologically or spiritually. For example, when we feel depressed we often do not feel like praying. Choosing not to pray can prolong or intensify feelings of despondency and hopelessness, which in turn causes us to feel even less like praying. It is at such times that we may feel far from God and separated from His love. It is precisely at these critical times, Bahá'u'lláh promises us, that we can count on His love and caring for us. He is always with us, in spite of what we may be doing to ourselves. 'And be thou so steadfast in My love that thy heart shall not waver, even if . . .' shines like a guiding light in the fog, telling us that even in the darkness of our personal hell, when we are our own worst enemy, we can count on His love. He assures us that He has not, nor will He ever abandon us. 'Forget not My bounties while I am absent,' He says. If we pause to ask ourselves who is absent from whom, we find that it is only we who absent ourselves from Him; He never absents Himself from us. The choice we have to make is to turn back to Him:

> Turn thy sight unto thyself, that thou mayest find Me standing within thee, mighty, powerful and self-subsisting.[446]

# 59

# A Flame of Fire to My Enemies

*Be thou as a flame of fire to My enemies*
*and a river of life eternal to My loved ones,*
*and be not of those who doubt.*

Shoghi Effendi gave several interpretations of the significance of this verse. 'The "flame of fire" in the Tablet of Aḥmad,' he wrote, 'should be taken figuratively.'[447] On another occasion he stated that 'The words "Be thou as a flame of fire to My enemies and a river of life eternal to My loved ones" should not be taken in their literal sense.'[448] He said that it means that we must be uncompromising in our loyalty to the Cause of Bahá'u'lláh and also emphasized that to be 'a flame of fire to My enemies' defines what our attitude should be towards Covenant-breaking and those who attack the Bahá'í Faith:

> The 'flame of fire' in the Tablet of Aḥmad should be taken figuratively. In other words, we must not tolerate the evil of Covenant-breakers or enemies of the Faith, but be uncompromising in our loyalty, in our exposure of them and in our defence of the Faith.[449]

Similarly he wrote:

> The admonition to be 'a flame of fire to My enemies' is figurative, and means the friends should be firm in their stand against the enemies of the Faith and not compromise with them in any way.[450]

Notice that Shoghi Effendi uses the word 'uncompromising' to describe two different facets of the same quality. On the one hand he says that we must be 'uncompromising in our *loyalty*' to the Cause of Bahá'u'lláh and on the other he asserts that we should 'not compromise with' the enemies of the Faith 'in any way'. The implication is that not compromising with enemies of the Faith is an important demonstration of our sincere loyalty to Bahá'u'lláh's teachings. It has been suggested that such an uncompromising attitude – even towards sworn enemies of the Faith or Covenant-breakers – is somehow at variance with Bahá'u'lláh's admonition to 'Consort with all men, O people of Bahá, in a spirit of friendliness and fellowship'.[451] This view fails to take into account other basic spiritual principles. Bahá'u'lláh tells us that we must learn to *discern* the signs of God:

> The essence of all that We have revealed for thee is Justice, is for man to free himself from idle fancy and imitation, discern with the eye of oneness His glorious handiwork, and look into all things with a searching eye.[452]

Although we are not to act judgementally towards others, we must be keenly aware of those we can trust and who is not trustworthy. We are not meant to walk blindly and naively through life, being abused or manipulated by people who are dishonest and insincere. The Bahá'í writings make a sharp distinction between those who are sincere in their actions and those who behave maliciously or treacherously towards others. Bahá'u'lláh and 'Abdu'l-Bahá warn us that such individuals, if given free rein, can harm the spiritual condition of others. Bahá'u'lláh, in the Hidden Words, admonishes us:

> Beware! Walk not with the ungodly and seek not fellowship with him, for such companionship turneth the radiance of the heart into infernal fire.[453]

'Abdu'l-Bahá further clarifies this basic principle in His Will and Testament:

> O ye beloved of the Lord! Strive with all your heart to shield the Cause of God from the onslaught of the insincere, for souls such as these cause the straight to become crooked and all benevolent efforts to produce contrary results.[454]

This is the heart of the matter. 'Abdu'l-Bahá explains that if an individual, from the goodness of his own heart, acts in a way that leads to compromise with enemies of the Faith or with those who harbour treacherous intentions, *all* his noble actions – 'all benevolent efforts' – will be misused and will result in the exact opposite of what he intended by his kindness. Bahá'u'lláh warns that even the kindness of one's own heart can be converted into bitterness and evil qualities by the confusion and treachery stirred up by malicious behaviour on the part of those whom we trust. We must not ignore this fundamental principle. It is a source of divine protection for us, for our family and friends and for the Cause of God. 'Abdu'l-Bahá declares:

> O ye beloved of the Lord! The greatest of all things is the protection of the True Faith of God, the preservation of His Law, the safeguarding of His Cause and service unto His Word.[455]

Nowhere is this principle more forcefully upheld than in the Bahá'í attitude towards Covenant-breaking. A point of clarification must be made. Covenant-breaking is not the breaking of Bahá'í laws through our mistakes and weakness. No one is perfect; we are all in the process of spiritual development and are bound to fail and make mistakes.

Covenant-breaking is the most malicious and sinister behaviour imaginable. It is the attempt by one-time Bahá'ís to tear apart the fabric of the Bahá'í community with the intention of creating permanent divisions in the Cause of God. Such behaviour attempts to subvert the Bahá'í community through conscious disobedience and disregard for the explicit commands of Bahá'u'lláh to follow His appointed successors and institutions which He established for the divine, infallible guidance of the sacred Cause of God. In His Will and Testament, a document designed to eternally protect the Bahá'í community from the attacks of such Covenant-breakers, 'Abdu'l-Bahá warns us:

> And now, one of the greatest and most fundamental principles of the Cause of God is to shun and avoid entirely the Covenant-breakers, for they will utterly destroy the Cause of God, exterminate His Law and render of no account all efforts exerted in the past.[456]

As we reflect on this principle, it becomes clear that to be 'a flame of fire to My enemies' implies that we must be unswerving in our loyalty to Bahá'u'lláh and His Cause, steadfast in our obedience to His teachings and uncompromising in our determination to protect His sacred Cause from the attacks of its enemies.

This illustrates a distinctive facet of the Tablet of Aḥmad. It is not only a call of the Beloved One to turn our hearts to Him and arise to teach His Cause; it is also a call to defend and protect the Faith of God against its enemies. Ever the wise Father, Bahá'u'lláh guides and instructs us, showers us with love and encouragement and protects His family from harm.

# 60

# The Fire of the Love of God

*Be thou as a flame of fire . . .*
*and a river of life eternal*

A 'flame of fire' may also mean being on fire with the love of God. This expression appears throughout the writings of Bahá'u'lláh. For example He says, 'Let the flame of the love of God burn brightly within your radiant hearts.'[457] In this sense to be a flame of fire suggests that the love of God should burn so brightly in our hearts and souls that we will become pillars of strength in the Cause of God and examples of true love, devotion and steadfastness to other Bahá'ís and to those who are seeking God.

The fire of the love of God burning within the heart of the individual is the motivating force for personal transformation and spiritual growth. It is the fire of such love that is changing the life of society. In one of His Tablets Bahá'u'lláh exhorts us to be ablaze with the fire of His love:

> You must all be so ablaze in this day with the fire of the love of God that the heat thereof may be manifest in all your veins, your limbs and members of your body, and the peoples of the world may be ignited by this heat and turn to the horizon of the Beloved.[458]

It is the fire of the love of God that enables us to arise and accomplish seemingly impossible tasks in the service of the Cause of God. It is the power of this love that is referred to in these words attributed to 'Abdu'l-Bahá:

> There is a power in this Cause – a mysterious power – far, far, far away from the ken of men and angels; that invisible power is the cause of all these outward activities. It moves the hearts. It rends the mountains. It administers the complicated affairs of the Cause. It inspires the friends.[459]

There is no limit to the power of this love. It is the fire of the love of Bahá'u'lláh, once fully kindled in the heart of the believer, that mystically weds him to his Lord and attracts to him the 'limitless effusions of His grace'.[460]

In the Tablet of Aḥmad Bahá'u'lláh urges us to be so on fire with His love that we will arise and dedicate our lives to serving His Cause. In this half of the Tablet of Aḥmad, He emphasizes that we should not let anything deter us from fulfilling this sacred task.

## 61

# Teach Ye the Cause of God

*Be thou as a flame of fire*
*to My enemies*
*and a river of life eternal*
*to My loved ones*

If a person is deeply in love with another it cannot be hidden. It becomes evident and obvious to all who see him. Likewise, if a believer is truly on fire with the love of his Lord, he cannot hide or contain his love; he must share it with others. This seems to be one of the implications of 'Be thou as a flame of fire . . . and a river of life eternal'. On one level it appears to be a command to arise and teach.

Bahá'u'lláh often couples His advice to be on fire with His love with an appeal to teach. For example He says:

> Let thy soul glow with the flame of this undying Fire . . . in such wise that the waters of the universe shall be powerless to cool down its ardour. Make, then, mention of thy Lord, that haply the heedless among Our servants may be admonished through thy words, and the hearts of the righteous be gladdened.[461]

> If he be kindled with the fire of His love, if he forgoeth all created things, the words he uttereth shall set on fire them that hear him . . . Happy is the man that hath heard Our voice, and answered Our call.[462]

Looked at in another way, being 'a flame of fire' could mean to be a beacon of guidance to all people. In the darkness of the night, a solitary flame of fire burns brightly and clearly; it is a guiding light to those who have lost their way.

A river flows continuously, freely and generously imparting its abundance to all living things. Thus to be 'a river of life eternal' could mean to be a source of spiritual life to all people, to teach them the knowledge of God and nourish their souls with the divine teachings and the Word of God.

'My loved ones' may refer to those who have recognized Bahá'u'lláh. His appeal to be a 'river of life eternal to My loved ones' implies that we must become a source of joy and spiritual life to the friends of God through our loving actions and the example of our lives, as well as by our words. It also implies that we study and deepen with each other in His teachings. It is essential for those who understand to share their knowledge with others, especially as there is no clergy in the Bahá'í Faith.

'My loved ones' may also refer to people who are seeking the knowledge of God. In this sense, to be 'a flame of fire . . . and a river of life eternal to My loved ones' means that we must teach all those who are seeking to find the truth.

In the *Book of Certitude* Bahá'u'lláh links the symbolism of the terms 'fire' and 'river' with the creative power of the Word of God. He says that the 'river' is the 'river of divine knowledge' and the term 'fire' means the fire of divine wisdom:

> Through them [the divinely-revealed verses] floweth the river of divine knowledge, and gloweth the fire of His ancient and consummate wisdom. This is the fire which, in one and the same moment, kindleth the flame of love in the breasts of the faithful, and induceth the chill of heedlessness in the heart of the enemy.[463]

Since the Word of God is the source of spiritual life for every human being, to be 'a flame of fire . . . and a river of life eternal' implies that we must share the pure teachings of Bahá'u'lláh. Bahá'u'lláh emphasizes the vital importance of using the Word of God in teaching and deepening. He says that His divine verses exert the greatest influence on people's hearts and describes them as the 'most potent elixir' for the transformation and upliftment of the souls of men:

> The sanctified souls should ponder and meditate in their hearts regarding the methods of teaching. From the texts of the wondrous, heavenly Scriptures they should memorize phrases and passages bearing on various instances, so that in the course of their speech they may recite divine verses whenever the occasion demandeth it, inasmuch as these holy verses are the most potent elixir, the greatest and mightiest talisman. So potent is their influence that the hearer will have no cause for vacillation.[464]

## 62

# Burn Away the Veil of Self

*Be thou as a flame of fire to My enemies*
*and a river of life eternal to My loved ones,*
*and be not of those who doubt.*

The fundamental purpose of our lives is to develop our spiritual qualities and acquire virtues. It is the responsibility of every individual believer to transform his own character in conformity with the teachings of Bahá'u'lláh. From this perspective, 'My enemies' may refer to those qualities within each one of us which are not God-like. In this sense to be 'a flame of fire to My enemies' suggests that we should burn away, through the power of the love of God, all those qualities which are unworthy of our true, spiritual nature. To be 'a river of life eternal to My loved ones', then, suggests that we should nurture the spiritual qualities within us and seek to perfect our virtues. In an inspiring passage Bahá'u'lláh counsels us:

> O friends! Be not careless of the virtues with which ye have been endowed, neither be neglectful of your high destiny. Suffer not your labours to be wasted through the vain imaginations which certain hearts have devised. Ye are the stars of the heaven of understanding, the breeze that stirreth at the break of day, the soft-flowing waters upon which must depend the very life of all men, the letters inscribed upon His sacred scroll. With the utmost unity, and in a spirit of perfect fellowship, exert yourselves, that ye may be enabled to achieve that which beseemeth this Day of God.[465]

It requires strength and courage for an individual to burn away the egotistical, negative qualities within him. To gain that strength, one must kindle the love of God within his heart. In the Seven Valleys Bahá'u'lláh says:

> Wherefore must the veils of the satanic self be burned away at the fire of love, that the spirit may be purified and cleansed and thus may know the station of the Lord of the Worlds.
>
> Kindle the fire of love and burn away all things,
> Then set thy foot into the land of the lovers.[466]

How does one kindle the fire of love? The Bahá'í writings tell us that it is through earnest prayer and constant striving, even under adverse conditions, to turn wholly to God. In the *Book of Certitude* Bahá'u'lláh advises the true seeker to

> . . . consume every wayward thought with the flame of His loving mention, and, with the swiftness of lightning, pass by all else save Him.[467]

In one of Bahá'u'lláh's prayers we find this supplication:

> Ignite, then, O my God, within my breast the fire of Thy love, that its flame may burn up all else except my remembrance of Thee, that every trace of corrupt desire may be entirely mortified within me, and that naught may remain except the glorification of Thy transcendent and all-glorious Being. This is my highest aspiration, mine ardent desire . . .[468]

In this sense, then, 'be not of those who doubt' implies that we should not doubt that God will assist us to accomplish the purpose of our lives, which is to perfect our characters. Bahá'u'lláh admonishes us to persevere in the daily struggles of life and encourages us to overcome all obstacles in our efforts to arise and serve Him.

## 63

# Be Not of Those Who Doubt (I)

*and be not of those who doubt*

In the sense that 'be thou as a flame of fire . . . and a river of life eternal' means to be a teacher of the Cause of God, Bahá'u'lláh may be telling us to 'be not of those who doubt' that this is the mission He has given us. In a Tablet in which He emphasizes the importance of personal teaching, He declares:

> Say: To assist Me is to teach My Cause. This is a theme with which whole Tablets are laden. This is the changeless commandment of God, eternal in the past, eternal in the future. Comprehend this, O ye men of insight.[469]

In the Tablet of Aḥmad Bahá'u'lláh challenges each one of us to 'choose the path to his Lord'. He then clearly encourages us to become dedicated teachers of His Cause. 'Be not of those who doubt' is an exhortation not to give up, not to turn away from this choice of service to His Cause. Elsewhere He says:

> Spread abroad the sweet savours of thy Lord, and hesitate not, though it be for less than a moment, in the service of His Cause.[470]

In the Tablet of Aḥmad, Bahá'u'lláh twice points out that He is writing to Aḥmad from prison. He declares that His mission is 'to deliver this clear message' yet He has been imprisoned by His enemies, who repeatedly exiled Him in a never-ending attempt to prevent Him from carrying out His God-given task. We know that Bahá'u'lláh did not allow Aḥmad to share this exile and imprisonment. In the Tablet of Aḥmad Bahá'u'lláh gives him a different mission. By repeating the fact that He is a prisoner, Bahá'u'lláh implies that since Aḥmad is free, he can best use his freedom to teach on behalf of his Lord. In this verse from the Tablet Bahá'u'lláh seems to tell Aḥmad not to doubt that this is the mission He has entrusted to him.

In the Hidden Words Bahá'u'lláh explains that He has created us out of love. And He asks us to love Him in return:

> O Son of Man! Veiled in My immemorial being and in the ancient eternity of My essence, I knew My love for thee; therefore I created thee . . .[471]

> O Son of Man! I loved thy creation, hence I created thee. Wherefore, do thou love Me . . .[472]

How does one return the love of the supreme Manifestation of God? The greatest gift an individual can receive from his Lord is the priceless privilege and honour of serving Him. And the greatest service one can offer is to be a teacher of His Cause. Bahá'u'lláh tells us to 'be not of those who doubt' that this is why we were created and called into being. In another Tablet He clearly affirms this:

> We call aloud unto thee saying: In truth there is no God but Me, the All-Knowing, the All-Wise. We have brought thee into being to serve Me, to glorify My Word and to proclaim My Cause. Centre thine energies upon that wherefor thou hast been created by virtue of the Will of the supreme Ordainer, the Ancient of Days.[473]

64

# Be Not of Those Who Doubt (II)

*Be thou as a flame of fire to My enemies*
*and a river of life eternal to My loved ones,*
*and be not of those who doubt.*

'Be not of those who doubt' seems to apply to each of the meanings of the verse 'Be thou as a flame of fire . . . and a river of life eternal'. In the sense that this verse means to burn away the veils of self, Bahá'u'lláh is telling us not to doubt that the purpose of our lives is to fight our own spiritual battles, to overcome our lower nature and to develop our virtues. This is the task He has given every believer. It is up to each one of us to choose this path to our Lord, to seek the shelter and care of His infinite love and to win the victory over our own selves. Do not doubt that you will succeed, He promises every devoted follower.

In the sense that to 'be a flame of fire . . . and a river of life eternal' means to be a tower of strength against the attacks of the enemies of the Cause of God and a source of comfort and assurance to the believers, especially in times of opposition and persecution, Bahá'u'lláh is telling us not to doubt His aid and assistance. He assures us that He will strengthen us through the power of His divine might.

In one of His Tablets Bahá'u'lláh urges us on to greater heights of service with these words of encouragement:

> There lay concealed within the Holy Veil, and prepared for the service of God, a company of His chosen ones who shall

> be manifested unto men, who shall aid His Cause, who shall be afraid of no one, though the entire human race rise up and war against them. These are the ones who, before the gaze of the dwellers on earth and the denizens of heaven, shall arise and, shouting aloud, acclaim the name of the Almighty, and summon the children of men to the path of God, the All-Glorious, the All-Praised. *Walk thou in their way, and let no one dismay thee. Be of them whom the tumult of the world, however much it may agitate them in the path of their Creator, can never sadden, whose purpose the blame of the blamer will never defeat.*[474]

'Be not of those who doubt' may also refer to His admonition to 'be thou so steadfast in My love that thy heart shall not waver, even if' everything in one's life seems to be going wrong. To be steadfast in Bahá'u'lláh's love is such a fundamental principle of His Faith that He exhorts us never to doubt the sincerity of His love and concern for each one of us. In one of His Tablets He admonishes us to be of those who are 'confident in their belief'.[475] He is 'the Most Trusted' and 'the Best Lover'. In one of His prayers He reminds us:

> No God is there save Thee, the Strong, the Faithful.
>
> Thou art He Who changeth through His bidding abasement into glory, and weakness into strength, and powerlessness into might, and fear into calm, and doubt into certainty. No God is there but Thee, the Mighty, the Beneficent.[476]

Because there is such a close interconnectedness among the verses of the Tablet of Aḥmad, we may apply Bahá'u'lláh's entreaty to 'be not of those who doubt' to every one of its exhortations. Reflect on the implications of each of these combinations:

> Bear thou witness that verily He is God . . . and be not of those who doubt.

> . . . be obedient to the ordinances of God . . . and be not of those who doubt.
>
> . . . let him choose the path to his Lord . . . and be not of those who doubt.
>
> Forget not My bounties while I am absent . . . and be not of those who doubt.
>
> . . . be thou so steadfast in My love that thy heart shall not waver . . . and be not of those who doubt.
>
> Rely upon God, thy God . . . and be not of those who doubt.
>
> Be thou assured in thyself . . . and be not of those who doubt.
>
> Learn well this Tablet . . . and be not of those who doubt.
>
> . . . be of those who are grateful . . . and be not of those who doubt.
>
> Read this Tablet with absolute sincerity . . . and be not of those who doubt.

'Be not of those who doubt' is one of the spiritual principles of the Faith of Bahá'u'lláh. To attain the state of certitude, it implies, it is necessary to truly recognize Bahá'u'lláh's station and sincerely believe in the truth of His words. He is the supreme Manifestation of God. His voice is the voice of God. His command is the command of God. All His actions are a reflection of the will of God. Whatever He says and does can never be separated from the will of God Himself. It is not for us to question His authority or the wisdom of the laws and institutions He has revealed for the guidance of individuals and the advancement of the Cause of God. Rather, it is our duty to beseech His assistance so that we can more fully understand and follow His teachings. This is what Bahá'u'lláh defines as the essence of belief in and recognition of His true station. He explains this principle in the Kitáb-i-Aqdas, His Most Holy Book:

> Blessed is the man that hath acknowledged his belief in God and in His signs, and recognized that 'He shall not be asked of His doings.'. . .
>
> Were He to decree as lawful the thing which from time immemorial had been forbidden, and forbid that which had, at all times, been regarded as lawful, to none is given the right to question His authority . . .
>
> Whoso hath not recognized this sublime and fundamental verity, and hath failed to attain this most exalted station, the winds of doubt will agitate him, and the sayings of the infidels will distract his soul. *He that hath acknowledged this principle will be endowed with the most perfect constancy* . . . Such is the teaching which God bestoweth on you, a teaching that will deliver you from all manner of doubt and perplexity, and enable you to attain unto salvation in both this world and the next. He, verily, is the Ever-Forgiving, the Most Bountiful.[477]

To be 'a flame of fire to My enemies and a river of life eternal to My loved ones, and be not of those who doubt' suggests that we should be pillars of steadfastness in the love of Bahá'u-'lláh, an example of devotion and love to all and a rock of assurance and beacon of guidance in explaining and defending the truths of His Cause to those who raise doubts or question the wisdom of what He has revealed.

Bahá'u'lláh has not left us alone to fend for ourselves. He promises us the grace of His invisible aid and assistance. He has revealed the ocean of His words for our guidance and assurance and has given us many prayers to help us attain the station of certitude and steadfastness. In one of His Tablets He urges us:

> Hearken thou unto the Words of thy Lord and purify thy heart from every illusion so that the effulgent light of the remembrance of thy Lord may shed its radiance upon it, and it may attain the station of certitude.[478]

He revealed this supplication to assist us in attaining this station:

> Magnified be Thy name, O my Lord, for Thou hast enabled me to recognize the Manifestation of Thine own Self, and hast caused me to be assured of the truth of the verses which have descended upon Thee. Empower me, I implore Thee, to cling steadfastly unto whatsoever Thou hast bidden me observe. Help me to guard the pearls of Thy love which, by Thy decree, Thou hast enshrined within my heart. Send down, moreover, every moment of my life, O my God, that which will preserve me from any one but Thee, and will set my feet firm in Thy Cause.
>
> Thou art, verily, the God of glory, the God of power, the God of knowledge and wisdom. No God is there beside Thee, the Great Giver, the All-Bountiful, the Almighty, the Ever-Forgiving.
>
> Praised be God, the All-Glorious, the All-Compelling.[479]

65

# Affliction in My Path

*And if thou art overtaken by affliction in My path,*
*or degradation for My sake, be not thou troubled thereby.*
*Rely upon God, thy God and the Lord of thy fathers.*

In one of His Tablets Bahá'u'lláh reveals the following principle:

> Whatever befalleth in the path of God is the beloved of the soul and the desire of the heart. Deadly poison in His path is pure honey, and every tribulation a draught of crystal water.[480]

This verse is similar to one found in the Long Obligatory Prayer:

> Whatsoever is revealed by Thee is the desire of my heart and the beloved of my soul. O God, my God! Look not upon my hopes and my doings, nay rather look upon Thy will that hath encompassed the heavens and the earth.[481]

It is a fact of human nature that we often fail to realize our own best interests. We all know that we have lessons to learn that we do not wish to go through. God in His wisdom and love causes us to experience what we need for our own spiritual growth and personal development. In the Hidden Words Bahá'u'lláh explains this principle more fully:

> O Son of Man! My calamity is My providence, outwardly it is fire and vengeance, but inwardly it is light and mercy. Hasten thereunto that thou mayest become an eternal light and an immortal spirit.[482]

When we are suffering the agony of an excruciating experience, we often cannot imagine that any possible benefit can be had from being forced to endure the pain of such an ordeal. And yet, much later, in the calm of hindsight, we feel glad and even thankful for having endured and overcome the difficulty. In the long run we can usually see how beneficial, or even necessary and indispensable, such ordeals are for our own growth and development. It is a reality of the human spirit that beyond the pain there is a feeling of triumph, and sometimes even sweetness, in having endured and overcome intense suffering. All the luxuries and comforts of the world can never compare to this.

Such experiences demonstrate the fact that events in this material world are not what they seem on the surface. If we concern ourselves only with outward appearances and allow ourselves to be battered and ruled by circumstances, then we will interpret such difficulties as 'fire and vengeance'. But once we begin to look beyond surface appearances and seek to understand the significance of such happenings for our own growth, we begin to discover that these ordeals are the bounties and favours of God. 'Abdu'l-Bahá explains that:

> Whatsoever may happen is for the best, because affliction is but the essence of bounty, and sorrow and toil are mercy unalloyed, and anguish is peace of mind, and to make a sacrifice is to receive a gift, and whatsoever may come to pass hath issued from God's grace.[483]

> Not until man is tried doth the pure gold distinctly separate from the dross. Torment is the fire of test wherein the pure gold shineth resplendently and the impurity is burned and blackened.[484]

That 'anguish is peace of mind' and torment beneficial to the soul is not easily accepted, particularly by this generation that desires instant gratification. Yet it is one of the fundamental themes of the Tablet of Aḥmad that events are not to be judged by their outward appearances. Bahá'u'lláh points out that His own imprisonment and the cruelties He was forced to endure are prime examples of this spiritual truth. It is also an historical fact that the advancement of the religion of God has been closely linked with the fire of ordeal. 'Abdu'l-Bahá explains that the attacks of the fanatical clergy have caused the religion of God to become widely known. Were it not for such attacks, He says, the Faith of God would not have been spread among the peoples of the world. Once we comprehend this, He says, we will not be troubled by such persecutions:

> Indeed, the attacks and the obstructiveness of the ignorant but cause the Word of God to be exalted, and spread His signs and tokens far and wide. Were it not for this opposition by the disdainful, this obduracy of the slanderers, this shouting from the pulpits, this crying and wailing of great and small alike, these accusations of unbelief levelled by the ignorant, this uproar from the foolish – how could news of the advent of the Primal Point and the bright dawning of the Day-Star of Bahá ever have reached to east and west? How else could the planet have been rocked from pole to pole? . . .
>
> . . . All these blessings and bestowals, the very means of proclaiming the Faith, have come about through the scorn of the ignorant, the opposition of the foolish, the stubbornness of the dull-witted, the violence of the aggressor. Had it not been for these things, the news of the Báb's advent would not, to this day, have reached even into lands hard by. Wherefore we should never grieve over the blindness of the unwitting, the attacks of the foolish, the hostility of the low and base, the heedlessness of the divines, the charges of infidelity brought against us by the empty of mind.[485]

In the Tablet of Aḥmad, Bahá'u'lláh tells us that we *can expect* to encounter afflictions in the path of God. But He admonishes us to 'be not thou troubled thereby' for such ordeals are the bounties and blessings of God and play an important role in the development of the life of the soul. This can be more easily understood by considering the suffering of the Manifestations of God.

The suffering borne by the Manifestations is a prime factor in the development of humanity and the evolution of society. The Manifestation of God trains the world through the crucible of His own suffering. For example, Bahá'u'lláh describes the inner significance of His suffering in these words:

> The shame I was made to bear hath uncovered the glory with which the whole of creation had been invested, and through the cruelties I have endured, the Day Star of Justice hath manifested itself, and shed its splendour upon men.[486]

The Manifestation of God is responsible for the advancement of humankind. His mission is to create a peaceful and unified society and to uplift humanity from its present condition to a higher level of spiritual development. The suffering He endures is providentially transformed into a grace which revolutionizes the life of society and causes humanity to grow and develop.

We as individuals are responsible to God for ourselves. Our mission in life is to perfect our own character and develop our own spiritual capacities. What the Bahá'í writings explain is that the personal suffering we experience is the crucible for the development of our own souls. The fact that the suffering of the Manifestation of God has profound meaning for the future life of humanity is in itself an assurance – a testimony from the Manifestation – that the suffering each individual experiences will have similar meaning for the development of his own soul.

# *Section 8: The Paths of Delusion*

## 66

## The Paths of Delusion

*For the people are wandering in the paths of delusion,*
*bereft of discernment to see God with their own eyes,*
*or hear His Melody with their own ears.*
*Thus have We found them,*
*as thou also dost witness.*

In this and the following paragraph of the Tablet of Aḥmad Bahá'u'lláh emphasizes the plight of humanity. They may be understood as a profound appeal to arise and rescue humanity from its state of ignorance and superstition. It is as if He says: Witness the condition of the people. They are helplessly wandering in the maze of their own delusions, wrapped in the thick fog of their superstitions and imaginations. They are lost and unable to find the path to God.

The implication is that they must be helped. God's purpose for humanity is to enable every human being to recognize his Lord, the Promised One of all ages. Bahá'u'lláh says that God has 'endowed every soul with the capacity to recognize the signs of God'.[487] He promises that those individuals who are open-minded and sincerely seeking God will be assisted by God to 'find and embrace the Truth' of His Revelation.[488] But, as both the Báb and Bahá'u'lláh point out, the people have allowed themselves to be shut out as by a veil from this most great bounty.[489] In the Tablet of Tajallíyát, Bahá'u'lláh says that it was God's intention that all people would be ready to accept His supreme Manifestation:

It was intended that at the time of the manifestation of the One true God the faculty of recognizing Him would have been developed and matured and would have reached its culmination. However, it is now clearly demonstrated that in the disbelievers this faculty hath remained undeveloped and hath, indeed, degenerated.[490]

Because people have not fully developed their inherent spiritual capacities, they need assistance. Bahá'u'lláh counsels us:

We cherish the hope that you, who have attained to this light, will exert your utmost to banish the darkness of superstition and unbelief from the midst of the people.[491]

The Báb explains that most people are spiritually helpless and need assistance to find their Lord. He tells us that our role is to open their hearts and dispel their doubts:

Wert thou to open the heart of a single soul by helping him to embrace the Cause of Him Whom God shall make manifest, thine inmost being would be filled with the inspirations of that august Name. It devolveth upon you, therefore, to perform this task . . . inasmuch as most people are helpless, and *wert thou to open their hearts and dispel their doubts, they would gain admittance into the Faith of God*. Therefore, manifest thou this attribute to the utmost of thine ability in the days of Him Whom God shall make manifest.[492]

As mentioned previously, Bahá'u'lláh twice points out in the Tablet of Aḥmad that He is a prisoner. He cannot help the people Himself. 'The people are wandering in the paths of delusion.' Who will arise and help them, He seems to ask. 'Be thou as a flame of fire . . . and a river of life eternal.' Be a teacher of the Cause. Guide the people to this new revelation and help them to recognize the Promised One of God.

For everyone who understands, it is his duty to guide others.

Later Bahá'u'lláh says 'Be thou assured in thyself', implying: be assured that this is the path of service in the Cause of God. Elsewhere He declares:

> Say: Teach ye the Cause of God, O people of Bahá, for God hath prescribed unto every one the duty of proclaiming His Message, and regardeth it as the most meritorious of all deeds.[493]

It is important to realize that Bahá'u'lláh's injunction to be a guide to others applies equally to teaching and assisting our fellow Bahá'ís. People are at different stages of development and all of us need help to grow and advance. It may be that the 'people [who] are wandering in the paths of delusion' also refers to we Bahá'ís who presently have a limited knowledge of the Bahá'í teachings. If this is so, it may be that Bahá'u'lláh is suggesting that those Bahá'ís who have a greater understanding of the Faith should share their knowledge with their fellow believers. His exhortation to be a 'river of life eternal to My loved ones' suggests that Bahá'ís must help and support each other and share their understanding of Bahá'u'lláh's life-giving teachings.

## 67

# Their Superstitions Have Become Veils

*Thus have their superstitions become veils*
*between them and their own hearts*
*and kept them from the path of God,*
*the Exalted, the Great.*

Bahá'u'lláh says that 'it is the veil of idle imaginations' which prevents people in every age from recognizing the new Manifestation of God.[494] Elsewhere He says, 'people for the most part delight in superstitions'. He continues:

> By holding fast unto names they deprive themselves of the inner reality and by clinging to vain imaginings they are kept back from the Dayspring of heavenly signs.[495]

It is not God who prevents people from recognizing His Manifestation. On the contrary, people shut themselves out from this promised grace of God.

> The One true God may be compared unto the sun and the believer unto a mirror. No sooner is the mirror placed before the sun than it reflects its light. The unbeliever may be likened unto a stone. No matter how long it is exposed to the sunshine, it cannot reflect the sun.[496]

The Báb explains that if it were up to God, He would cause everyone to become a believer; He would transform 'the stone into a mirror' of His light. But, He says, 'the person himself remaineth reconciled to his state'. His own attitude veils him from the glory of God's revelation. Had he wished to become a believer, the Báb adds, God would have enabled him to do so.[497]

Bahá'u'lláh says that the human heart 'is the seat of the revelation of the inner mysteries of God'.[498] But the superstitions and imaginations which people choose to believe block the inspiration of their own hearts from guiding them to the truth and the recognition of God's revelation. It is their own conscious choices which shut them out from this source of guidance.

The teachings of Bahá'u'lláh are centred around the principle of the oneness of the human race. Their purpose is to unite all the peoples and nations into one human family so that the Kingdom of God may be established on earth. In the Tablet of Maqsúd Bahá'u'lláh declares:

> If any man were to meditate on that which the Scriptures . . . have revealed, he would readily recognize that their purpose is that all men shall be regarded as one soul, so that . . . the light of Divine bounty, of grace, and mercy may envelop all mankind.[499]

In the same Tablet He says:

> The tabernacle of unity hath been raised; regard ye not one another as strangers. Ye are the fruits of one tree, and the leaves of one branch.[500]

The essence of being a Bahá'í is to love all humanity and to devote one's life to the service of the human race. Unfortunately, at the present time many people do not love humanity. If a person is steeped in prejudice and regards people who are different from himself as his enemies, then his attitude towards others veils him from recognizing that he has been created to be a member of the one human family. Owing to his outlook, he will not be attracted to those who are different from himself and his behaviour will naturally result in their lack of attraction to him. Since the bounties of God depend on one's love and service to humanity, the behaviour of such an individual will not attract the favours of God. His own suspicions and hostility towards others will tend to repel God's bounties. It is extremely difficult for a person who harbours such hatreds and prejudices to understand that he has been created by God to love others and be of service to them. Such attitudes become serious obstacles which veil an individual from recognizing the love of God in his own heart. These prejudices prevent him from understanding the purpose of Bahá'u'lláh's Revelation. No wonder that Bahá'u'lláh declares, 'Lack of a proper education hath, however, deprived him of that which he doth inherently possess.'[501] In another Tablet He asserts:

> The Cause is manifest, it shineth resplendent as the sun, but the people have become veils unto themselves. We entreat God that He may graciously assist them to return unto Him.[502]

*Section 9: The Second Warning*

# 68

# Be Thou Assured in Thyself (I)

*Be thou assured in thyself*

Bahá'u'lláh gives Aḥmad very specific advice. Early in the Tablet He admonishes him to bear witness to the truth of this promised Day of God. He tells him to deliver the clear message of the Cause of God. He assures him of the bounties of His love. He warns him that no matter how severe the trials and difficulties he encounters in carrying out his teaching mission, he must be so steadfast in His love that nothing will cause him to waver.

Bahá'u'lláh continues to reassure Aḥmad of His deep and abiding love throughout the remainder of the Tablet. He cautions him not to doubt the promises He has given him and again warns him not to be troubled by affliction or adversity in the path of God but to rely upon God under all conditions. He points out to Aḥmad that he should be a witness to the sorry condition of humanity and arise to relieve the helpless people of the world from the burden of their superstitions and idle imaginings. After all these words of advice and encouragement, Bahá'u'lláh then tells Aḥmad to be assured in himself of the absolute truth of all that has been revealed to him.

Bahá'u'lláh's appeal is in reality a command – 'Be thou assured in thyself' – and expresses a fundamental spiritual principle: the purpose of our lives is to know and to love God. To truly know and love Him, we must become assured of His love and care for us. The more confident we become of God's unfailing assistance in our daily lives, the greater will be our devotion and love for Him. This is why we are encouraged to pray regularly. God wants us to be fully conscious of His love and assistance. Our goal, Bahá'u'lláh tells us, is the station of certitude, to 'remain steadfast in the Cause of God – exalted be His glory – and to be unswerving in His love'.[503] His exhortation that we become assured within our own selves is a promise that this is indeed possible. In one of His Tablets He advises:

> Such should be thy certitude that if all mankind were to advance such claims as no man hath ever advanced, or any mind conceived, thou wouldst completely ignore them, wouldst cast them from thee, and would set thy face towards Him Who is the Object of the adoration of all worlds.[504]

# 69

## Be Thou Assured in Thyself (II)

*Be thou assured in thyself that verily,*
*he who turns away from this Beauty*
*hath also turned away from the Messengers of the past*
*and showeth pride towards God*
*from all eternity to all eternity.*

This is another instance in which Bahá'u'lláh appears to be reminding us of two important principles in the same phrase. In telling us to be assured that 'he who turns away from this Beauty hath also turned away from the Messengers of the past', He is also telling us to be assured that the converse of this statement must likewise be true. Those who do not turn away – those who believe in Bahá'u'lláh and remain faithful to His Cause – are the ones who have truly recognized the purpose of the religion of God and have bowed down to the will of God and humbled themselves before Him. More specifically, Bahá'u-'lláh is telling each one of us that if we cleave unto His love and become steadfast in His Cause, we may be assured within our own hearts of His unfailing love and protection for us. This is a divine promise and is itself a fundamental principle of His Revelation. In the Hidden Words He asserts:

> O Son of Being! Thy Paradise is My love; thy heavenly home, reunion with Me. Enter therein and tarry not. This is that which hath been destined for thee in Our kingdom above and Our exalted Dominion.[505]

And again in the Hidden Words He affirms:

> O Son of Being! My love is My stronghold; he that entereth therein is safe and secure, and he that turneth away shall surely stray and perish.[506]

In one of His Tablets Bahá'u'lláh elaborates on this theme and gives us a vision of what it truly means to be a believer in the supreme Manifestation of God in this promised day:

> Whoso hath, in this Day, refused to allow the doubts and fancies of men to turn him away from Him Who is the Eternal Truth, and hath not suffered the tumult provoked by the ecclesiastical and secular authorities to deter him from recognizing His Message, such a man will be regarded by God, the Lord of all men, as one of His mighty signs, and will be numbered among them whose names have been inscribed by the Pen of the Most High in His Book. Blessed is he that hath recognized the true stature of such a soul, that hath acknowledged its station, and discovered its virtues.[507]

## 70

# He Who Turns Away from This Beauty

*Be thou assured in thyself that verily,*
*he who turns away from this Beauty*
*hath also turned away from the Messengers of the past*
*and showeth pride towards God*
*from all eternity to all eternity.*

In this verse Bahá'u'lláh invokes a fundamental principle of the eternal covenant of God which is that every Manifestation of God makes an agreement with His followers that they will accept the next Manifestation when He appears.[508]

'Abdu'l-Bahá explains that every divine Messenger has established a covenant with the believers living in His time, on behalf of future generations of His followers, that the believers living at the time of the appearance of the next Manifestation of God will accept Him. He asserts that this is a basic principle of every religion and that the followers of all religions are bound by the terms of this covenant.[509]

There is another principle of the covenant of God which applies specifically to the Revelation of Bahá'u'lláh. All the Messengers in the prophetic cycle that began with Adam were commissioned by God to make a separate covenant with their followers concerning God's promise of the day that would witness the appearance of the Lord Himself. All the Messengers of God have promised this.

The Báb leaves no doubt about the existence of this special covenant. In the Qayyumu'l-Asmá', which He began revealing on the very night of His declaration to the first person to believe in Him, He states:

> With each and every Prophet Whom We have sent down in the past, We have established a separate Covenant concerning the Remembrance of God and His Day.[510]

> . . . We have established a separate covenant regarding Him with every Prophet and His followers. Indeed, We have not sent any Messenger without this binding covenant . . .[511]

Bahá'u'lláh also testifies to the existence of this binding covenant. Referring to His own manifestation, He affirms:

> . . . Thou didst manifest Him Who is the Revealer of Thyself and the Treasury of Thy wisdom and the Dawning-Place of Thy majesty and power. *Thou didst establish His covenant with every one who hath been created* in the kingdoms of earth and heaven and in the realms of revelation and of creation.[512]

Thus the believers of all existing Faiths, by their allegiance to their own Prophet, are under the obligation to accept the Promised One of God. No follower of any existing religion can claim to have fully and completely followed the teachings of his own Prophet unless and until he accepts Bahá'u'lláh. Bahá'u'lláh Himself makes this abundantly clear. He warns the clergy of other Faiths, and all their followers, that if they reject Him they have denied the truth of their own religions:

> Say: O concourse of the foolish! If ye reject Him, by what evidence can ye prove your allegiance to the former Messengers of God or vindicate your belief in that which He hath sent down from His mighty and exalted Kingdom?[513]

We may well ask how a person can claim to be faithfully following his own religion when he has ignored and disobeyed such a fundamental commandment of every religion.

Bahá'u'lláh's answer is that he cannot justify such a claim. When He says 'he who turns away from this Beauty [Bahá'u-'lláh Himself] hath also turned away from the Messengers of the past', He is stating that if an individual rejects Him, in the sight of God he has also rejected his own Prophet. In one of His Tablets Bahá'u'lláh declares:

> No man can obtain everlasting life, unless he embraceth the truth of this inestimable, this wondrous, and sublime Revelation.[514]

In the *Book of Certitude* Bahá'u'lláh explains that re-birth has always meant recognition of and belief in the new Manifestation of God when He appears. Death, He says, is the death of unbelief.[515] Whoever rejects the Promised One of God is spiritually dead, no matter what position he occupies in this world.

One meaning of 'eternity' is the duration of the dispensation of a Manifestation of God. Showing 'pride towards God from all eternity to all eternity' thus suggests that if an individual rejects Bahá'u'lláh, he has, in effect, denied all the Manifestations of the past and all the divine Messengers yet to be manifested in the future.

# *Section 10: Learn Well This Tablet*

## 71

## Learn Well This Tablet

*Learn well this Tablet, O Aḥmad.*
*Chant it during thy days*
*and withhold not thyself therefrom.*

In the final paragraphs of the English translation of the Tablet of Aḥmad, Bahá'u'lláh gives us two distinct reasons to use this Tablet in our prayers. First, He advises anyone who is experiencing 'affliction or grief' to 'read this Tablet with absolute sincerity' and promises that this will bring the reader special assistance.

Second, He says to 'chant [*iqrá'*] it during thy days and *withhold not* thyself therefrom' (emphasis added), specifically, it seems, telling us not to wait for difficulties or special circumstances to read the Tablet. Rather He advises us to use it often.[516]

Why does He suggest that we read this particular Tablet regularly?

All the evidence suggests that the Tablet itself is one of Bahá'u'lláh's special bounties. The Guardian asserts that the Tablet of Aḥmad has been 'invested by Bahá'u'lláh with a special potency and significance'. He goes on to say that it 'should therefore be accepted as such' by the believers. He explains that it has a two-fold purpose. The first, he says, is that through its use we 'may enter into a much closer communion with God'. This implies using it regularly. Its second purpose, he says, is that through its use the believers may 'identify themselves more fully with His laws and precepts'.[517]

How can reading this Tablet help us do this?

Bahá'u'lláh tells us to 'learn well this Tablet'. The Arabic from which 'learn well' has been translated is *aḥfaḍ*, which literally means 'memorize' and which also means 'preserve' or 'protect'.[518]

We must follow the example of Aḥmad, memorize the Tablet and study it many times to find out what Bahá'u'lláh desires us to do. His appeal suggests that within the Tablet He has placed many mysteries which He wants us to discover. He implies that no matter how much we may find, there will always be more. Through reading and persistent study of the Tablet, striving to understand its many meanings, we can uncover the priceless gems of divine wisdom it contains. Such study will draw us closer to Bahá'u'lláh and help us become firmer in His Faith.

As mentioned earlier, the Tablet's appeal is very personal. The potency of this Tablet is so great, and the creative range of the Word of God so vast, that an individual may often find that its exhortations relate to his own personal circumstances. Bahá'u'lláh's advice to 'withhold not thyself therefrom' seems to indicate a promise that the Tablet can provide spiritual guidance for personal problems. Whoever studies the Tablet earnestly and 'with unquestioning faith and confidence' will find many clear messages from Bahá'u'lláh.

## 72

# The Reward of a Hundred Martyrs

*For verily,*
*God hath ordained for the one who chants it,*
*the reward of a hundred martyrs*

The final paragraphs of the Tablet of Aḥmad contain two astounding promises. Here we consider the first of these, the promise that if we chant the Tablet we will receive 'the reward of a hundred martyrs and a service in both worlds'. What is the significance of this promise?

Martyrs are those who sacrifice their lives in the path of God. Bahá'u'lláh seems to be telling us that we do not need to become martyrs in order to receive their reward. He appears to be clearly saying that all we have to do to receive the same reward as the martyrs is to chant this Tablet.

Bahá'u'lláh sent Aḥmad the Tablet because He wished him to teach the Bábís. Had He wished Aḥmad to become a martyr, surely He would not have promised Aḥmad the 'reward of a hundred martyrs' simply for reading the Tablet. It seems clear that Bahá'u'lláh was telling Aḥmad that he did not want him to become a martyr but to serve in another capacity.

What is so special about the Tablet of Aḥmad that Bahá'u-'lláh would promise Aḥmad the 'reward of a hundred martyrs' for reading it? It may well have been the imperative needs of the teaching work that merited this reward. Recall that at the time Bahá'u'lláh revealed this Tablet most of the followers of the Báb in Persia were unaware of the claim of Bahá'u'lláh to be the one promised by the Báb. Bahá'u'lláh chose some of His most trusted disciples to travel to Persia to teach the Bábís the truth of His Cause. Aḥmad became one of these disciples through his response to the Tablet. Bahá'u'lláh clearly valued this service so highly that He offered Aḥmad this reward for fulfilling this teaching mission. Those who taught the Bábís in Persia accomplished a tremendous feat. Through the dedicated efforts of Aḥmad and others like him, within a few years almost all the followers of the Báb accepted Bahá'u'lláh and became Bahá'ís.

Why is it that Bahá'u'lláh offers the reward of a *hundred* martyrs? The answer may be that this is the pure bounty of God. The scriptures indicate that God often rewards one act of valued service a hundredfold. For example, 'Abdu'l-Bahá cites a verse from the Qur'án:

> God says in the Qur'án: 'The example of the people of faith is like unto a field which obtains freshness and verdancy from the rain descending from the clouds, attaining to full fruition and finding the blessings of the Kingdom. There is no doubt that day by day it will grow and develop and in the end the ears of the sheaves will be laden with God's benediction bringing forth one hundred fold.'[519]

This statement has several implications. On one level it seems to tell us that the blessing of God on the people of faith is a hundredfold. On another it may also be telling us that the fruits produced by 'the people of faith', meaning the development of their spiritual characters and the fruits of their lives, will be one hundredfold. On yet another level this verse from the Qur'án implies that the efforts of the 'the people of faith' will be multiplied by God to produce the results that are a hundred times their own efforts.

The implications of this Quranic verse may also apply to Bahá'u'lláh's promise in the Tablet of Aḥmad. On one level it implies that the bounty of God will reward Aḥmad one hundredfold for his faithfulness in reciting the Tablet and arising to serve the Cause of Bahá'u'lláh. On another level it also seems to imply that the fruit of his life will be increased by a hundredfold for his faithfulness and service to the Cause of God. Bahá'u'lláh may also be implying that if Aḥmad is faithful to Him and if he arises to carry out the service Bahá'u-'lláh has asked of him, the results of his efforts in the Cause of His Lord will be magnified one hundred times.

This seems to be supported by the Báb. In one of His Tablets He tells us that the efforts of a single person of true faith are magnified by God a hundredfold:

> Say, God hath, according to that which is revealed in the Book, taken upon Himself the task of ensuring the ascendancy of any one of the followers of the Truth, over and above one hundred other souls, and the supremacy of one hundred believers over one thousand non-believers . . . [520]

The Báb's statement may also apply to Bahá'u'lláh's promise in the Tablet of Aḥmad. In this sense Bahá'u'lláh may be telling Aḥmad that if he arises to serve Him, God will inspire him and enable him to successfully teach the Bábís. It also implies that God will protect him and make him victorious over the enemies of the Cause of God.

What is the reward that Bahá'u'lláh promises Aḥmad? What is the reward of those who offer themselves as martyrs in the path of God? Those who offer their lives as a sacrifice for the Cause of God are so filled with the love of Bahá'u'lláh that their only desire is to please Him. Their goal is to be united with their Lord, so they regard this life as nothing in comparison to winning the good pleasure of God. From the Bahá'í writings we learn that a martyr's reward is reunion with His Lord. For example, 'Abdu'l-Bahá says:

> Therefore do the lovers of the Abhá Beauty wish for no other recompense but to reach that station where they may gaze upon Him in the Realm of Glory, and they walk no other

> path save over desert sands of longing for those exalted heights.[521]

It seems that the gift of Bahá'u'lláh's presence may be the priceless bounty that Bahá'u'lláh offers Aḥmad in this Tablet. The paradox, again, is that by obeying Bahá'u'lláh and returning to Persia, willingly giving up his one chance to visit Bahá'u'lláh, Aḥmad attains the presence of his Lord. Bahá'u'lláh seems to confirm this in the next verse of the Tablet:

> These favours have we bestowed upon thee as a bounty on Our part and a mercy from Our presence, that thou mayest be of those who are grateful.

What greater gift can the Manifestation of God bestow on any of us than the gift of His presence? Aḥmad, through the choices he made, seems to have clearly understood the promise Bahá'u'lláh made him. What greater demonstration of gratefulness could Aḥmad have made than giving up his opportunity to be with Bahá'u'lláh? All Aḥmad ever asked was to be in the presence of his Lord and this Bahá'u'lláh seems to have bountifully given him as a reward for his faithfulness, steadfastness and wholehearted dedication to the teaching work. On yet another level, the 'reward of a hundred martyrs' may signify that if Aḥmad arises to serve his Lord, Bahá'u'lláh will inspire him with the courage and strength of the martyrs. It may also imply that Bahá'u'lláh is promising Aḥmad that the spirit of the martyrs will be with him as he strives to fulfil his teaching mission.

Notice that Bahá'u'lláh does not restrict this reward to Aḥmad alone. In the Tablet Bahá'u'lláh unequivocally states:

> For verily, God hath ordained *for the one who chants it* the reward of a hundred martyrs and a service in both worlds. (emphasis added)

How are we to understand this promise for ourselves?

We should first note that Bahá'u'lláh does not promise us the *station* of the martyrs for chanting this Tablet. Rather He promises us the *reward* of the martyrs. This is a profound distinction. We also note that in order for us to receive this promised reward it seems that we must fulfil the conditions Bahá'u'lláh has set down for us. In this one paragraph of the Tablet He appears to have given us four conditions. First He tells us to 'learn well this Tablet'. As we have seen, this also has the implication of memorizing it. It certainly suggests that we must study the Tablet to find out for ourselves what advice Bahá'u'lláh may be giving to us. It also suggests that we use the Tablet of Aḥmad to inspire our souls in the path of service to His Cause and that we let the spirit of the Tablet flood our souls with the love of Bahá'u'lláh.

The next condition Bahá'u'lláh makes is that we do not 'withhold' ourselves from the Tablet. This suggests that He is advising us to use the Tablet on a regular basis. Taking this advice together with the first condition suggests that we study the Tablet often enough to find the guidance of Bahá'u'lláh for us and to ensure that the spirit contained within this Tablet can inspire us.

The third condition Bahá'u'lláh sets out is that we 'chant' the Tablet. The verb chant means to sing or to recite in a melodious voice. The Guardian states that the prayer should be 'recited by the believers with unquestioning faith and confidence'.[522] Recite means to speak aloud from memory.[523] Both verbs suggest that this prayer be read aloud.[524] This implies that we can help inspire ourselves and that we can more easily evoke the spirit and power of this Tablet and more fully reap its benefits by reading it aloud.

The final condition Bahá'u'lláh gives us in this paragraph is that we are 'grateful'. Each of us will have our own feelings on how we can personally demonstrate our gratefulness to Bahá'u'lláh. In general we can say that being grateful to Bahá'u'lláh suggests that we thank Him for all His bounties and favours to us, that we accept from Him all that He offers us and that we demonstrate our gratefulness to Him by arising to serve His Cause.

As we strive to fulfil these conditions in our lives, what may we possibly expect as 'the reward of a hundred martyrs and a service in both worlds'? We first note that Bahá'u'lláh's counsels to us throughout the Tablet of Aḥmad seem to be focused on service to the Cause of God. The fact that Bahá'u-'lláh links 'the reward of a hundred martyrs' with 'a service in both worlds' suggests that reward and service go hand in hand. On one level Bahá'u'lláh is telling us that when we use the Tablet of Aḥmad as He has advised us to do, He will inspire our souls in service to His Cause. Earlier in the Tablet Bahá'u'lláh advised us to 'choose the path' to our Lord. In one sense this means to choose the path of service to Him. The implication of this advice, when considered together with His promise of 'a service in both worlds', is that if we are steadfast in His Cause and we devotedly and faithfully carry out the service He has inspired us to do, Bahá'u'lláh will accept from us this service.

Bahá'u'lláh also promises us 'a service in *both* worlds' (emphasis added): if we are faithful in reciting the Tablet of Aḥmad and we devotedly arise to serve His Cause, He will reward us by enabling us to serve Him in the next world as well.[525] On another level the promised rewards of the Tablet of Aḥmad suggest that if we recite this Tablet as Bahá'u'lláh has counselled us to do and we faithfully arise to serve His Cause, He will magnify our efforts one hundred times and bountifully enrich our lives a hundredfold. On yet another level the 'reward of a hundred martyrs' may imply that as we strive to serve His Cause Bahá'u'lláh will inspire us with the spirit of the martyrs and with their strength and courage. It also suggests that He will magnify our feeble efforts a hundred times and will enrich the harvest of our efforts a hundredfold. What greater guarantee of divine assistance can He give us?

On a very personal level, Bahá'u'lláh's promise of 'the reward of a hundred martyrs' suggests that when we say the Tablet of Aḥmad with our hearts turned to Him, He will reward us with the gift of His presence. Here in the Tablet of Aḥmad Bahá'u'lláh lovingly and freely offers this greatest reward to each one of us. All He seems to ask in return is that we love Him, that we remain steadfast in His love, that we recite this Tablet regularly and that we faithfully arise to serve Him.

In conclusion we see that the rewards Bahá'u'lláh promised Aḥmad in this Tablet also seem to be available to us. Just as Aḥmad used this Tablet to comfort himself in his absence from the presence of Bahá'u'lláh, so we too can read the Tablet of Aḥmad to comfort us in our absence from Bahá'u'lláh and inspire our souls with the spirit of His love and presence. Aḥmad read this Tablet many times to find out what Bahá'u'lláh desired of him. We, too, can read and study the Tablet to seek its guidance and to inspire us to arise to serve the Cause of our Lord. Just as Aḥmad recited this Tablet to strengthen, comfort and sustain him in carrying out the teaching mission he had been given, we, too, can use this Tablet to strengthen us, comfort us and sustain us in our dedication and service to the Cause of Bahá'u'lláh.

## 73

# A Service in Both Worlds

*God hath ordained for the one who chants it,*
*the reward of a hundred martyrs*
*and a service in both worlds.*

Aḥmad's life tells us that this Tablet is, above all else, an appeal to become a teacher of the Cause of God. Bahá'u'lláh characterizes teaching as 'the most meritorious of all deeds'.[526] In another Tablet He declares, 'To assist Me is to teach My Cause.'[527] What greater service can there be than guiding a soul to the supreme Manifestation of God?

Shoghi Effendi equates the value of teaching in this day with being a martyr in the early days of the Faith:

> The Cause at present does not need martyrs who would die for the faith, but servants who desire to teach and establish the Cause throughout the world. To live to teach in the present day is like being martyred in those early days. It is the spirit that moves us that counts, not the act through which that spirit expresses itself; and that spirit is to serve the Cause of God with our heart and soul.[528]

This statement suggests that the reward for dedicating our lives to the teaching work will be the same as if we had been martyred. It is interesting to note in this regard that the Arabic of the phrase 'path to his Lord' is *sabíl*, which connotes martyrdom.

Bahá'u'lláh tells us that if we could truly appreciate the

bounty of serving the Cause of God in this promised day, we would sacrifice a myriad lives in our longing to attain this station. In one of His Tablets He counsels us:

> Please God ye may all be strengthened to carry out that which is the Will of God, and may be graciously assisted to appreciate the rank conferred upon such of His loved ones as have risen to serve Him and magnify His name. Upon them be the glory of God, the glory of all that is in the heavens and all that is on the earth, and the glory of the inmates of the most exalted Paradise, the heaven of heavens.[529]

# 74

# Be of Those Who are Grateful

*These favours have We bestowed upon thee*
*as a bounty on Our part*
*and a mercy from Our presence,*
*that thou mayest be of those who are grateful.*

The essential point of this verse seems to be that these are favours from Bahá'u'lláh. These favours are the bounty and mercy 'bestowed' by the Most Bountiful, All-Merciful Lord; we cannot earn them. He gives them to us as gifts. All we can do is demonstrate our appreciation by accepting them from Him. It is said that accepting a gift honours the gift-giver. To humbly turn to Bahá'u'lláh and beseech His grace and bounty and to be thankful to Him for all His gifts and favours is a demonstration of gratitude. This is what He asks of us. 'Abdu'l-Bahá says, 'Try with all your hearts to be willing channels for God's Bounty.'[530]

God loves every human being and desires to shower His blessings on every soul. The Long Obligatory Prayer says:

> Thou seest, O my Lord, this wretched creature knocking at the door of Thy grace, and this evanescent soul seeking the river of everlasting life from the hands of Thy bounty.[531]

He desires to instil in us an attitude such that we will constantly knock at the door of His grace and always seek assistance from the hands of His bounty. His words are a reflection of the words of Christ, who exhorted us to:

> Ask, and it shall be given you; seek, and ye shall find; knock, and it shall be opened unto you: For every one that asketh receiveth; and he that seeketh findeth; and to him that knocketh it shall be opened.[532]

God has created us to be dependent upon Him. If we truly recognize and appreciate this relationship, we will always turn to Him and ask Him for His help and assistance. What Bahá'u-'lláh asks us to do is to open our hearts and turn to Him in love, to recite this prayer with sincerity and to graciously accept all the bounties He desires to bestow on us. In one of His prayers He says:

> For the poor can find no refuge unless he knocketh at the door of Thy wealth, and the outcast can find no peace until he be admitted to the court of Thy favour.[533]

We can best demonstrate the sincerity of our love for Him and our gratitude for His endless bounties by striving to obey His laws and teachings and by dedicating our lives to the service of His sacred Cause. In one of His talks, 'Abdu'l-Bahá advises us:

> In thanksgiving for [the bestowals and favours of God] ye must act in accordance with the teachings of Bahá'u'lláh. Ye must read the Tablets . . . and act according to them. This is real thanksgiving, to live in accord with these utterances.[534]

And in one of His Tablets He counsels us:

> The time hath come when, as a thank-offering for this bestowal, ye should grow in faith and constancy as day followeth day, and should draw ever nearer to the Lord, your God, becoming magnetized to such a degree, and so aflame, that your holy melodies in praise of the Beloved will reach upward to the Company on high; and that each one of you,

even as a nightingale in this rose garden of God, will glorify the Lord of Hosts, and become the teacher of all who dwell on earth.[535]

## 75

# Steps in Spiritual Problem-Solving

*By God! Should one who is in affliction or grief*
*read this Tablet with absolute sincerity,*
*God will dispel his sadness,*
*solve his difficulties*
*and remove his afflictions.*

This verse, with its promise of divine assistance, may be one of the best known and most appealing sections of the Tablet of Aḥmad. Of all the bounties Bahá'u'lláh has placed within this Tablet, His promise of unfailing help and assistance is the bounty most often remembered by the friends. How many of us have been drawn to the Tablet of Aḥmad in times of difficulties or in a serious crisis or emergency by this promise of divine assistance? How many personal accounts attest to the power of this Tablet to bring aid and relief? This promise draws us to the Tablet of Aḥmad like a magnet and it is a sign of the 'special potency and significance' with which Bahá'u'lláh has endowed it.

Learning to cope with and overcome tests and difficulties is one of the most profound learning experiences of human life. Most of us experience 'tests' which are given to us as part of our school work or as part of job training and employment advancement. These tests are generally predictable and we usually have the opportunity to prepare for them. In contrast, difficulties and ordeals of daily living are unpredictable. We cannot study in preparation for an unknown test. Such tests catch us off guard and unprepared. This is their essential nature. The only way we learn to cope with and overcome these tests is to experience them and live through them, drawing on the power of divine assistance. Our experience also indicates that once we have successfully overcome a particular situation the next set of tests we face is usually different and requires us to go through a new learning process. We might even call this God's school of life training! Is there a reason for the tests we experience? Are there any tools we can use to help us deal with and overcome them?

Let us first consider why we experience so many tests and difficulties. Then we will examine the steps that Bahá'u'lláh has given us in the phrase 'God will dispel his sadness, solve his difficulties and remove his afflictions'. Understanding these steps may help us deal more effectively and productively with the tests we experience.

Why, we may often wonder, are we forced to endure hardships and ordeals? 'Abdu'l-Bahá explains that if we did not experience such tests and difficulties, we would not progress. He explains that God sends us trials and ordeals for our own training and perfecting:

> The mind and spirit of man advance when he is tried by suffering. The more the ground is ploughed the better the seed will grow, the better the harvest will be. Just as the plough furrows the earth deeply, purifying it of weeds and thistles, so suffering and tribulation free man from the petty affairs of this worldly life until he arrives at a state of complete detachment. His attitude in this world will be that of divine happiness. Man is, so to speak, unripe: the heat of the fire of suffering will mature him.[536]

Notice that 'Abdu'l-Bahá says that the purpose of such tests and difficulties is to help us become completely detached from the 'petty affairs' of this world and to enable us to attain 'divine happiness'. Of course, when we are struggling through an excruciating ordeal it is hard to imagine how the suffering we are experiencing is supposed to help us. However, this is God's training for us. Quite mysteriously and to our own surprise, we may find that once we have endured an ordeal we can appreciate and value the experience it gives us. This suggests that in the middle of such struggles we should not lose sight of the fact that God is helping us to become detached and to feel divine happiness.

In the Tablet of Aḥmad Bahá'u'lláh assures us that 'God will dispel his sadness, solve his difficulties and remove his afflictions'. In this verse He gives us three specific promises of divine assistance. The order and sequence of these three promises may be particularly significant. He may be suggesting that God leads us through a spiritual process, a series of steps in helping us overcome problems. If this is so, then He says the initial step is for God to help us *dispel* our sadness. Next He will help us *solve* our difficulties and finally He will assist us to *remove* our afflictions. Bahá'u'lláh appears to be suggesting a specific approach to spiritual problem-solving.

This passage suggests that Bahá'u'lláh is telling us that we must first gain control over our own emotions and mental state. This frees us to figure out what the real problem is and take appropriate action.

In practical terms, how can we overcome a difficult situation if we are sad, down-hearted and in a negative frame of mind? It is very difficult for us to be healed or helped if we feel that what has happened to us is the worst thing in the world or if our attitude is that the whole world has conspired against us. Such emotions and attitudes make it extremely difficult, if not impossible, for us to perceive what needs to be done and to have the strength to take action and make necessary changes in our lives. We must free ourselves from the grip of negative attitudes which trap us in the situation and emotions which weigh us down. We find this clearly spelled out by 'Abdu'l-Bahá in the prayer He has given us for these situations:

> O God! Refresh and gladden my spirit. Purify my heart. Illumine my powers. I lay all my affairs in Thy hand. Thou art my Guide and my Refuge. I will no longer be sorrowful and grieved; I will be a happy and joyful being. O God! I will no longer be full of anxiety, nor will I let trouble harass me. I will not dwell on the unpleasant things of life.
>
> O God! Thou art more friend to me than I am to myself. I dedicate myself to Thee, O Lord.[337]

In the Tablet of Aḥmad, Bahá'u'lláh promises us that when we are in distress God will help *dispel* our sadness. To dispel something means to disperse or scatter it. When this happens, generally something else comes to take its place. In His prayer 'Abdu'l-Bahá says, 'I will no longer be sorrowful and grieved; I will be a happy and joyful being.' This suggests that we have the power to choose to replace sadness with joy and happiness and peace of heart. We must strive to be joyous in our relationship with God. This usually requires prayer and it seems that the Tablet of Aḥmad is one meant to be used for this purpose.

Becoming happy and light of heart frees us emotionally and mentally. This enables us to find the strength to examine dispassionately the obstacles confronting us and to assess all possibilities with an open mind. All things happen for a reason and it is up to each of us to figure out what lesson we are being given. The real problem may be very different from the one we first imagined.

The next step in this problem-solving process, Bahá'u'lláh seems to be telling us, is for God to help us *solve* our difficulties. Some difficulties can only be solved if we are willing to adopt alternative solutions and make decisions that we otherwise would not have considered. Reaching such decisions is a momentous step and requires strength and courage. Prayer is essential and we may infer that Bahá'u'lláh is telling us that using the Tablet of Aḥmad will give us the inner strength we need.

Taking positive action often produces a feeling of being freed from a hopeless problem. This is the case even if the outward situation has not changed and illustrates an important step in solving difficulties, which is to overcome the feeling of being trapped. The *internal* change that we must go through in coming to grips with a serious problem enables us to successfully overcome the situation. The real tests we face are not the outward circumstances confronting us but the inner challenges to the way we think about ourselves and how we respond to our problems. Once this internal change has taken place, the affliction is removed, no matter what the outward circumstances may be.

Bahá'u'lláh says that God never tests any soul beyond its capacity.[538] Yet how often do we feel stretched to the limit before help arrives! Surely God sees in each one of us an inner strength that we fail to recognize in ourselves. There is a sweetness on the other side of suffering but it is not easy to reach this distant shore. Once we have stood upon these sands and felt the breeze of gladness blowing from our own hearts, we will forever be assured of God's unfailing aid and favours.

In the Tablet of Aḥmad, Bahá'u'lláh says, 'Be thou assured in thyself'. On one level He may be counselling us to be assured of His love, mercy and assistance to us. It is this feeling of confidence and assurance which may be our reward for enduring steadfastly through the storms of tests. The inner strength we gain and the inner assurance we feel in Bahá'u-'lláh's love are the foundation of that feeling of divine happiness promised to us by 'Abdu'l-Bahá.

# 76

# Read This Tablet with Absolute Sincerity

*By God! Should one who is in affliction or grief*
*read this Tablet with absolute sincerity,*
*God will dispel his sadness,*
*solve his difficulties*
*and remove his afflictions.*

What is the significance of Bahá'u'lláh's injunction to 'read this Tablet with absolute sincerity'?[539] Is Bahá'u'lláh issuing us an all-or-nothing ultimatum, meaning that if we are not *absolutely* sincere we will not receive any benefit or any assistance from reading this precious Tablet? Or is Bahá'u'lláh seeking to guide us to a deeper understanding of profound spiritual significance?

Let us examine the relationship between sincerity and the promise of divine assistance. Sincerity is the quality of being sincere. 'Sincere' is defined as being without pretence or hypocrisy, to be the same in reality as in appearance. To be sincere means to be real, to be genuine, to be honest and to be truthful. Sincerity, then, is genuineness. Sincerity is truthfulness in all aspects of life. It is the virtue of being honest in mind and intention. *Absolute* sincerity implies that we become more sincere than we are at present. Since sincerity is a spiritual attribute, its development requires effort, practice and patience with ourselves. Because sincerity is a quality that we are always in the process of developing, we may infer that the clause about absolute sincerity in the Tablet of Aḥmad is not an all-or-nothing, pass-or-fail test of whether we qualify to receive assistance from Bahá'u'lláh in our times of need. He will not forget us or turn away from us. It is simply not in the nature of a Manifestation of God to turn His back on any human being and it is contradictory to everything in the writings of Bahá'u'lláh to think that He would deny our plea for help simply because we do not possess 'absolute' sincerity. Emphasizing this point, Hand of the Cause of God William Sears remarked that if we were only one per cent sincere, wouldn't it be wonderful if God solved even one per cent of our difficulties and removed one per cent of our afflictions![540]

In the context of the verse in the Tablet of Aḥmad to 'read this Tablet with absolute sincerity', absolute sincerity may have special significance for our relationship with Bahá'u'lláh. Being absolutely sincere with Bahá'u'lláh suggests that we must practise confiding in Him. It suggests that we must also practise trusting and relying more completely on Bahá'u'lláh in our daily lives.

In another sense it may be that 'absolute sincerity' is synonymous with absolute need. When we are faced with a crisis that truly requires quick relief, we may cry out to Bahá'u'lláh from the depth of our being for His help. In that moment of prayer, our desperate need may cause us to become absolutely sincere in our request for assistance. Having truly met Bahá'u'lláh's criterion in the Tablet of Aḥmad, we may find that we receive a swift answer to our cry for help.

It may also be significant that Bahá'u'lláh uses the term 'absolute' in the Seven Valleys when He describes the final stage of the lover's journey back to God. He calls this stage the 'Valley of true poverty and absolute nothingness':

> This station is the dying from self and the living in God, the being poor in self and rich in the Desired One.[541]

This suggests that the word 'absolute' in the phrase 'absolute sincerity' refers to the spiritual life of our soul. By contrast, everything in the material world is relative; nothing on this earthly plane can be characterized as absolute. Only the attributes of God are absolute. Qualities which are described in absolute terms must therefore refer to the spiritual worlds of God. Absolute sincerity may thus refer to the spiritual realm of our life in God. Becoming absolutely sincere may indicate an essential requirement for us to turn – genuinely, completely and wholeheartedly – to Bahá'u'lláh. It may be telling us not to neglect our inner life, to treasure our connection with God and nurture this connection at all times.

In Bahá'u'lláh's discussion of the Valley of true poverty and absolute nothingness, He points out that each season is given a special bounty and virtue. In the following passage Bahá'u-'lláh alludes to the divine springtime symbolizing His own Manifestation; it may also have relevance to the sufferings we experience:

> O My friend, listen with heart and soul to the songs of the spirit, and treasure them as thine own eyes. For the heavenly wisdoms, like the clouds of spring, will not rain down on the earth of men's hearts forever; and though the grace of the All-Bounteous One is never stilled and never ceasing, yet to each time and era a portion is allotted and a bounty set apart, this in a given measure . . . The cloud of the Loved One's mercy raineth only on the garden of the spirit, and bestoweth this bounty only in the season of spring.[542]

In one of His Tablets 'Abdu'l-Bahá explains how the storms of winter and spring bring the rich harvests of the summer. He likens these physical storms to the difficulties and trials we experience in our lives:

> O ye beloved of God! When the winds blow severely, rains fall fiercely, the lightning flashes, the thunder roars, the bolt

> descends and storms of trial become severe, grieve not; for after this storm, verily, the divine spring will arrive, the hills and fields will become verdant, the expanses of grain will joyfully wave, the earth will become covered with blossoms, the trees will be clothed with green garments and adorned with blossoms and fruits. Thus blessings become manifest in all countries. These favours are results of those storms and hurricanes.[543]

'The cloud of the Loved One's mercy' which 'bestoweth this bounty only in the season of spring' may also allude to the special mercy of God which is showered on us during our times of tests and ordeals. It is in this 'season', the times when we are faced with excruciating trials and difficulties, when we feel anguish and even desperation, that we may truly open ourselves to God's love and assistance. It is at such times that we have the greatest potential for our own spiritual growth and development. So it may be that these afflictions are the 'springtimes' of God's most tender favours and mercies to us.

We may expect, therefore, that through the wisdom and favours of God, He knows when it is in our best interest to alleviate and remove our suffering and difficulties quickly. He also knows when it is not in our best interest to do so. We may expect, therefore, that when we use the Tablet of Aḥmad to pray for God's assistance in our times of need, sometimes we may be relieved from our afflictions quickly and sometimes we may not. We may be certain that He will use these occasions to purify us and to help us to become more sincere and more reliant on Him. This will enable us to draw closer to Him, to trust Him more completely and to feel near to Him at all times.

'Abdu'l-Bahá tells us that when life is going well for us and we have no problems, we tend to forget God. But when we experience tests and difficulties, He says, we remember God and turn to Him for help and comfort:

> While a man is happy he may forget his God; but when grief comes and sorrows overwhelm him, then will he remember his Father who is in Heaven, and who is able to deliver him from his humiliations.[544]

As we have seen, in the Hidden Words, Bahá'u'lláh tells us that 'the healer of all thine ills is remembrance of Me'.[545] Thus for us to receive the assistance promised in the verse 'God will dispel his sadness, solve his difficulties and remove his afflictions', it is first necessary for us to turn wholeheartedly to Bahá'u'lláh. Because tests are given to us for our own perfecting, it is the sincerity of this relationship which is tested and purified by the ordeals we experience. It is through these divinely sent trials and afflictions that our relationship with Bahá'u'lláh is strengthened and we are taught how to 'Make My love thy treasure and cherish it even as thy very sight and life'.[546]

We may conclude that when we use the Tablet of Aḥmad to pray for divine assistance in our times of need, the special bounties and favours of God are showered upon us. Although we may not be aware of His assistance, in spite of our feelings of inadequacy and unworthiness, God is with us. He will use the particular situation we find ourselves in to teach us to more fully rely upon Him so that we may reap the reward of His boundless love and experience the bounty of 'the Presence of the Generous One'. It is through this divine, sacred process, which is certainly an outpouring of His grace and mercy to us, that 'God will dispel his sadness, solve his difficulties, and remove his afflictions'.

## 77

# The Promise of Divine Assistance

*By God! Should one who is in affliction or grief*
*read this Tablet with absolute sincerity,*
*God will dispel his sadness,*
*solve his difficulties*
*and remove his afflictions.*

The promise of divine assistance in the Tablet of Aḥmad makes it a favourite prayer for many of us when we are having difficulties. Our experience has shown that when we use the Tablet of Aḥmad to ask for help with our trials and ordeals, the responses we receive vary greatly. Sometimes we may even feel that we have not received any response at all to our request for help. Why is this so? Let us consider what appear to be the spiritual principles at work in these situations.

The promise of divine assistance in the Tablet of Aḥmad is by no means limited to emergencies or severe crises. We often read the Tablet to reach out to Bahá'u'lláh and ask for His help in general. Most of the times we use the Tablet of Aḥmad we are not having a life-or-death crisis that requires immediate assistance. We must realize that there is a significant difference between those crises that require quick relief and those situations in which we ardently want an immediate solution to our problems. The rapidity of the response we receive to our prayer seems to depend on the severity and nature of the crisis we are facing. It is often on those very occasions when we feel that our needs are so great that we desperately want a quick solution that the relief we seek is not swiftly forthcoming. At such times it is natural for us to have doubts. We may doubt whether we are being sincere in reciting the Tablet. We may doubt whether we are 'good enough' Bahá'ís to 'merit' receiving assistance. We may even wonder what is wrong with us that Bahá'u'lláh has not, apparently, responded to our pleas for help.

When we find ourselves in such situations, there appear to be several principles at work. The first is that Bahá'u'lláh is surely helping us, even though we may not be aware of the assistance He is providing. Bahá'u'lláh Himself assures us of this:

> No man that seeketh Us will We ever disappoint, neither shall he that hath set his face towards Us be denied access unto Our court.[547]

The second principle of assistance concerns Bahá'u'lláh's promise that 'God will dispel his sadness'. Notice that this is the first of three specific promises. The fact that dispelling our sadness precedes the promises of solving our difficulties and removing our afflictions strongly suggests that dispelling sadness may be a precondition for solving difficulties and removing afflictions. If this is so, it implies that it is our spiritual attitude towards the test we are going through that is the major factor in resolving the situation. However, if we are experiencing severe stress or agony because of the test we are dealing with, we may not be at all concerned with our own attitudes. Our major concern may simply be that God relieves us from the ordeal. So when the problem does not go away, we wonder what is wrong. It may be that in spite of ourselves God is assisting us, as promised, to dispel our sadness and improve our own attitudes about the situation. He may be using the ordeal to help us become more detached from the experience and more accepting of His will for us. In such circumstances, it is not until we give up our insistence on how we 'expect' to be helped that the situation can change.

As hard as we try not to do so, it is surprising how often we find ourselves attempting to 'make a deal' with God. The fact that Bahá'u'lláh sometimes refers to God as the Ever-Abiding may help us understand that God can always out-wait us! In the Hidden Words Bahá'u'lláh explains:

> O Son of Man! Thou dost wish for gold and I desire thy freedom from it. Thou thinkest thyself rich in its possession, and I recognize thy wealth in thy sanctity therefrom. By My life! This is My knowledge, and that is thy fancy; how can My way accord with thine?[548]

The word 'gold' often symbolizes material riches and material well-being. Let us generalize this to include anything material which we feel makes us rich or provides for our well-being when we possess it. In this sense we could even say that our well-being is greatly enhanced when our lives are free from difficulties and ordeals. If we allow ourselves this broader meaning of the term 'gold' then we may apply this Hidden Word to the tests we experience. From this point of view, Bahá'u'lláh may be indicating that it is our attachment to our desire to be free from difficult tests that stands in the way of His help. He says, 'Thou thinkest thyself rich in its possession, and I recognize thy wealth in thy sanctity therefrom.' This seems to say that it is not the 'gold' itself – not freedom from tests and difficulties – that is the problem. Rather, it is our desperate longing to be free from ordeals, our narrow-minded focus and attachment to this desire that prevents us from considering effective and productive means of dealing with the problem. It is this attachment that conflicts with His desire for us. We may infer that as we change our own attitudes and become detached from our preoccupation to be free of the ordeal we are experiencing that we will fulfil the first condition of dispelling our own sadness. This, in turn, opens the door to solve difficulties and remove afflictions.

This leads us to another fundamental principle of assistance with difficulties and ordeals. It may often be that the test itself is a gift from God. More often than not this is the key to understanding problems and predicaments. While we want only to be rid of such a test and free from its agonizing hold on us, God desires to help us grow spiritually stronger through the test itself. In one of His talks 'Abdu'l-Bahá explains:

> Tests are benefits from God, for which we should thank Him. Grief and sorrow do not come to us by chance, they are sent to us by the Divine Mercy for our own perfecting . . .
>
> Men who suffer not, attain no perfection. The plant most pruned by the gardeners is that one which, when the summer comes, will have the most beautiful blossoms and the most abundant fruit.
>
> The labourer cuts up the earth with his plough, and from that earth comes the rich and plentiful harvest. The more a man is chastened, the greater is the harvest of spiritual virtues shown forth by him. A soldier is no good General until he has been in the front of the fiercest battle and has received the deepest wounds.[549]

If the difficulty we are experiencing is a benefit and mercy from God, then this may be one reason why we sometimes do not receive quick relief in response to our prayers. If the test is a gift from God then we may be asking God to remove the very test He has given us as a bounty on His part. Then how should we respond to such situations? The first step in this process is recognizing that we are being tested. We may say that any difficult situation can be considered a personal test. If we feel that we are being tested, instead of asking God to remove the test, we can choose to pray for help in dealing effectively with the problem and benefiting from it.

Furthermore, if the test is God's gift to us, then it is our attitude towards the test that will determine its benefit. If we let ourselves think that we are victims of such a test, we may react by asking God, 'Why me?' But 'Why me?' is never the question to ask. The only true answer to 'Why me?' is that God loves us. If we react to a test as if it were the worst thing that had ever happened to us, then it is likely its effect on our lives will be devastating. But if we rise above that attitude and respond to the test as if it were the best thing that had ever happened to us, then it will truly become so. As a result of such a positive outlook we will grow spiritually stronger and gain confidence. By our own attitudes these tests become wonderful gifts.

As we have seen, in the Hidden Words Bahá'u'lláh tells us:

> O Son of Man! My calamity is My providence, outwardly it is fire and vengeance, but inwardly it is light and mercy. Hasten thereunto that thou mayest become an eternal light and an immortal spirit. This is My command unto thee, do thou observe it.[550]

Bahá'u'lláh tells us in no uncertain terms that if we only look at the outward circumstances of tests, we will always feel that they are but 'fire and vengeance' falling on us. However, He says that if we look at the inner significance of such tests we will see that they are truly 'light and mercy'. Notice that He asserts that this is His command to us and that we must observe it. He appears to be telling us that when we experience tests He wants us to find the inner lessons and bounties in them. It is this attitude, we may infer, that will enable us to conquer the test and benefit from it.

How do we do this? The first step is to accept that the situation is actually a test. Accepting the test for what it is means that we stop battling against it. This does not mean that we give up striving to solve the problem. There is a subtle yet profound difference here. If we are battling a test, we are constantly wasting our own time and energy complaining about being tested. We may even feel frustrated or angry at God for putting us into such a situation. Yet it is not wrong to feel this way. We often use anger and other emotions to hide or cover an underlying issue. So if we experience such feelings it simply means that Bahá'u'lláh has led us to confront some important personal issues. This suggests that if we find ourselves in these circumstances we need to sit down and have a heart-to-heart talk with Bahá'u'lláh and ask Him to help us resolve the issues we may be struggling with. In these situations, getting us to work on resolving these underlying issues may be the inner lesson and the 'light and mercy' of such a test.

This is not an easy lesson to learn, especially when the tests become more difficult. Experience is the best teacher in such matters. When we have to deal with an affliction or difficulty that will not go away, we may eventually learn to become detached from the situation, to let go of the problem and give it up to God. As part of the process of learning how to do this we are faced with having to become more reliant on Bahá'u-'lláh. We also have to develop greater trust in Bahá'u'lláh and what He is leading us through. Achieving this spiritual state of mind may also be the inner lesson and bounty of such a test and another reason why God may not relieve us from its burden immediately. He does not want to deprive us of achieving this victory.

We find examples of this attitude towards difficulties in the Bahá'í prayers. For instance we read:

> He is the Compassionate, the All-Bountiful!
>
> O God, my God! Thou seest me, Thou knowest me; Thou art my Haven and my Refuge. None have I sought nor any will I seek save Thee; no path have I trodden nor any will I tread but the path of Thy love. In the darksome night of despair, my eye turneth expectant and full of hope to the morn of Thy boundless favour and at the hour of dawn my drooping soul is refreshed and strengthened in remembrance of Thy beauty and perfection.[551]

By invoking an image of living through a long, dark night, waiting for the break of day, 'Abdu'l-Bahá seems to be telling us that we must develop patience and reliance if we are to endure through our own nights of despair to reach the promised dawn of relief. There are times when we pray for relief from an agonizing situation and apparently do not receive any help. In such circumstances we may pray and pray, may become more and more desperate and reach the point where we feel we cannot bear any more. Just when we are ready to give up altogether, assistance arrives and we experience relief from the torment. Such experiences carry profound, mysterious lessons for us. How slowly the night passes and how long the darkness seems to last! It may be that in these moments, when the dawning light of divine assistance floods our drooping souls, that we develop greater trust and reliance on God. Having lived through our own 'darksome night of despair' to the morning light of divine assistance, the next time we experience such a situation we can have more faith and confidence that we will make it through the night to the promised dawn. Having lived through it ourselves, we are more able to offer comfort and compassion to others who are going through their own ordeals.

Notice how well the analogy of the darkness of night and the break of day describes the spiritual process we often experience. Indeed, it is an old adage that the night is darkest just before the dawn. Just as in the physical world every night is followed by the light of a new day, so too is the darkness of our nights of despair followed by the spiritual light of divine mercy and the flood of God's grace.

When we find ourselves in difficult situations and we pray for assistance, we bring with us certain expectations and desires. These can easily become obstacles and barriers to solving difficulties and removing afflictions. Looking at a problem in only one way prevents us from seeing other options and accepting an alternative solution. God has to prepare us so that we are ready to accept His will for us. Since He desires only the best for us, when we pray and ask Him to help us we may, in effect, be asking Him to purify us so that His grace and loving kindness can reach us. In this sense it may be that

God tests the sincerity of our prayer to see if we are willing to accept His remedy. This, too, may be another reason why we sometimes do not experience immediate relief from ordeals. This testing and purifying fire that we go through is the crucible of His love. It seems to be one of the spiritual processes whereby He recreates us. Bahá'u'lláh alludes to this crucible in one of His prayers:

> The companions of all who adore Thee are the tears they shed, and the comforters of such as seek Thee are the groans they utter, and the food of them who haste to meet Thee is the fragments of their broken hearts.[552]

There are many other passages in the writings that allude to this divine process. For example:

> O Son of Man! If thou lovest Me, turn away from thyself; and if thou seekest My pleasure, regard not thine own; that thou mayest die in Me and I may eternally live in thee.[553]

We do not easily give up our own notions and expectations. How can we die to our own opinions and self-imposed limitations? What personal experiences must we have so that we might confront these barriers and overcome them? The Bahá'í writings suggest that many of us must endure and grow through difficulties and ordeals, especially if we desire to draw closer to Bahá'u'lláh:

> O Thou Whose tests are a healing medicine to such as are nigh unto Thee . . .[554]

It is through the fire of the ordeals we experience that we are taught how to become detached from our difficulties and problems. Through this purifying fire we become more sincere in our devotion to God and resigned to His will. Through this fire He prepares us to accept His remedy. Through the particular circumstances of the ordeals we have to endure we are led to scale the otherwise insurmountable walls of the limitations we impose on ourselves and to consider new possibilities for our lives. Through this providential process He makes us worthy of His love and He recreates us. Thus we may say that Bahá'u'lláh has given us the Tablet of Aḥmad with its promise of divine assistance so that we may call upon Him for help in our struggles and He may empower us to achieve victory over ourselves.

# 78

# The Merciful, the Compassionate

*Verily,*
*He is the Merciful,*
*the Compassionate.*

Mercy is showing kindness in excess of that which may be expected by fairness. Compassion is sorrow for the distress or misfortunes of another human being, with the desire to help. Compassion derives from two root words, one meaning 'to suffer with' and the other meaning 'sympathy'. It is significant that immediately following His promise that 'God will dispel his sadness, solve his difficulties and remove his afflictions' Bahá'u'lláh asserts that 'He is the Merciful, the Compassionate'. Bahá'u'lláh is the one we can trust to be full of mercy, who always shows us infinitely greater kindness than we can reasonably expect by our own actions. He is the one who is full of compassion, sympathizing with us in our distress and hardships, suffering with us and ever ready to help. In one of His Tablets He says:

> If tribulation touch thee for My sake, call thou to mind My ills and troubles, and remember My banishment and imprisonment.[555]

He reminds us that whatever ordeals we may face, we are not alone. He has been there before us and has borne the misfortunes of the world for our sake. In this Tablet He promises divine assistance so that we may be assured that we can succeed in our struggles. With tenderness and love He invites us to turn to Him for succor and comfort.

# 79

# The Lord of All the Worlds

*Praise be to God,*
*the Lord of all the worlds.*

In chapter 6 above we discussed how Bahá'u'lláh fulfils the promise of the appearance of the 'King of the day of reckoning' mentioned in the fourth verse of the opening súrih of the Qur'án. There is a well-known tradition in Islam from Imám 'Alí that the Qur'án contains the essence of all the holy scriptures and the essence of the Qur'án is contained in the first súrih, the essence of the first súrih is contained in the first verse, the essence of the first verse is contained in the first word and the essence of the first word is contained in the first letter.[556]

In Arabic the first verse of the Qur'án is '*Bismi'lláh ar-raḥmán ar-raḥím*', which translates as 'In the name of God, the Compassionate, the Merciful'. Hand of the Cause of God Zikrullah Khadem pointed out that the opening word, '*Bismi'lláh*' begins with the letter 'B'. He explained that in the traditions of Islam there are specific statements by the Imáms that '"*El-Bá Bahá'u'lláh*" (B means Bahá'u'lláh)'.[557]

If the essence of the Qur'án is contained within the letter 'B', might there be a prophetic significance to the verses of the first chapter? The opening súrih of the Qur'án is called the 'Mother of the Book'. As we have seen, its first four lines are:

> In the Name of God, the Compassionate, the Merciful.
> Praise be to God, Lord of the worlds!
> The compassionate, the merciful!
> King of the day of reckoning![558]

The Báb declared:

> The Lord of the Day of Reckoning will be manifested at the end of Váḥid (19) and the beginning of eighty (1280 A.H.).[559]

Mr Khadem discussed this prophecy of the Báb.[560] Váḥid has a numerical value of 19. 'The end of Váḥid' means 19 years after the declaration of the Báb in 1844, which is the year 1863. 1863 is also the beginning of the Islamic year 80, meaning 1280 AH. Bahá'u'lláh's declaration of His divine mission took place in the Garden of Riḍván in late April 1863. His declaration was the fulfilment of this prophecy of the Báb and demonstrates that the verse from the opening chapter of the Qur'án, 'King of the day of reckoning', was a prophetic allusion to His advent. Bahá'u'lláh confirms this in one of His Tablets:

> Unto this beareth witness He Who under all conditions proclaimeth, 'Verily He is God, the sovereign Ruler of the Day of Reckoning and the Lord of the mighty Throne.'[561]

If we set the opening phrase of the Tablet of Aḥmad, 'He is the King', against the final verses of the Tablet, we find a remarkable similarity between these verses and the opening verses of the Qur'án:

> *Tablet of Aḥmad*
>
> He is the King . . .
> Verily, He is the Merciful, the Compassionate. Praise be to God, the Lord of all the worlds.

*Qur'án*

In the Name of God, the Compassionate, the Merciful.
Praise be to God, Lord of the worlds!
The compassionate, the merciful!
King of the day of reckoning!

It appears that in concluding His Tablet, Bahá'u'lláh is telling us that He is the King of the day of reckoning promised by Muḥammad and by the Báb. It is one more proof that He is the Promised One of all ages, He whose advent was foretold by all the Messengers of the past.

Lift up thy voice and say: All praise be to Thee, O Thou, the Desire of every understanding heart![562]

# 80

# Epilogue: O Aḥmad!

A particular feature of this Tablet is its call to Aḥmad. 'Aḥmad' derives from the Arabic verb 'to praise', 'to exalt'[563] and is translated 'most praiseworthy'. So when Bahá'u'lláh calls out 'O Aḥmad!' He is addressing Aḥmad of Yazd, for whom the Tablet was revealed, and, at the same time, each one of us.

'O Aḥmad' may be understood as an appeal to the person reading the Tablet, meaning 'O thou who desires to be most praiseworthy in the sight of God'. For example, when Bahá'u-'lláh says 'O Aḥmad! Bear thou witness that verily He is God', He may be telling us that if we desire to be most praiseworthy in the sight of God, then *we* must bear witness in our own lives to the fact that 'there is no God but Him'. Similarly, when He calls out 'O Aḥmad! Forget not My bounties while I am absent', He may be telling us that if we truly want to be most praiseworthy in His sight, then we must never forget how much He loves us and cares for us. We must also never forget His bounties to us and how He is ever ready and willing to pour His grace upon us. And finally, when He counsels 'Learn well this Tablet, O Aḥmad', He may be counselling each one of us to read and study this Tablet regularly so that we, too, like Aḥmad before us, may find out what our Lord desires of us.

In a very real sense each one of us is an Aḥmad. Aḥmad was devoted to Bahá'u'lláh and earnestly desired to serve Him. Bahá'u'lláh wrote to Aḥmad that the mission God had given Him was to suffer imprisonment and exile and to take on the sufferings of the world in order to transform humankind. He urged Aḥmad to 'choose the path to his Lord'. From this

Tablet Aḥmad learned that Bahá'u'lláh desired him to teach the Bábís, to be 'a flame of fire to My enemies and a river of life eternal to My loved ones'.

We do not live in the time of Bahá'u'lláh and so we cannot render service to Him in exactly the same way that Aḥmad did. But the message of the Tablet of Aḥmad is universal and its appeal is for all time. Bahá'u'lláh calls upon each one of us to 'choose the path' to our Lord. He urges us to find out what service He desires of us and to arise and fulfil in our own lives, to the best of our ability, this task.

There will always be teaching needs of the Cause of God. Each of us is called upon to be 'a flame of fire' to His enemies and 'a river of life eternal' to His loved ones and not to be 'of those who doubt'. Do not doubt that He is addressing this Tablet to us. Do not doubt that He is calling us to choose to arise and serve Him. And do not doubt that as we arise in service, His bounties will be poured out upon us, that we can always call upon Him for help and assistance in our lives and that He will be there for us.

Every plan given to the Bahá'ís of the world by the Universal House of Justice has its particular goals. It is 'the message which hath been revealed by God' for the specific needs of the world at the time in which it is given. Each of us can arise and render service to Bahá'u'lláh by assisting in the fulfilment of the particular goals of the current plan.

This is the mission Bahá'u'lláh has given us. We, like Aḥmad before us, can demonstrate our devotion and love for Bahá'u'lláh by arising to serve the Universal House of Justice. There will always be needs of the Cause of God to be met. There will always be services to render. As in the time of Bahá'u'lláh, there will always be a need for believers who, like Aḥmad, will arise with devotion and dedication.

We all live in the shadow of Aḥmad and the other early disciples and apostles of the Báb and Bahá'u'lláh. Because Aḥmad arose with absolute sincerity, devotion and dedication to fulfil the wishes of his Lord, he has released the power of this sacred Tablet for each one of us.

As we strive in our own lives, to the best of our ability and capacity, to follow Aḥmad's example, we too reap the immeasurable benefits and bounties Bahá'u'lláh has promised in the Tablet of Aḥmad and we release more of its healing power to flow out to all humankind.

# Bibliography

'Abdu'l-Bahá. *The Promulgation of Universal Peace*. Wilmette, Ill.: Bahá'í Publishing Trust, 1982.
— *Selections from the Writings of 'Abdu'l-Bahá*. Haifa: Bahá'í World Centre, 1978.
— *Some Answered Questions*. Wilmette, Ill.: Bahá'í Publishing Trust, 1981.
— *Tablets of Abdul-Baha Abbas*. New York: Bahá'í Publishing Committee; vol. 1, 1930; vol. 2, 1940; vol. 3, 1930.
— *The Will and Testament of 'Abdu'l-Bahá*. Wilmette, Ill.: Bahá'í Publishing Trust, 1971.
*The American Bahá'í*, vol. 23, no. 14, 27 September 1992.
The Báb. *Selections from the Writings of the Báb*. Haifa: Bahá'í World Centre, 1976.
*Bahá'í Prayers: A Selection of Prayers revealed by Bahá'u'lláh, the Báb and 'Abdu'l-Bahá*. Wilmette, Ill.: Bahá'í Publishing Trust, 1991.
*Bahá'í World Faith*. Wilmette, Ill.: Bahá'í Publishing Trust, 2nd edn. 1976.
Bahá'u'lláh. *Epistle to the Son of the Wolf*. Wilmette, Ill.: Bahá'í Publishing Trust, 1988.
— *Gleanings from the Writings of Bahá'u'lláh*. Wilmette, Ill.: Bahá'í Publishing Trust, 1983.
— *The Hidden Words*. Wilmette, Ill.: Bahá'í Publishing Trust, 1990.
— *The Kitáb-i-Aqdas*. Haifa: Bahá'í World Centre, 1992.
— *Kitáb-i-Íqán*. Wilmette, Ill.: Bahá'í Publishing Trust, 1989.
— *Prayers and Meditations*. Wilmette, Ill.: Bahá'í Publishing Trust, 1987.
— *The Proclamation of Bahá'u'lláh*. Haifa: Bahá'í World Centre, 1967.
— *The Seven Valleys and the Four Valleys*. Wilmette, Ill.: Bahá'í Publishing Trust, 1991.
— *Tablets of Bahá'u'lláh revealed after the Kitáb-i-Aqdas*. Haifa: Bahá'í World Centre, 1978.

Balyuzi, H. M. *Bahá'u'lláh, The King of Glory*. Oxford: George Ronald, 1980.

*Compilation of Compilations, The*. Prepared by the Universal House of Justice 1963–1990. 2 vols. [Sydney]: Bahá'í Publications Australia, 1991.

*The Concise Oxford Dictionary*. R.E. Allen (ed.). 8th edn. Oxford: Clarendon Press, 1992.

*The Covenant of Bahá'u'lláh: A Compilation*. Manchester: Bahá'í Publishing Trust, 1950.

*Encyclopedia of Religion*. Mircea Eliade, et al. (eds.). MacMillan and Free Press: New York, 1987.

Faizi, A. Q. 'A Flame of Fire: The Story of the Tablet of Ahmad', Part I, in *Bahá'í News*, March 1967; Part II, April 1967.

Garrida, Gertrude (compiler). *Directives from the Guardian*. New Delhi: Bahá'í Publishing Trust, 1973.

Goodall, Helen S. and Cooper, Ella Goodall. *Daily Lessons Received at 'Akká*. Wilmette, Ill.: Bahá'í Publishing Trust, 1979.

Haneef, Suzanne. *What Everyone Should Know About Islam and Muslims*.

*Holy Bible. King James Version*. London: Collins, 1839.

*Japan Will Turn Ablaze*. Japan: Bahá'í Publishing Trust, 1974.

Khadem, Zikrullah. 'Bahá'u'lláh and His Most Holy Shrine', in *Bahá'í News*, no. 540, March, 1976; reprinted in Khadem, Javidukht. *Zikrullah Khadem*, pp. 303–4.

*The Koran*. Trans. J. M. Rodwell. London: Dent (Everyman's Library), 1963.

Lawson, Todd. 'Seeing Double', in Momen, *The Bahá'í Faith and Other Religions*, Oxford: George Ronald, forthcoming.

*Lights of Guidance: A Bahá'í Reference File*. Compiled by Helen Hornby. New Delhi: Bahá'í Publishing Trust, 2nd edn. 1988.

Maxwell, May. *An Early Pilgrimage*. Oxford: George Ronald, 1976.

Momen, Moojan. ''Abdu'l-Bahá's Commentary on the Islamic Tradition: "I was a Hidden Treasure . . ." (A Provisional Translation)', *Bulletin of Bahá'í Studies*, vol. 3, no. 4, Dec. 1985, pp. 4–64.

— *An Introduction to Shi'i Islam*. London: Yale University Press, 1985.

Nabíl-i-A'ẓam. *The Dawn-Breakers: Nabíl's Narrative of the Early Days of the Bahá'í Revelation*. Wilmette, Ill.: Bahá'í Publishing Trust, 1970.

Pickthall, Marmaduke. *The Meaning of the Glorious Koran*, New York: Dorset Press, no date.

*Seeking the Light of the Kingdom*. A Compilation of the Universal House of Justice. London: Bahá'í Publishing Trust. 1977.

Shoghi Effendi. *The Advent of Divine Justice*. Wilmette, Ill.: Bahá'í Publishing Trust, 1990.

— *Dawn of a New Day: Messages to India 1923–1957*. New Delhi: Bahá'í Publishing Trust, 1970.

— *God Passes By*. Wilmette, Ill.: Bahá'í Publishing Trust, rev. edn. 1974.

— *Messages to the Bahá'í World*. Wilmette, Ill.: Bahá'í Publishing Trust, 1971.

— *The World Order of Bahá'u'lláh*. Wilmette, Ill.: Bahá'í Publishing Trust, 1991.

*Shorter Encyclopaedia of Islam*. H. A. R. Gibb and J.H. Kramers (eds). Leiden: E.J. Brill, 1974.

Taherzadeh, Adib. *The Covenant of Bahá'u'lláh*. Oxford: George Ronald, 1992.

— *The Revelation of Bahá'u'lláh*, vol. 2. Oxford: George Ronald, 1977.

*Webster's Unabridged Dictionary*, 2nd edn.

# Notes and References

1. Shoghi Effendi, *Advent of Divine Justice*, p. 49.
2. Shoghi Effendi, *God Passes By*, p. xii.
3. Taherzadeh, *Revelation of Bahá'u'lláh*, vol. 2, p. 109.
4. Faizi, 'A Flame of Fire', part 1, in *Bahá'í News*, March 1967, pp. 2–3.
5. Mullá Ṣádiq was one of the outstanding believers during the ministries of both the Báb and Bahá'u'lláh.
6. Taherzadeh, *Revelation of Bahá'u'lláh*, vol. 2, pp. 109–10.
7. Faizi, 'A Flame of Fire', part 1, in *Bahá'í News*, March 1967, p. 3.
8. ibid. pp. 3–4.
9. Taherzadeh, *Revelation of Bahá'u'lláh*, vol. 2, p. 111.
10. ibid. These are not the exact words of Bahá'u'lláh.
11. ibid. pp. 111–12.
12. Faizi, 'A Flame of Fire', part 2, *Bahá'í News*, April, 1967, p. 2.
13. Quoted in Shoghi Effendi, *God Passes By*, p. 137.
14. Ḥájí Muḥammad-Ṭáhir-i-Málmírí, quoted in Taherzadeh, *Revelation of Bahá'u'lláh*, vol. 2, p. 113.
15. ibid. p. 112.
16. Faizi, 'A Flame of Fire', part 2, *Bahá'í News*, April, 1967, p. 2.
17. ibid.
18. The Bábís were in constant danger of being discovered by fanatical Muslims. If it was found that someone was a Bábí, the individual could be imprisoned, tortured and even killed for his beliefs. To protect themselves the early believers often placed the holy writings in containers which they hid in the ground or inside the walls of their homes.
19. Taherzadeh, *Revelation of Bahá'u'lláh*, vol. 2, pp. 114–15.
20. Faizi, 'A Flame of Fire', part 2, *Bahá'í News*, April, 1967, p. 3.
21. Ḥájí Muḥammad-Ṭáhir-i-Málmírí, quoted in Taherzadeh, *Revelation of Bahá'u'lláh*, p. 115.

22 Faizi, 'A Flame of Fire', part 2, *Bahá'í News*, April, 1967, pp. 3–4.
23. Faizi, 'A Flame of Fire', part 2, in *Bahá'í News*, April 1967, p. 2.
24. This is reported in a pilgrim's note.
25. These teachers were very successful. It was estimated that 99 per cent of the Bábís recognized Bahá'u'lláh and became Bahá'ís. See figures given by Mírzá Ḥaydar-'Alí, in Taherzadeh, *Covenant of Bahá'u'lláh*, pp. 87–8.
26. Faizi, 'A Flame of Fire', part 2, *Bahá'í News*, April, 1967, p. 2.
27. ibid.
28. Bahá'u'lláh, *Tablets*, p. 196.
29. From a letter written on behalf of Shoghi Effendi, in *Bahá'í Prayers*, p. 209.
30. Bahá'u'lláh, *Gleanings*, pp. 141–2.
31. ibid. p. 175.
32. Bahá'u'lláh, *Kitáb-i-Íqán*, p. 255.
33. ibid. p. 33.
34. Quoted in ibid. p. 255.
35. 'Abdu'l-Bahá, *Promulgation*, p. 155.
36. Bahá'u'lláh, *Prayers and Meditations*, p. 231.
37. Bahá'u'lláh, *Gleanings*, p. 60.
38. ibid. p. 211.
39. Ps. 24:9–10.
40. Shoghi Effendi, *God Passes By*, pp. 94, 95.
41. Bahá'u'lláh, *Tablets*, p. 239.
42. Qur'án 1:1–4.
43. See Shoghi Effendi, *God Passes By*, p. 29; see the discussion in chapter 79 of the present volume.
44. Rev. 21:3.
45. See Bahá'u'lláh, *Gleanings*, p. 244.
46. See Bahá'u'lláh, *Tablets*, p. 185, and Bahá'u'lláh, *Prayers and Meditations*, p. 119.
47. Bahá'u'lláh, *Gleanings*, p. 101.
48. The Báb, *Selections*, p. 59.
49. Bahá'u'lláh, *Kitáb-i-Íqán*, p. 252.
50. Nabíl, *Dawn-Breakers*, pp. 372–3.

51. *Warqátu'l-firdaws*. Literally, this means the 'pigeon' or 'dove of paradise', 'nightingale' being *bulbul*. See Lawson, 'Seeing Double', in Momen, *The Bahá'í Faith and Other Religions*.
52. Bahá'u'lláh, *Kitáb-i-Aqdas*, para. 139.
53. Bahá'u'lláh, *Tablets*, p. 15.
54. *Concise Oxford Dictionary*.
55. Bahá'u'lláh, *Gleanings*, pp. 27–8.
56. Bahá'u'lláh, *Tablets*, p. 107.
57. Bahá'u'lláh, *Kitáb-i-Íqán*, p. 78.
58. Bahá'u'lláh, *Epistle to the Son of the Wolf*, p. 40.
59. Bahá'u'lláh, *Tablets*, p. 261.
60. Bahá'u'lláh, in *Compilation*, vol. 2, p. 337.
61. Bahá'u'lláh, *Gleanings*, p. 104.
62. Gen. 2:9, 17; 3:22, 24. The 'Tree of Life' also emerges as an important symbol in the Book of Revelation (Rev. 22:2; also see the discussion in chapter 10 of the present volume).
63. 'Abdu'l-Bahá, *Some Answered Questions*, pp. 123–4.
64. Isa. 11:1. See also Shoghi Effendi, *God Passes By*, p. 94.
65. Matt. 7:17.
66. Qur'án 53:14, 16; Shoghi Effendi, *God Passes By*, p. 94.
67. The Báb, *Selections*, p. 155.
68. Bahá'u'lláh, *Tablets*, p. 208.
69. ibid. p. 53.
70. The Báb, *Selections*, p. 112.
71. ibid. pp. 112–13.
72. Gen 17:7.
73. 'Abdu'l-Bahá, *Selections*, p. 309.
74. 'Abdu'l-Bahá, in *Bahá'í World Faith*, p. 429.
75. Bahá'u'lláh, *Tablets*, pp. 208–9.
76. Bahá'u'lláh, *Kitáb-i-Íqán*, p. 207.
77. Bahá'u'lláh, *Gleanings*, p. 195.
78. Bahá'u'lláh, *Prayers and Meditations*, p. 83.
79. Bahá'u'lláh, *Gleanings*, p. 343.
80. ibid. p. 298.
81. The Báb, *Selections*, p. 138.
82. Bahá'u'lláh, *Gleanings*, p. 132.
83. 'Súrih' means 'chapter'. The Súrih of Joseph is the twelfth súrih of the Qur'án.

84. The Báb, *Selections*, p. 49.
85. ibid. p. 52.
86. Qur'án 12:19.
87. Qur'án 12:96.
88. See Bahá'u'lláh, *Gleanings*, p. 208.
89. ibid. p. 38.
90. Qur'án 12:20.
91. 'Abdu'l-Bahá, *Selections*, p. 34.
92. Rom. 13:10–12.
93. Joel 2:1.
94. Bahá'u'lláh, *Gleanings*, p. 40.
95. Qur'án 70:5–9.
96. Bahá'u'lláh, *Gleanings*, pp. 44–5.
97. Qur'án 56:87–8.
98. Qur'án 81:10–14.
99. Qur'án 50:29–34.
100. Qur'án 26:87–90.
101. Bahá'u'lláh, *Gleanings*, pp. 45–6.
102. Taherzadeh, *Revelation of Bahá'u'lláh*, vol. 2, pp. 65–75.
103. The Báb, *Selections*, p. 79; emphasis added.
104. ibid. p. 85 (from the Persian *Bayán*).
105. ibid. p. 104 (from the Persian *Bayán*).
106. ibid. p. 148 (from the *Kitáb-i-Asmá'*).
107. ibid. p. 168.
108. ibid. pp. 82–3 (from the Persian *Bayán*).
109. Momen, *Introduction to Shi'i Islam*, p. 176.
110. Qur'án 5:77.
111. Qur'án 6:102–3.
112. Qur'án 4:80.
113. The Báb, *Selections*, pp. 200–1.
114. Bahá'u'lláh, *Gleanings*, p. 166.
115. ibid. p. 185.
116. ibid. p. 195.
117. Bahá'u'lláh, in *Bahá'í Prayers*, p. 96.
118. Bahá'u'lláh, *Gleanings*, p. 186.
119. ibid. p. 50.
120. ibid. p. 78.
121. Bahá'u'lláh, *Tablets*, p. 41.

122. Bahá'u'lláh, in *Bahá'í Prayers*, p. 218.
123. Bahá'u'lláh, *Gleanings*, p. 79; emphasis added.
124. ibid.
125. ibid. p. 59.
126. ibid. p. 167.
127. John 14:9.
128. Bahá'u'lláh, *Tablets*, p. 14.
129. Bahá'u'lláh, *Proclamation*, p. 95.
130. Bahá'u'lláh, *Tablets*, pp. 209–10.
131. The Báb, *Selections*, pp. 164–5; emphasis added.
132. Rev. 21:3.
133. Bahá'u'lláh, *Kitáb-i-Íqán*, p. 139.
134. ibid. p. 138.
135. ibid. pp. 142–3.
136. Bahá'u'lláh, *Gleanings*, p. 70.
137. ibid.
138. Bahá'u'lláh, *Kitáb-i-Íqán*, p. 138.
139. However, it must be pointed out that the Arabic word *adkhala*, which means 'caused to enter', is a frequent Quranic idiom and is found in various prayers, as, for example, in the phrase 'Cause me to enter'.
140. Bahá'u'lláh, *Gleanings*, p. 211. It is interesting to note that in the Arabic phrase He refers to Himself as the 'clothing' of the King of Kings.
141. Bahá'u'lláh, *Tablets*, p. 28.
142. Bahá'u'lláh, *Gleanings*, p. 291.
143. ibid. pp. 271–2.
144. ibid. pp. 289–90.
145. ibid. p. 289.
146. Bahá'u'lláh, *Prayers and Meditations*, p. 250.
147. Bahá'u'lláh, *Tablets*, p. 155.
148. Bahá'u'lláh, *Kitáb-i-Íqán*, pp. 3–4.
149. Bahá'u'lláh, *Seven Valleys*, pp. 21–2.
150. Qur'án 54:54–5. It is important to recognize that most Muslims would see this verse as a reference to the afterlife.
151. Qur'án 39:68–9.
152. Bahá'u'lláh, *Gleanings*, p. 44.
153. Rev. 1:8; emphasis added.

154. See Bahá'u'lláh, *Kitáb-i-Íqán*, p. 179.
155. The original idea for this interpretation of Rev. 1:8 was provided by the late Ruth Moffett in a talk she gave in Alamogordo, New Mexico, in the late 1970s.
156. The Báb, *Selections*, pp. 105–6.
157. Bahá'u'lláh, *Prayers and Meditations*, p. 208.
158. Bahá'u'lláh, *Gleanings*, p. 241.
159. ibid. p. 143.
160. 'Abdu'l-Bahá, *Selections*, p. 245.
161. Bahá'u'lláh, *Prayers and Meditations*, p. 155.
162. ibid. p. 261.
163. Bahá'u'lláh, *Gleanings*, p. 264.
164. ibid. p. 186.
165. ibid. p. 304.
166. ibid. p. 82.
167. ibid. p. 67.
168. ibid. p. 68.
169. Bahá'u'lláh, *Hidden Words*, Arabic no. 59.
170. ibid. Persian no. 8.
171. Bahá'u'lláh, *Seven Valleys*, pp. 21–2.
172. Bahá'u'lláh, *Hidden Words*, Persian no. 32.
173. Bahá'u'lláh, *Gleanings*, p. 145.
174. Bahá'u'lláh, *Tablets*, p. 4.
175. ibid.
176. Bahá'u'lláh, *Kitáb-i-Aqdas*, para. 1.
177. Bahá'u'lláh, *Gleanings*, p. 241.
178. Bahá'u'lláh, *Epistle to the Son of the Wolf*, p. 63.
179. Bahá'u'lláh, *Proclamation*, p. 89.
180. The Báb, *Selections*, p. 54.
181. ibid. pp. 156–7.
182. Ps. 50:2–3.
183. Bahá'u'lláh, *Gleanings*, pp. 320–1.
184. Bahá'u'lláh, *Epistle to the Son of the Wolf*, p. 11.
185. ibid.
186. Bahá'u'lláh, *Gleanings*, p. 13.
187. Shoghi Effendi, *God Passes By*, p. 94.
188. 'Abdu'l-Bahá, quoted in Shoghi Effendi, *World Order*, pp. 127–8.

189. Bahá'u'lláh, quoted in Shoghi Effendi, *God Passes By*, p. 100.
190. Bahá'u'lláh, quoted in Shoghi Effendi, *World Order*, p. 104.
191. Ex. 6:3.
192. Ps. 83:18.
193. Isa. 26:4.
194. John 14:15–17.
195. John 15:26.
196. John 16:12–13.
197. The Arabic word *Nabá* is often translated as 'the Tidings' or 'the News'. Shoghi Effendi, in the *Epistle to the Son of the Wolf*, page 143, translates it as the 'Great Announcement'.
198. Qur'án 78:1–2.
199. Bahá'u'lláh, *Gleanings*, p. 50.
200. Bahá'u'lláh, *Kitáb-i-Aqdas*, para. 99.
201. John 16:13.
202. Bahá'u'lláh, *Tablets*, p. 12.
203. The Báb, *Selections*, p. 142.
204. ibid.
205. Bahá'u'lláh, *Tablets*, p. 161.
206. Bahá'u'lláh, *Gleanings*, p. 290.
207. 'Abdu'l-Bahá, *Some Answered Questions*, p. 47.
208. 'Abdu'l-Bahá, quoted in Shoghi Effendi, *Advent of Divine Justice*, p. 26.
209. Bahá'u'lláh, *Gleanings*, p. 80. In this context wisdom, *ḥikmat*, is always associated with the practice of medicine and the healing arts. A physician is a *ḥakím*. The terminology assumes that a physician worthy of the name will also be well versed in other sciences including philosophy, astronomy, law, exegesis and so on.
210. ibid. p. 213.
211. ibid. p. 81.
212. ibid. p. 286.
213. ibid. p. 213.
214. ibid. pp. 39–40.
215. Shoghi Effendi, *World Order*, p. 34.
216. ibid. pp. 42–3.
217. Bahá'u'lláh, *Gleanings*, p. 255.
218. Bahá'u'lláh, *Hidden Words*, Persian no. 69.

219. Qur'án 44:2–4 (Pickthall, *Meaning of the Glorious Koran*); emphasis added. The Arabic of this verse of the Qur'án and of the verse 'the wisdom of every command shall be tested' is exactly the same, i.e. Bahá'u'lláh is quoting from the Qur'án.
220. Qur'án 44:5–6.
221. Qur'án 44:9–13.
222. Bahá'u'lláh, *Gleanings*, p. 40.
223. Bahá'u'lláh, *Kitáb-i-Íqán*, p. 76.
224. ibid. p. 255.
225. ibid. pp. 8–9.
226. Qur'án 44:11.
227. Qur'án 44:12–13.
228. The Báb, *Selections*, p. 46.
229. Bahá'u'lláh, *Gleanings*, p. 5.
230. 'Abdu'l-Bahá, *Selections*. p. 57.
231. Gen. 2:9; 3:22.
232. Rev. 22:2, 14.
233. 'Abdu'l-Bahá, *Some Answered Questions*, pp. 67–8.
234. Rev. 21:23; emphasis added.
235. Rev. 22:2; emphasis added.
236. Bahá'u'lláh, quoted in Shoghi Effendi, *God Passes By*, p. 99.
237. 'Abdu'l-Bahá, *Some Answered Questions*, p. 124.
238. Bahá'u'lláh, *Gleanings*, p. 79.
239. Muḥammad, quoted in Bahá'u'lláh, *Epistle to the Son of the Wolf*, p. 42.
240. 'Abdu'l-Bahá, quoted in Shoghi Effendi, *World Order*, pp. 102, 110.
241. Bahá'u'lláh, *Tablets*, pp. 33–4.
242. 'Abdu'l-Bahá, *Some Answered Questions*, p. 124.
243. ibid. p. 161.
244. From a letter written on behalf of Shoghi Effendi to an individual believer, 14 November 1935, in *Lights of Guidance*, p. 473.
245. Bahá'u'lláh, *Kitáb-i-Íqán*, pp. 103–4.
246. ibid. p. 104.
247. Bahá'u'lláh, *Gleanings*, p. 104.
248. 'Abdu'l-Bahá, quoted in Shoghi Effendi, *World Order*, p. 111.

249. Bahá'u'lláh, quoted in ibid. p. 104.
250. Bahá'u'lláh, *Gleanings*, p. 30.
251. ibid. p. 65.
252. ibid. p. 68.
253. ibid. p. 215.
254. Bahá'u'lláh, *Epistle to the Son of the Wolf*, p. 26.
255. Bahá'u'lláh, in *Compilation*, vol. 1, p. 247.
256. See Bahá'u'lláh, *Gleanings*, pp. 67–8.
257. Bahá'u'lláh, *Kitáb-i-Íqán*, pp. 240–1.
258. Bahá'u'lláh, quoted in Shoghi Effendi, *Advent of Divine Justice*. p. 31.
259. 'Abdu'l-Bahá, *Some Answered Questions*; emphasis added.
260. Bahá'u'lláh, *Tablets*, p. 189.
261. Shoghi Effendi, *Messages to the Bahá'í World*, p. 84.
262. *Webster's Unabridged Dictionary*, 2nd ed.
263. The Arabic phrase is '*Lá Iláha Illa'lláh*', literally meaning 'no god but Alláh'.
264. The daily prayer includes this declaration of faith: '*Lá Iláha Illa'lláh, Muḥammadu rasul'u'lláh*', literally meaning 'no god but Alláh, Muḥammad is [the] Messenger (or Prophet) of Alláh'.
265. 'Here [in the *shaháda*] the word deity is used in the broad sense which the Arabic word *Ilah* [*Iláh*] conveys: that is, anyone or anything who is worshipped, to whom one's love and devotion are given and one's goal is directed . . . Thus it becomes clear that this declaration has a far broader meaning than the words conveyed in English. It is, in effect, a proclamation that the one who believes and utters it cancels from his heart loyalty, devotion, obedience, submission to and worship of anything other than God, praised and exalted – not merely of man-made idols of wood or stone, but also of any conceptions, ideologies, ways of life, desires, love, preoccupations and authority-figures which claim his supreme devotion, loyalty, obedience and worship' (Haneef, *What Everyone Should Know About Islam and Muslims*, p. 42).
266. 'He is God, there is no god but Him' is a *dhikr* formula used in many Islamic devotional settings.
267. The Báb, *Selections*, p. 144.

268. Bahá'u'lláh, *Gleanings*, p. 272.
269. John 14:6–7.
270. Bahá'u'lláh, *Gleanings*, p. 66.
271. ibid. pp. 67–8.
272. The Báb, *Selections*, p. 81.
273. Bahá'u'lláh, *Gleanings*, p. 49; emphasis added.
274. ibid.
275. 'Abdu'l-Bahá, *Some Answered Questions*, pp. 146–7.
276. 'Abdu'l-Bahá, *Tablets*, vol. 3, p. 485.
277. Bahá'u'lláh, *Gleanings*, p. 6.
278. ibid. p. 108.
279. Bahá'u'lláh, quoted in Shoghi Effendi, *Advent of Divine Justice*, p. 77.
280. Bahá'u'lláh, quoted in Shoghi Effendi, *God Passes By*, p. 101.
281. Bahá'u'lláh, *Gleanings*, pp. 248–9.
282. Bahá'u'lláh, *Tablets*, p. 33; emphasis added.
283. For the source of the ideas presented here, see the discussion by Adib Taherzadeh in *Revelation of Bahá'u'lláh*, vol. 2, pp. 286–9.
284. Bahá'u'lláh, quoted in Shoghi Effendi, *Advent of Divine Justice*, p. 79.
285. ibid.
286. Bahá'u'lláh, *Gleanings*, p. 341.
287. ibid.
288. Bahá'u'lláh, quoted in Shoghi Effendi, *World Order*, p. 106.
289. ibid.
290. 'This is the first letter of "Thamarih" which means "fruit". Shoghi Effendi, in his writings, refers to the Báb as the "Thamarih" (fruit) of the Tree of God's successive Revelations.' Footnote to The Báb, *Selections*, p. 3.
291. The Báb, *Selections*, p. 3; emphasis added.
292. Bahá'u'lláh, *Gleanings*, p. 101.
293. The Báb, *Selections*, p. 6; emphasis added.
294. ibid. pp. 6–7; emphasis added.
295. Shoghi Effendi, *World Order*, p. 97.
296. The Báb, *Selections*, pp. 6–7.
297. The Báb, quoted in Bahá'u'lláh, *Gleanings*, p. 147.
298. Bahá'u'lláh, *Gleanings*, p. 179.

299. ibid. p. 74.
300. Bahá'u'lláh, *Kitáb-i-Íqán*, p. 103.
301. ibid. p. 243.
302. The Báb, quoted in Shoghi Effendi, *God Passes By*, p. 25.
303. Bahá'u'lláh, *Gleanings*, p. 91.
304. Bahá'u'lláh, *Tablets*, p. 53.
305. Shoghi Effendi, *God Passes By*, p. 25.
306. Shoghi Effendi, quoted in Introduction to Bahá'u'lláh, *Kitáb-i-Aqdas*, p. 8.
307. Shoghi Effendi, *God Passes By*, p. 25.
308. The Báb, *Selections*, p. 101.
309. ibid. p. 138.
310. ibid. p. 155.
311. ibid. pp. 155–6.
312. Bahá'u'lláh, *Gleanings*, pp. 244–5.
313. The Báb, *Selections*, p. 12.
314. Bahá'u'lláh, *Kitáb-i-Aqdas*, para. 1.
315. See Momen, ''Abdu'l-Bahá's Commentary on the Islamic Tradition: "I was a Hidden Treasure. . ." (A Provisional Translation)', *Bulletin of Bahá'í Studies*, vol. 3, no. 4, Dec. 1985, pp. 4–64.
316. Bahá'u'lláh, *Tablets*, p. 268.
317. Bahá'u'lláh, *Gleanings*, p. 78.
318. ibid. p. 59.
319. ibid. p. 79.
320. ibid. p. 50.
321. Shoghi Effendi, *World Order*, p. 102.
322. ibid. p. 123.
323. Bahá'u'lláh, quoted in ibid. pp. 124–5.
324. 'Abdu'l-Bahá, quoted in ibid. p. 127.
325. 'Abdu'l-Bahá, quoted in ibid. p. 128.
326. Bahá'u'lláh, *Kitáb-i-Íqán*, pp. 243–4.
327. Shoghi Effendi, *World Order*, p. 123.
328. See Eliade, et al. (eds.), *Encyclopedia of Religion* and Gibb and Kramers (eds.). *Shorter Encyclopaedia of Islam*. The Arabic term *umm* means 'mother' and connotes comprehensiveness.
329. Bahá'u'lláh, *Kitáb-i-Íqán*, p. 153.
330. Bahá'u'lláh, *Gleanings*, pp. 78–9.

331. Bahá'u'lláh, *Kitáb-i-Íqán*, p. 243.
332. The Báb, *Selections*, p. 11.
333. ibid. p. 12.
334. Qur'án 43:2–4.
335. See Bahá'u'lláh, *Gleanings*, pp. 141–2, 199; Bahá'u'lláh, *Tablets*, p. 247.
336. Bahá'u'lláh, *Tablets*, p. 173.
337. Bahá'u'lláh, *Gleanings*, p. 141.
338. ibid. p. 142.
339. Bahá'u'lláh, *Tablets*, p. 141.
340. Aḥmad is en route to Bahá'u'lláh; Bahá'u'lláh tells him: 'We are reminding you (the root of the word translated as "call" is "remind") that the essence of the message is: it is up to you to follow the advice given here and if you do, this will be the true path to your Lord, even though your Lord is asking you not to visit Him.'
341. Bahá'u'lláh, *Gleanings*, p. 137.
342. Qur'án 5:92. Translation of Yusuf Ali.
343. Qur'án 16:35.
344. Qur'án 24:54.
345. Qur'án 3:20. Translation of Yusuf Ali.
346. Indeed, Aḥmad would have had difficulty reading this passage in his Tablet without thinking of such Quranic statements, Muḥammad and His Covenant and associating these with Bahá'u'lláh and His message. See Lawson, 'Seeing Double', in Momen, *The Bahá'í Faith and Other Religions*.
347. Qur'án 3:138; 55:4; 75:19.
348. Shoghi Effendi, *God Passes By*, p. 94.
349. Isa. 9:6.
350. Bahá'u'lláh, *Tablets*, p. 42.
351. Bahá'u'lláh, *Epistle to the Son of the Wolf*, p. 144.
352. Bahá'u'lláh, *Tablets*, p. 163.
353. ibid. p. 44.
354. ibid. p. 71.
355. ibid.
356. ibid. p. 86.
357. Bahá'u'lláh, *Kitáb-i-Aqdas*, para. 184.
358. Bahá'u'lláh, *Gleanings*, p. 148.

359. Bahá'u'lláh, *Tablets*, p. 189.
360. Bahá'u'lláh, *Gleanings*, p. 299.
361. ibid. p. 117.
362. ibid. p. 149.
363. ibid. pp. 196–7.
364. The term occurs 116 times in the Qur'án. See Lawson, 'Seeing Double', in Momen, *The Bahá'í Faith and Other Religions*.
365. Bahá'u'lláh, quoted in Balyuzi, *King of Glory*, p. 152.
366. Bahá'u'lláh, *Gleanings*, p. 129.
367. 'Abdu'l-Bahá, *Selections*, p. 238.
368. Bahá'u'lláh, *Gleanings*, p. 259.
369. Bahá'u'lláh, *Tablets*, p. 74.
370. Bahá'u'lláh, *Epistle to the Son of the Wolf*, p. 115.
371. Bahá'u'lláh, *Gleanings*, p. 105.
372. The Báb, *Selections*, p. 120.
373. Bahá'u'lláh, *Kitáb-i-Íqán*, p. 219.
374. Bahá'u'lláh, *Epistle to the Son of the Wolf*, pp. 42–3.
375. Bahá'u'lláh, *Kitáb-i-Íqán*, p. 205.
376. ibid. p. 207.
377. ibid. pp. 91–2.
378. ibid. p. 206.
379. Bahá'u'lláh, *Gleanings*, p. 195.
380. The Báb, quoted in Bahá'u'lláh, *Epistle to the Son of the Wolf*, p. 159.
381. The Báb, *Selections*, p. 104.
382. ibid. p. 91.
383. The Báb, *Selections*, p. 100.
384. Bahá'u'lláh, *Kitáb-i-Aqdas*, paras. 99, 101.
385. See Lawson, 'Seeing Double', in Momen, *The Bahá'í Faith and Other Religions*, for the Quranic background of the challenge to produce verses 'like it'. In Quranic studies they are referred to as the 'challenge verses' and are an important part of the Quranic message. Bahá'u'lláh is invoking these here.
386. John 14:6.
387. John 14:10.
388. Qur'án 2:21–2.
389. The Báb, *Selections*, p. 58.

390. Bahá'u'lláh, *Gleanings*, p. 259.
391. Bahá'u'lláh, quoted in Shoghi Effendi, *Advent of Divine Justice*, p. 78.
392. Bahá'u'lláh, *Gleanings*, p. 108.
393. ibid. p. 8.
394. ibid. p. 320.
395. ibid. p. 213.
396. Bahá'u'lláh, *Epistle to the Son of the Wolf*, p. 38.
397. Bahá'u'lláh, *Prayers and Meditations*, pp. 304, 307.
398. Bahá'u'lláh, *Gleanings*, pp. 45–6; emphasis added.
399. ibid. p. 32.
400. ibid. p. 33; emphasis added.
401. Forgetting and remembering (as in 'Thus doth the Nightingale "utter His call"', the Arabic of which is, literally, 'remind you'– of something which you might have forgotten) are part of this tradition as well. See Lawson, 'Seeing Double', in Momen, *The Bahá'í Faith and Other Religions*.
402. 'Abdu'l-Bahá, quoted in Shoghi Effendi, *Advent of Divine Justice*, p. 33.
403. Bahá'u'lláh, *Prayers and Meditations*, p. 241.
404. Bahá'u'lláh, in *Compilation*, vol. 2, p. 358.
405. Bahá'u'lláh, *Gleanings*, pp. 13–14.
406. Bahá'u'lláh, in *Seeking the Light of the Kingdom*, p. 21.
407. Bahá'u'lláh, *Prayers and Meditations*, p. 265.
408. Bahá'u'lláh, *Bahá'í Prayers*, pp. 143–4.
409. The Báb, *Selections*, p. 191.
410. Deut. 6:5–6.
411. Matt. 22:36–7.
412. The Báb, *Selections*, p. 190.
413. Bahá'u'lláh, *Hidden Words*, Arabic no. 5.
414. Bahá'u'lláh, *Tablets*, p. 71.
415. Bahá'u'lláh, *Gleanings*, pp. 326–7.
416. ibid. p. 186; emphasis added.
417. ibid.
418. 'While I am absent' (*ghaybatí*) is one of the most powerful concepts in Shí'ism: the absence of hiddenness (*ghayba*) of the Hidden Imám. See also the first three verses of suríh 2

regarding those who believe in the absent/unseen g͟hayb. (Todd Lawson)

419. See discussion of *qurb*/nearness and the 'Presence of the Generous One' in chapter 17.
420. Bahá'u'lláh, *Hidden Words*, Arabic no. 16.
421. Bahá'u'lláh, *Gleanings*, p. 186; emphasis added.
422. Bahá'u'lláh, *Hidden Words*, Arabic no. 6; emphasis added.
423. ibid. Arabic no. 36.
424. 'Abdu'l-Bahá, quoted in Maxwell, *Early Pilgrimage*, p. 40.
425. Bahá'u'lláh, *Gleanings*, p. 203.
426. ibid. pp. 119–20.
427. John 15:13.
428. Bahá'u'lláh, *Gleanings*, p. 85.
429. Bahá'u'lláh, quoted in Shoghi Effendi, *Advent of Divine Justice*, p. 76.
430. Bahá'u'lláh, *Gleanings*, pp. 99–100.
431. ibid. p. 42.
432. ibid. p. 119.
433. ibid. p. 42.
434. Bahá'u'lláh, *Prayers and Meditations*, p. 14.
435. Bahá'u'lláh, *Bahá'í Prayers*, pp. 218–19.
436. Bahá'u'lláh, *Gleanings*, p. 79.
437. Bahá'u'lláh, *Hidden Words*, Arabic no. 51.
438. See chapter 17.
439. Qur'án 70:5–7.
440. Qur'án 50:15.
441. Bahá'u'lláh, in *Compilation*, vol. 1, p. 171.
442. Bahá'u'lláh, *Gleanings*, p. 261.
443. Letter of Shoghi Effendi to an individual, 19 December 1943.
444. See, for example, Bahá'u'lláh, *Kitáb-i-Íqán*, p. 48.
445. Bahá'u'lláh, in *Compilation*, vol. 1, p. 169.
446. Bahá'u'lláh, *Hidden Words*, Arabic no. 13.
447. From a letter written on behalf of Shoghi Effendi, 21 July 1955.
448. From a letter written on behalf of Shoghi Effendi, 27 March 1938, in Shoghi Effendi, *Dawn of a New Day*, p. 200.
449. Letter of Shoghi Effendi, 21 July 1955.
450. Letter of Shoghi Effendi, 19 December 1943.

451. Bahá'u'lláh, *Gleanings*, p. 289.
452. Bahá'u'lláh, *Tablets*, p. 157.
453. Bahá'u'lláh, *Hidden Words*, Persian no. 57.
454. 'Abdu'l-Bahá, *Will and Testament*, p. 22.
455. ibid. p. 4.
456. ibid. p. 20.
457. Bahá'u'lláh, *Gleanings*, p. 325.
458. Bahá'u'lláh, in *Compilation*, vol. 2, p. 293.
459. 'Abdu'l-Bahá, in *Covenant of Bahá'u'lláh*, p. 70. The Research Department of the Universal House of Justice has noted that 'This passage is from Ahmad Sohrab's diary and should be considered as interesting material, but not as scripture' (in *American Bahá'í*, vol. 23, no. 14, 27 September 1992).
460. Bahá'u'lláh, *Gleanings*, p. 58.
461. Bahá'u'lláh, *Gleanings*, p. 38.
462. ibid. p. 335.
463. Bahá'u'lláh, *Kitáb-i-Íqán*, p. 205.
464. Bahá'u'lláh, *Tablets*, p. 200.
465. Bahá'u'lláh, *Gleanings*, p. 196.
466. Bahá'u'lláh, *Seven Valleys*, p. 11.
467. Bahá'u'lláh, *Kitáb-i-Íqán*, p. 194.
468. Bahá'u'lláh, *Prayers and Meditations*, p. 161.
469. Bahá'u'lláh, *Tablets*, p. 196.
470. Bahá'u'lláh, *Gleanings*, p. 43.
471. Bahá'u'lláh, *Hidden Words*, Arabic no. 3.
472. ibid. Arabic no. 4.
473. Bahá'u'lláh, *Tablets*, p. 246.
474. Bahá'u'lláh, *Gleanings*, pp. 280–1; emphasis added.
475. ibid. p. 245.
476. Bahá'u'lláh, in *Bahá'í Prayers*, p. 119.
477. Bahá'u'lláh, *Kitáb-i-Aqdas*, paras. 161–3; emphasis added.
478. Bahá'u'lláh, *Tablets*, p. 183.
479. Bahá'u'lláh, *Prayers and Meditations*, pp. 176–7.
480. Bahá'u'lláh, *Epistle to the Son of the Wolf*, p. 17.
481. Bahá'u'lláh, in *Bahá'í Prayers*, pp. 8–9.
482. Bahá'u'lláh, *Hidden Words*, Arabic no. 51.
483. 'Abdu'l-Bahá, *Selections*, p. 245.
484. ibid. pp. 120–1.

485. ibid. pp. 234–5.
486. Bahá'u'lláh, *Gleanings*, p. 100.
487. Bahá'u'lláh, *Gleanings*, pp. 105–6.
488. Nabíl, *Dawn-Breakers*, p. 586.
489. See The Báb, *Selections*, p. 103; Bahá'u'lláh, *Gleanings*, p. 11; and Bahá'u'lláh, *Tablets*, p. 244.
490. Bahá'u'lláh, *Tablets*, pp. 52–3.
491. Nabíl, *Dawn-Breakers*, p. 586.
492. The Báb, *Selections*, p. 133; emphasis added.
493. Bahá'u'lláh, *Gleanings*, p. 278.
494. Bahá'u'lláh, *Gleanings*, p. 82.
495. Bahá'u'lláh, *Tablets*, p. 58.
496. The Báb, *Selections*, p. 103.
497. ibid.
498. Bahá'u'lláh, *Kitáb-i-Íqán*, p. 192.
499. Bahá'u'lláh, *Tablets*, p. 162.
500. ibid. p. 164.
501. ibid. p. 161.
502. ibid. p. 79.
503. Bahá'u'lláh, *Tablets*, p. 51.
504. Bahá'u'lláh, *Gleanings*, p. 245.
505. Bahá'u'lláh, *Hidden Words*, Arabic no. 6.
506. ibid. Arabic no. 9.
507. Bahá'u'lláh, *Gleanings*, p. 159.
508. See Lawson, 'Seeing Double', in Momen, *The Bahá'í Faith and Other Religions*.
509. See Goodall and Cooper, *Daily Lessons*, pp. 90–1.
510. The Báb, *Selections*, p. 68.
511. ibid. p. 46.
512. Bahá'u'lláh, *Prayers and Meditations*, p. 36; emphasis added.
513. Bahá'u'lláh, *Tablets*, p. 248.
514. Bahá'u'lláh, *Gleanings*, p. 183.
515. Bahá'u'lláh, *Kitáb-i-Íqán*, p. 118.
516. It is interesting to note that *iqrá'* was the very first word revealed by God to Muḥammad: *iqrá' bismi rabbika* (suríh 96). It is frequently translated as 'recite' but a better translation is 'intone' or 'chant'. A professional chanter of the Qur'án is a *qárí*, which is derived from the same word. (Todd Lawson)

517. From a letter written on behalf of Shoghi Effendi, in *Bahá'í Prayers*, p. 209.
518. '*Aḥfaḍ* is also used in the form *Ḥafiḍ* (which is also the name of the famous poet Hafez) to describe a person who has memorized the entire Qur'án. The idea is that the Qur'án is protected in the hearts of the believers, since writing and writing materials were underdeveloped at the time of its revelation, and it also protects the hearts of the believers. The believer thus becomes an "embodiment" of the Qur'án.' (Todd Lawson)
519. 'Abdu'l-Bahá, *Japan Will Turn Ablaze*, p. 13. The verse of the Qur'án is probably 2:261.
520. The Báb, *Selections*, p. 153.
521. 'Abdu'l-Bahá, *Selections*, p. 184.
522. From a letter written on behalf of Shoghi Effendi, in *Bahá'í Prayers*, p. 209.
523. Compare this with the original use of this verb in the Qur'án: Gabriel said to Muḥammad, '*Iqrá*'! (recite)'. Muḥammad, puzzled, asked, 'What shall I recite?' This exchange occurred three times. Finally Gabriel said, 'Recite in the name of thy Lord . . . (suríh 96). Thus this recitation was not necessarily from memory. (Todd Lawson)
524. This is not to imply that reading the prayer aloud is inherently superior to or will bring more reward than reading it silently. It simply defines the verbs 'chant' and 'recite'. As with other aspects of prayer and meditation, it is up to each individual to determine for himself those practices which are most beneficial to him, bearing in mind these words from Bahá'u'lláh: 'Intone, O My servant, the verses of God . . . that the sweetness of thy melody may kindle thine own soul, and attract the hearts of all men' (Bahá'u'lláh, *Gleanings*, p. 295).
525. See the treatment of this in Lawson, 'Seeing Double', in Momen, *The Bahá'í Faith and Other Religions*. The point that may be taken from the article is that the Guardian, through his translation, transformed the Shí'í symbol of the covenant into a more universal one.
526. Bahá'u'lláh, *Gleanings*, p. 278.

527. Bahá'u'lláh, *Tablets*, p. 196.
528. From a letter written on behalf of Shoghi Effendi to an individual believer, 3 August 1932, in *Compilation*, vol. 2, p. 5.
529. Bahá'u'lláh, *Gleanings*, p. 197.
530. 'Abdu'l-Bahá, *Paris Talks*, p. 68.
531. Bahá'u'lláh, in *Bahá'í Prayers*, p. 11.
532. Matt 7:7–8.
533. Bahá'u'lláh, *Prayers and Meditations*, p. 176.
534. 'Abdu'l-Bahá, *Promulgation*, p. 237.
535. 'Abdu'l-Bahá, *Selections*, p. 19.
536. 'Abdu'l-Bahá, *Paris Talks*, p. 178.
537. 'Abdu'l-Bahá, in *Bahá'í Prayers*, p. 152.
538. Bahá'u'lláh, *Gleanings*, p. 106.
539. 'The Arabic for "absolute sincerity" is *ṣidq mubín*. *Mubín*, "absolute", is usually translated as "clear", "evident", "obvious", "patent", "final" or "irrevocable". It might also be translated as "undeniable". The usual word for absolute is *muṭlaq*, which is used in philosophy and so on. *Mubín* has a more "human" and existential "feel".

    'Sincerity is *ṣidq*, frequently translated as "truthfulness". It could also mean "faithfulness" or "with integrity".

    'Interestingly, "sincere" comes from the Latin for "clean" or "pure", meaning "without wax". This refers to the practices of Roman statue repairers. The dishonest ones used wax, the honest ones used "no wax" (sincere).' (Todd Lawson)
540. Talk given at the Bahá'í Youth Conference in Oklahoma City, June 1973.
541. Bahá'u'lláh, *Seven Valleys*, p. 36.
542. ibid. pp. 37–8.
543. 'Abdu'l-Bahá, in *Compilation*, vol. 2, p. 139.
544. 'Abdu'l-Bahá, *Paris Talks*, pp. 50–1.
545. Bahá'u'lláh, *Hidden Words*, Persian no. 32.
546. ibid.
547. Bahá'u'lláh, *Gleanings*, pp. 271–2.
548. Bahá'u'lláh, *Hidden Words*, Arabic no. 56.
549. 'Abdu'l-Bahá, *Paris Talks*, pp. 50–1.
550. Bahá'u'lláh, *Hidden Words*, Arabic no. 51.
551. 'Abdu'l-Bahá, in *Bahá'í Prayers*, pp. 31–2.

552. Bahá'u'lláh, *Prayers and Meditations*, p. 155.
553. Bahá'u'lláh, *Hidden Words*, Arabic no. 7.
554. Bahá'u'lláh, *Prayers and Meditations*, p. 220.
555. Bahá'u'lláh, *Gleanings*, p. 313.
556. Khadem, 'Bahá'u'lláh and His Most Holy Shrine', in Khadem, *Zikrullah Khadem*, pp. 303–4.
557. ibid. p. 303.
558. Qur'án 1:1–4.
559. The Báb, quoted in Shoghi Effendi, *God Passes By*, p. 29.
560. Khadem, 'Carmel: The Mountain of God and the Tablet of Carmel', in Khadem, *Zikrullah Khadem*, pp. 289.
561. Bahá'u'lláh, *Tablets*, p. 74.
562. Bahá'u'lláh, *Gleanings*, p. 195.
563. Bahá'u'lláh, *Seven Valleys*, p. 2, footnote 2.